THE NEW HARP OF COLUMBIA

• TENNESSEANA EDITIONS •

THE NEW HARP OF COLUMBIA

BY M. L. SWAN

A FACSIMILE EDITION WITH AN INTRODUCTION BY

Dorothy D. Horn, Ron Petersen, and Candra Phillips

THE UNIVERSITY OF TENNESSEE PRESS : KNOXVILLE

Nathalia Wright, General Editor

Clothbound editions of University of Tennessee Press books are printed on paper designed for an effective life of at least 300 years, and binding materials are chosen for strength and durability.

Library of Congress Cataloging in Publication Data

Main entry under title:

The New harp of Columbia.

(Tennesseana editions)
Hymns, with music.
Reprint of the 1867 ed.
1. Hymns, English. I. Swan, Marcus Lafayette. II. Series.
M2117.N52 1978 783.9′52 78–5504
ISBN 0–87049–251–9

CONTENTS

INTRODUCTION TO THE NEW EDITION

I. *The New Harp of Columbia* AND ITS MUSIC IN THE SINGING-SCHOOL TRADITION

By Dorothy D. Horn

The New Harp of Columbia was originally a singing-school manual. Many people have never heard of singing schools, but the schools began in New England in the 1730s as an effort to improve congregational singing in the churches. For a considerable number of years before this time, psalm tunes had been sung from memory, and numerous worshippers had interpreted "freedom of conscience" to mean that they could embellish a tune as the spirit moved them. By all accounts the result was musical chaos. A group of progressive clergymen decided that the remedy was to teach people to "sing by note," and to this end the group proposed to start singing schools, each under the direction of a master who was able to teach the rudiments of sight singing.

There was much opposition to this plan, but the schools were established and almost at once became very popular, probably because they provided an acceptable social outlet. By 1770 nearly every village, town, and city had its singing school, sometimes on a permanent basis, sometimes only for a few weeks in the winter.

Because singing schools constantly required new material on which to practice, the masters themselves turned composer to satisfy the need and incidentally to earn a little extra money. Although untrained in the conventional harmony of the day, these men were frequently extremely musical. The best of this group, whose compositions became well loved and were reprinted in countless other manuals, became our first truly American composers. In many ways they quite unconsciously retraced the development of music in medieval Europe, and because they largely escaped the prevalent Germanic influence that held both European and American composed music in a vise until nearly the twentieth century, their music has a charm for the musician of today that the music of their better trained contemporaries does not have.

These early Americans wrote in three forms: (1) the hymn tune, usually in long, common, or short meter and designed to be used with any rhymed text written in the same meter; (2) the anthem, generally in unrhymed text from scripture and containing sections of both block harmony and polyphony (essentially the plan of the English anthem and the Italian motet); and (3) the fuguing piece, in rhymed text, with the first two or four phrases in straight four-part harmony before ending with a strong cadence; the piece continues with the "fuguing" section, in which each voice enters alone, somewhat in the manner of a round; this section too ends with a strong cadence.

There had been, of course, music of a more European kind in America long before the Revolution, some of it composed by gentleman amateurs such as Francis Hopkinson, lawyer, judge, and signer of the Declaration of Independence. There were also musicians of foreign birth and training who had cast their lot with that of the colonies; among these men was Charles Theodore Pachelbel, organist at Trinity Church in Newport, Rhode Island. In 1736 in New York, Pachelbel gave the first public concert of which a record exists.

After the Revolution, more and more well-trained musicians came to this country. The native-born American composer, in the words of Gilbert Chase,

> occupied a sort of no-man's land between the privileged security of the gentleman amateur and the acknowledged competence of the professional emigrant. Salaried positions in church or theater were almost invariably filled by the foreign musicians. Our native musical pioneers, being self-taught empiricists with more zeal than skill, could not at this early stage hope to compete with the imported professionals on their own ground. Nevertheless . . . they managed to stake out an area for themselves . . . [that] enabled them to supply with considerable effectiveness a large portion of the country's rapidly growing musical needs.[1]

The area they staked out was a rural one: the isolated districts of the Northeast and the new settlements along the rapidly expanding frontier. In these areas, singing schools remained popular for years; when the writer first began attending Old Harp sings in the early 1940s, many of the older singers spoke nostalgically of attending singing schools held by T.J. Lawson, who seems to have been the last master in the Maryville-Blount County area.[2] So, although dates may vary for the last singing school in different parts of East Tennessee, today the Old Harp singings are all that remain of an honorable tradition. Indeed, this is true throughout the South.[3]

Shortly after 1800 two innovations were introduced into the singing-school books. The first of these changes was shaped notes (sometimes called character notes, buckwheat notes, or patent notes), one shape for each syllable of the solmization used. Opinions vary over whether it was Andrew Law (who did not use a staff) or William Little and William Smith (who placed their shaped notes on a staff) who first introduced shaped notes. Only four shapes were used, for the scale in those days was sung fa-sol-la-fa-sol-la-mi-fa.[4]

The advantages of the system were obvious: one no longer had to teach key signatures. The student had only to find the key note—fa for major, la for minor—and go on from there. Although various singing-school masters experimented with all

[1] Gilbert Chase, *America's Music* (New York: McGraw-Hill, 1955), p. 123.

[2] Thomas J. Lawson, 1843–1917, was born in Cades Cove in the Great Smoky Mountains, but in later years he lived in Dry Valley and held his schools mostly in Tuckaleechee Methodist Church. This information was furnished by his grandson, Lloyd Wells.

[3] I have heard that singing schools using the Stamps-Baxter books are still occasionally held. Since these books are largely devoted to gospel music of the foot-stamping variety, such singing schools can only be considered an off-shoot of the older tradition.

[4] See *A Plaine and Easie Introduction to Practical Musick* (London: Thomas Morley, 1597) or see my own book, *Sing to Me of Heaven* (Gainesville: Univ. of Florida Press, 1970), pp. 5–7.

kinds of shapes (some even used animal figures), eventually the four shapes used both by Law and by Little and Smith became standard: a triangle for fa, a circle for sol, a square for la, and a diamond for mi. These notes were placed on a staff, as Little and Smith had done, and the system survives to this day in *The Original Sacred Harp*, which is still very much in use in parts of the South.

The second innovation of the early nineteenth century was the inclusion of folk hymns in the manuals. So far as we know, these hymns first appeared in any number in Jeremiah Ingalls's *Christian Harmony* of 1805. Folk hymns had been around for a long time, perhaps since the First Great Awakening movement of 1734; certainly new ones came out of the Kentucky Revival of 1800.

George Pullen Jackson thought folk hymns were secular English folk tunes to which sacred words had been grafted. It is quite true that numerous American folk hymns are based on English secular tunes, but even Jackson, though he devoted many years to the task, could not find English folk song origins for a great number of the tunes he recognized as folk hymns, or, as he called them, "white spirituals." His musician colleague, John Powell, offered two other possibilities.[5] First, some hymns were actually composed in the style of folk music; presumably these were by folk musicians imbued with the folk idiom. Second, some hymns were pieced together from motives or entire phrases taken from preexisting tunes; this process, known as *centonization*, is by no means uncommon in the history of music.[6]

One other source of folk hymns was the camp meeting. Following the Kentucky Revival, camp meetings became popular. These gatherings, like the early singing schools, satisfied both a religious and a social need, though the "goings on" shocked some people.[7] The refrain and chorus or simply chorus became a feature of the camp-meeting tune.

During the 1830s two trends emerged which had direct effect on the singing schools. The first of these was what Gilbert Chase called the "genteel tradition," which resulted from a rather pathetic yearning for culture. The genteel tradition is characterized by an emulation of the elegant—striving for "good taste"—and by a prevailing sentimentality. Unfortunately, this tradition prevailed throughout the nineteenth century and affected all phases of life, including that within the singing schools.

I once drove to a rural section of Indiana to hear a widely publicized yearly singing in which the descendants of the original pioneers met to recreate the singing school that had played an important part in the lives of their ancestors. What I heard was the most unmitigated musical tripe: songs celebrating the beautiful spring, true love, or whatever, and tearjerkers relating the death of a loved one, all set to the tritest of tunes. On inquiry I found that the original singing school had used the wholly

[5] See George Pullen Jackson, *Spiritual Folksongs of Early America* (Locust Valley, N.Y.: J.J. Augustin, 1937), pp. vii, ix, and 19.

[6] See *The Harvard Dictionary of Music*, article on "Melody Types." It may be noted also that many of the German chorales have so-called "wandering phrases" and that English folk-song is full of the same sort of thing, except that here they are called "commonplaces."

[7] Mrs. Frances Trollope, for instance. See *Domestic Manners of the Americans*, 1832, chs. VIII, IX, and XV.

admirable *Missouri Harmony*, but in the 1880s the younger members had demanded something more elegant (I cannot even remember the name of the book used). The number of manuals of the same kind published during the latter half of the century indicates that this "genteel tradition" was happening all over the country. Only in the more isolated sections of the Midwest and North and in the conservative rural South did manuals of the older type continue to be popular.

A second ideal emerging about the 1830s was that of the sanctity of progress: one's self and one's country improved through progress; therefore it behooved one to be up-to-date.

These two ideals, gentility and progress, were combined in a remarkable man, Lowell Mason. Born in Medfield, Massachusetts, in 1792, he was the son of a member of the state legislature and the grandson of a singing-school master from whom he apparently inherited his musical talent. As a young man Mason went as a bank teller to Savannah, Georgia, where he also played the organ and conducted the choir at the Independent Presbyterian Church. Soon he had compiled a collection of sacred music that included some of his own tunes as well as tunes of European composers to which sacred words had been adapted. This collection was copyrighted in 1822 as *The Boston Handel and Haydn Society Collection of Church Music*; it immediately became popular and went through many editions.

By the 1830s Mason's stature as an authority on church music was well established. At the beginning of the decade he had already started a campaign to have music taught in the Boston public schools, and by 1838 he had succeeded. In 1832 Mason was one of the founders of the Boston Academy of Music, whose purpose was to apply the Pestalozzian method to the teaching of music to children. By 1834 he had established teacher-training classes in music.

Until his death in 1872, Mason was busy in the field of music, mostly of an educational or sacred nature. He was compiler or co-compiler of more than twenty collections, many of which went into ten or more editions, and he composed or arranged hundreds of hymns. Mason had his prejudices, but they were in keeping with his times. He considered the music of the singing-school composers inferior, he disapproved of shaped notes, and he introduced the Italian method of solmization, in which each degree of the scale has a different syllable. Despite these strictures, the older tunes still continued to be loved, the four-shape notation has held its own to this day, and even some of Mason's own books had to be printed in shaped notes to find a market in certain parts of the country. Today Mason is honored more as an organizer than as a composer of sacred music; indeed his hymns, once so popular among Protestants of all denominations, are appearing in fewer and fewer numbers in modern hymnals.

In the late 1930s and early 1940s American musicologists became aware of our first truly American composers, beginning with William Billings and later Timothy Swan, Justin Morgan, Oliver Holden, and others. The shackles of conventional nineteenth-century harmony had been thrown off, and musicians were able to appreciate the strength and significance of the singing-school composers. Slightly earlier than this, George Pullen Jackson had become fascinated by folk hymns and devoted the rest of his life to research in this field. This work resulted in a series of books, of which *Spiritual Folksongs of Early America* (1937), *Down East Spirituals and Others* (1943), and *Another Sheaf of White Spirituals* (1952) are the most important for the researcher. Together they form a compendium of folk hymns: in each case the tune and words are given, there is a musical analysis of the scale and mode used, and there is a list of manuals in which the tune or its variants may be found. Included also are notes on the origin of the tune, particularly when the tune began as a secular English or Scottish folksong. Although the books contained a few mistakes and subsequent scholarship added to our knowledge of the folk hymn, Jackson's works still remain a valuable research tool.

The New Harp of Columbia, first published in 1867, has examples of all three types of folk hymns mentioned by George Pullen Jackson and John Powell, and it employs the solmization evolved by Lowell Mason. The book is a fairly late example of a typical American singing-school manual of the traditional type. Like its predecessors, its contents are largely sacred or patriotic; like its predecessors, it retains tried-and-true examples from the past, introduces the more popular newer hymns, and provides a showcase for the talents of the compiler.

The title page of the book gives M.L. Swan as compiler. The initials stand for Marcus Lafayette, and tradition says that he played the violin rather well. That he was a man of some education can be seen from the concise and lucid Preface. Incidentally in this section Swan says: "The parts are arranged as will be seen in Lesson VI [i.e., from the top: Treble, Alto or Counter, Tenor, and Bass].[8]"

As its name implies, *The New Harp of Columbia* was preceded by an earlier *Harp of Columbia*, printed in Knoxville in 1848, with W.H. and M.L. Swan listed as compilers. Since the first part of this introduction is concerned with a consideration of *The New Harp* in the context of the New England singing-school phenomenon and of the types of music associated with this movement, a discussion of more specific information about *The New Harp*, its earlier predecessor, and its compiler will be taken up in the next section.

The New Harp of Columbia was rather a modern book for its day. First, unlike many of its rivals, it was well printed, a circumstance that makes this and many earlier reprints possible. Second, it uses a seven-shape notation, following the seven-syllable solmization favored by Lowell Mason. Third, the book contains a larger percentage of standard hymns than most manuals—that is, it contains many hymn tunes included in contemporary hymnals approved by the leading Protestant churches, especially tunes by the then-popular Lowell Mason. Of course, as indicated previously, it follows tradition by including old psalm and hymn tunes, anthems and fuguing pieces by the early Americans, quite a lot of folk hymns, and numerous compositions by the compiler himself.

For the researcher wishing to study the authentic versions of the early American pieces it is best to go to the originals, for in the course of many reprintings over the years mistakes inevitably creep in. Frequently these errors are caused by a laudable desire on the part of the compiler to make the supporting parts more interesting. Thus in Kimball's "Invitation" (p. 178), the soprano and alto parts are more elaborate than in the original, whereas the tenor and bass segments have very few changes.

The following lists may give some idea of the contents of *The*

[8] Around Maryville the parts are referred to (from the top line down) as treble, counter, tenor, and bass. Ron Petersen found a different tradition, as explained in Section II of this Introduction.

New Harp of Columbia and of the remarkable variety of sources upon which it draws.

Psalm Tunes of European Origin

1. Devizes, 94. Of English origin, this psalm is by Isaac Tucker and dates from 1810.
2. Dublin, 129. This piece, frequently known as "Coleshill" in Northern books, is listed by Jackson, but even he admits that as a psalm tune it is of English origin. The tune is usually attributed to "Kirby" and occurs in the Scottish Psalter of 1615 under the title of "Dundee."
3. Dundee, 53. This song occurs in the Scottish Psalter of 1635 under the title "French Tune" and is probably by Guillaume Franc, c. 1615.
4. Mear, 14. There is some doubt about this psalm tune; some scholars think it is of American origin, but most say it comes from England. It is usually attributed to Aaron Williams, c. 1760.
5. Old Hundred, 11. This piece comes from the Huguenot Psalter, Geneva, 1551, where the tune was used for the 134th Psalm.
6. St. Martin's, 39. This is by William Tansur, a German who lived in England. The date usually given is 1740.

Early American Tunes

a. Hymn tunes.

1. China, 39. A hymn tune in common meter by Timothy Swan, from his *New England Harmony*, 1801.
2. Coronation, 117. A hymn tune in common meter by Oliver Holden. This is the only composition by an early American to appear in modern hymnals. It comes from Holden's *Union Harmony* of 1793.
3. Egypt, 150. A hymn tune but in 8's instead of one of the church meters. Though it is attributed only to "Swan" in the *New Harp* (*NH*), it is by Timothy and not M.L. and may be found in *The New England Harmony.*
4. Windham, 18. A hymn tune in long meter. Attributed to "Leed," it is really by Daniel Read and is from his *American Singing Book* of 1785.
5. Winter, 101. A hymn tune in common meter. Though no composer is given in the *NH*, it is by Daniel Read, and this tune too comes from the *American Singing Book*. The tune is sometimes called "Staughton" in other books, possibly to distinguish it from the "Winter" by Daniel Belknap, published in 1800.

b. Anthems

1. Easter Anthem, 195. No composer is given, but it is by William Billings and may be found in his *Suffolk Harmony* of 1786.
2. Farewell Anthem, 219. No composer is given here or in any other book I have examined. It is found as early as 1793 in *The Psalmodists Companion.*
3. Ode on Science, 208. No composer is given, but it is by Deacon Janaziah Summers. He composed it for the semicentennial of Stephen Daggett's Academy of Taunton, Massachusetts, in 1798. It is one of the few anthems to have a patriotic text.

4. Rose of Sharon, 199. Attributed correctly to "Billings"—William Billings of course. It is included in his *Singing Master's Assistant*, 1778.

c. Fuguing pieces

1. Ballstown, 161. No composer is given, but in earlier manuals it is attributed to Nehemiah Shumway. It may be found in *The Musical Instructor* of 1818, but it probably appeared much earlier. See "Creation" below.
2. Creation, 157. The composer is given as "Shumway," which of course is Nehemiah. Shumway published an *American Harmony* in 1793, though I have been unable to locate a copy. Certainly this piece appears in Holden's *Worcester Harmony* of 1803.
3. Exhortation, 155. No composer is given, but it is by Eliakim Doolittle (1772–1850) and appears in *The Easy Instructor* by William Little and William Smith in 1802.
4. Huntingdon, 175. No composer is given, but the piece is by Justin Morgan (1747–1798). Although Morgan is more famous as the originator of the famous Morgan breed of horses, he was also a singing-school master and composer. Unlike most of his contemporaries, he published no book.
5. Invitation, 178. The composer is given as "Kimbol." This is Jacob Kimball (1761–1826), and the tune appears in his *Rural Harmony* of 1793.
6. Lenox, 42. Attributed correctly to "Edson." This was Lewis Edson, Sr. (1748–1820). "Lenox" is one of the most popular fuguing pieces.
7. Liberty, 98. Attributed in the *NH* to "Wythe," *The Original Sacred Harp* gives "Stephen Jenks, 1803." *The Sacred Melodeon* gives (Nehemiah) Shumway, but it may be found, however, in Jenks' *Musical Harmonist* of 1800.
8. Middletown, 173. No composer given. In other manuals it is sometimes spelled "Middleton" and is attributed to "Ball" or "Bull." It is probably by Amos Bull and appears in Shumway's *American Harmony* of 1793.
9. Milford, 152. Attributed to "Stephenson." This was John Stephenson, and the work may be found in Holden's *American Harmony* of 1793.
10. Montgomery, 158. Attributed to "More," it is by Justin Morgan and dates from 1793.
11. Ninety-fifth, 35. Though attributed to "Chapin" in the *NH*, this popular fuguing piece is usually attributed to "Colton" or "Coulton." I have found it no earlier than *The Beauties of Harmony* (Freeman Lewis, 1814), but it has an implied modulation at the end of the first section which takes it out of the folk class.
12. Northfield, 115. The composer, misspelled "Ingols," is Jeremiah Ingalls, and the tune appears in his *Christian Harmony* of 1805.
13. North Salem, 110. No composer is given, but in many manuals it is attributed to Stephen Jenks. I have not verified this.
14. Ocean, 159. Attributed to "Swan," this tune is definitely by Timothy. The *Original Sacred Harp* gives the date as 1793.
15. Sutton, 113. Though the name of the composer is blurred in the *NH*, elsewhere it is given as "Goff." The piece appears in French's *Psalmodist Companion* of 1793.

Tunes Composed or Arranged by Lowell Mason

1. Antioch, 130. This is "Joy to the World" and the date usually given is 1830. No composer is credited in the *NH*.
2. Anvern, 34. No date is available. The *NH* says: "Arranged from the German by L. Mason"; older standard hymnals simply attribute the tune to him.
3. Ariel, 76. Attributed to "L. Mason." The date usually given is 1836.
4. Azmon, 63. Not attributed, but Mason arranged it from a German piece by Carl Glaser and introduced it in 1839.
5. Boylston, 181. Attributed. It dates from 1830.
6. Chimes, 72. No composer given. No date available.
7. Danvers, 23. Attributed. It dates from around 1839.
8. Fountain, 64. Attributed. No date available.
9. Haddam, 96. Attributed. This tune dates from 1839.
10. Harwell, 108. Not attributed. The date is 1841.
11. Hebron, 20. Attributed. The usual date is given as 1830.
12. Laban, 80. Not attributed. Composed about 1830.
13. Migdol, 34. Attributed. No date is available.
14. Missionary Hymn, 88. Not attributed. The date usually given is 1823, which seems very early.
15. Naomi, 63. Not attributed. The date usually given is 1836.
16. Nashville, 41. The credit line "Arranged from a Gregorian Chant by L. Mason" is also given in most hymnals, but the nature of the melody makes this most unlikely. Composed in 1839.
17. Oliphant, 145. Not attributed. The date is 1839.
18. Olney, 149. Not attributed. The date is usually given as 1830.
19. Orford, 22. Not attributed. This tune dates from 1839.
20. Rockingham, 21. Attributed. Again the date is 1839.
21. Shawmut, 80. Not attributed. No date is available.
22. Upton, 36. Not attributed, but this tune appears in Mason's first collection, *The Handel and Haydn Society's Collection of Church Music*, 1822.
23. Uxbridge, 20. Attributed. Composed in 1840.
24. Watchman, 184. Attributed. This also dates from 1840.
25. Zerah, 64. Not attributed. This tune is usually dated 1837.

Tunes by Thomas Hastings[9]

1. New Haven, 125. This appears in Hastings' *Presbyterian Psalmist* of 1849.
2. Ortonville, 128. The date is 1837.
3. Waynesville, 108. Composed in 1840.
4. Zion, 114. The date is 1830.

Other Standard Hymns Frequently Appearing in Hymnals of Various Denominations[10]

1. Amsterdam, 169. By James Nares. This hymn appears in the early Methodist *Foundery Collection* (London, 1742).
2. Arlington, 59. By Dr. Thomas Arne, an Englishman (1710–1788).

[9] None of the tunes are attributed to Hastings.

[10] Unless noted, no composers are given in the *NH*.

3. Bealoth, 82. This hymn appeared in Mason's *Sacred Harp* of 1840, but it is doubtful if Mason wrote it. He did not claim it.
4. Ballerma, 52. By Robert Simpson. The date is 1833.
5. Benevento, 50. Attributed. By Samuel Webbe (1740–1816). This standard hymn is incorrectly claimed as a folk hymn by Jackson (*Another Sheaf of White Spirituals* 68), one of his few errors. *The Music of the Methodist Hymn Book* says it was originally part of a mass by this English composer, with the words "Tantum ergo sacrementum."
6. Duke Street, 23. Attributed. By John Hatton, an Englishman. This hymn was published in *A Select Collection of Psalm and Hymn Tunes* (Glasgow: Henry Boyd, 1793).
7. Henry, 52. Attributed. By S.B. Pond, an American. Pond was a composer of popular hymns and Sunday-school songs and was a member of an American publishing house until 1850.
8. Lischer, 132. By Friedrich Schneider, a German (1786–1853). This hymn is sometimes attributed to Mason; he may have first published it in this country.
9. Lucas, 126. By James Lucas. Composed about 1762.
10. Marlow, 59. By John Chetham. The date is 1718.
11. Martyn, 120. Attributed. By Simeon B. Marsh (1798–1875). Probably written in 1834. This Easter hymn is "Jesus Lover of my Soul" and is interesting because it has its original words.
12. Mendon, 21. A German melody arranged by Samuel Dyer in 1814.
13. Miles' Lane, 116. Attributed. By William Shrubsole. The date is 1779.
14. Missionary Chant, 22. By Charles Zeuner. Composed in 1832.
15. Ornan, 182. This would seem to be "Jesus I my Cross Have Taken," with a few changes in rhythm. Modern hymnals attribute this to Mozart, as arranged by Hubert P. Main (1839–1926), and call it "Ellesdie."
16. Peterboro', 62. By the Reverend Ralph Harrison. The date is 1786.
17. Pleyel's Hymn, 151. By Ignaz Joseph Pleyel (1757–1831). It is often called "Brattle Street."
18. Portugal, 100. Attributed to "Thorley"—no first name given. Although this is no longer contained in modern hymnals, it was quite popular at the time of the *NH*.
19. Shirland, 81. Attributed to "Stanley," who was probably Samuel J. Stanley, of Birmingham, England. Another old favorite hymn.
20. Warwick, 53. Attributed also to Stanley. The date is 1767.
21. Wells, 19. Attributed to "Holdrad." This is Israel Holdroyd, who was born in England about 1690. The hymn dates from about 1746.
22. Wilmot, 96. The credit line reads: "From C.M. von Weber." I recall this from my youth as "Hark What Mean These Holy Voices." It was quite popular up to the middle of this century and is always attributed to Carl Maria von Weber (1786–1826), the German composer of "Der Freischutz."
23. Woodstock, 58. Attributed to "D. Dutton, Jr." This is Deodatus Dutton, Jr. (1808–1832). Written about 1830.

Folk Hymns[11]

Abbreviations for the Jackson references:
SF: *Spiritual Folksongs of Early America*
DE: *Down East Spirituals and Others*
AnS: *Another Sheaf of White Spirituals*

1. Anticipation, 75. *DE* 238.
2. Cardiphonia, 138. *AnS* 100.
3. Christian Contemplation, 48. This is sometimes called "Faithful Soldier." *SF* 59.
4. Christian Soldier, 120. This is not in Jackson, but it has many of the characteristics of a folk hymn: (1) it is modal (Aeolian); (2) it is in a gapped (hexatonic) scale; and (3) it is centonized from other folk hymns. For more on these musicological matters, see my own book *Sing to Me of Heaven*, Chs. III through VI.
5. Concord, 46. *DE* 161.
6. Deep Spring, 93. *SF* 35
7. Erie, 105, *DE* 68.
8. Farewell, 32. *SF* 25.
9. France, 148. *AnS* 329.
10. Golden Hill, 81. *DE* 86.
11. Gray Ridge, 78. *Ans* 136.
12. Greenfields, 16. *SF* 60.
13. Heavenly Armour, 56. Although Jackson does not list this, it is undoubtedly a folk hymn: (1) it is modal (mixolydian); (2) it is pentatonic; (3) it is centonized from two other folk hymns; and (4) it has the typical melodic shape of a folk hymn.
14. Holy Army, 119. Another not given by Jackson, but (1) it is in a hexatonic scale; (2) it is centonized; and (3) it has a refrain.
15. Holy Manna, 107. *SF* 114.
16. Hopewell, 37. Sometimes called "Columbus." *SF* 75.
17. Humility, 112. Sometimes called "Christian Soldier." *SF* 68.
18. Idumea, 44. *SF* 137.
19. Indian's Farewell, 134. *AnS* 332.
20. Jordan's Shore, 177. *DE* 241.
21. Kedron, 45. *SF* 57.
22. Kingwood, 83. *DE* 152.
23. Lancaster, 91. *DE* 162.
24. Leander, 61. *SF* 107.
25. Liverpool, 113. *SF* 7.
26. Lone Pilgrim, 49. *SF* 18.
27. Marietta, 90. Sometimes called "Sweet Heaven." *DE* 116.
28. Mexico, 147. *AnS* 108.
29. Middleton, 69. Usually called "New Britain." *SF* 135.
30. Midnight Cry, 84. *AnS* 69.
31. Morality, 89. *DE* 138.
32. Morning Trumpet, 99. *SF* 241.
33. Never Part Again, 74. *AnS* 191.
34. New Year, 67. *AnS* 318.
35. Ninety-third, 25. *DE* 146.

[11] Because space does not permit giving the entire background for each of these hymns, only the Jackson references (by song number, not page) have been noted. Some years ago I checked on these: most are correct, and some of the doubtful ones have already been mentioned in this Introduction. A few tunes not in Jackson have been added, but in each case the reason for the addition has been given.

36. Oh, Sing to Me of Heaven, 73. *DE* 205.
37. Paradise, 68. *DE* 276.
38. Parting Hand, 95. *DE* 16.
39. Pleasant Hill, 43. *DE* 91.
40. Promised Land, 47. *SF* 246. Called "Bound for the Promised Land."
41. Prospect, 15. *DE* 147.
42. Protection, 57. *DE* 145. Also called "Bellvue."
43. Rapture, 123. Not in Jackson, but it is basically pentatonic and is highly centonized.
44. Reflection, 13, *SF* 122.
45. Salvation, 24. *SF* 95.
46. Sion's Security, 30. Not in Jackson, but it is modal (Aeolian), has the folk-hymn shape, and is completely pentatonic.
47. Soda, 67. *SF* 121. Sometimes called "Tender Care."
48. Sudbury, 41. *AnS* 218.
49. Summer, 122. *DE* 79.
50. Warrenton, 56. *SF* 205.
51. Wondrous Love, 143. *SF* 88.

Contrafacti of Well-known Tunes

1. Bequest, 71. An oral tradition form of "The Vesper Hymn" by Bortniansky.
2. Bruce's Address, 109. This is "Scots What Hae Wi' Wallace Bled," a tune that was well known to our grandparents. Jackson counts it as a folk hymn.
3. Celebration, 118. This is "O Where and O Where has my Highland Laddie Gone."
4. Hamburg, 111. This is "Auld Lang Syne."
5. Home, 54. As might be expected, this is "Home Sweet Home."
6. Joyful, 141. This is the English carol "Joys Seven," although it has an added conclusion. Jackson includes it.
7. Long Ago, 183. This is "Long, Long Ago."
8. Marston, 131. This is an oral tradition form of "The Farmer in the Dell."

The rest of the tunes in *The New Harp* form a curious mixture. There are some forty-four that seem actually to have been composed by M.L. Swan. Unfortunately for his reputation as a composer, they seem never to have been very popular. "Come Ye Disconsolate" is included in Walker's *Southern Harmony* and in his *Christian Harmony*, but I have found no other tune by Swan used by another compiler, nor have I heard any of his compositions (as distinct from his arrangements) used in an Old Harp singing. Most of the rest of the material in the book I have been unable to trace. An exception is "Loving-Kindness" (p. 28), which has remained popular up to the present day. Although no composer is given in *The New Harp*, the fine old tune is attributed to William Caldwell in most of the many books and hymnals including it. The composer is probably the William Caldwell of *The Union Harmony*, printed in Maryville in 1837.

This, then, is *The New Harp of Columbia*, a song book that has retained its popularity in East Tennessee for over a hundred years. It is hoped that the purchaser of this reprint will join an Old Harp group and thus help to keep alive a remarkable tradition—you will find it is a rewarding experience.

II. EAST TENNESSEE HARP SINGING

By Ron Petersen and Candra Phillips

Shape-note singing in East Tennessee predates *The New Harp of Columbia*, presently used in the traditional "harp sings" of the area. *Union Harmony* by Caldwell and *Knoxville Harmony*, songbooks with shaped notes, were produced in East Tennessee before the Swans prepared *The Harp of Columbia*, the predecessor of *The New Harp*. There is every assurance that the music was not always religious in shape-note singing. In fact, two rounds included in *The Harp of Columbia* were not so. Now, however, from the Shenandoah Valley of Virginia through western North Carolina and East Tennessee to the Deep South, all books still in use are almost exclusively religious.

To examine the only book used for harp sings in this region, and its author, is to reflect some of the history of the area itself. The family of the authors of *The Harp of Columbia* came from the North with other early immigrants, settled in this area, and compiled a book which reached great popularity here. Moreover, although there has been a renascence of interest in southern Appalachian folk culture, little has been written about the harp tradition and its link to East Tennessee folk history.

At least three members of the Swan family apparently played roles in the history of singing schools and shape-note music. Timothy Swan (1758–1842) produced the *New England Harmony* (1801) and lived long enough to have had contact with W. H. Swan, but no direct connection of communication or lineage between the two is known. Included in *New England Harmony* were the songs "China," "Egypt," and "Solomon's Song"—all also in *The Harp of Columbia* and therein attributed merely to "Swan." Moreover, the first edition of *The Harp of Columbia* was published in 1848, six years after the death of Timothy Swan.

The predecessor of the book here reprinted was *The Harp of Columbia*, compiled by M.L. Swan and W.H. Swan. All accounts seem to agree that M.L. Swan was Marcus Lafayette Swan. George Pullen Jackson, in his introduction to the reprint of *The Sacred Harp*, cites the compilers of *The Harp of Columbia* as Markus [*sic*] Lafayette Swan and W. Harvey Swan. Census records for 1850 list Marcus as "author, music." Thus all in all, the identity of M.L. Swan seems certain. The identity of W.H. Swan, on the face of it, would also seem easily discerned, for Marcus's father was listed in various census records and count lists as William H. Swan; but a second W.H. Swan, this one William Harvey Swan, was present in Knoxville at the appropriate time to have participated in the publication of *The Harp of Columbia*. Which of these two W.H. Swans appears on the title page of the book we do not know. We can only relate the genealogy as we have pieced it together.

From records in the McClung Collection of the Lawson McGhee (Knoxville-Knox County) Public Library and estate books there, as well as probate and real estate records at the Knox County Courthouse, the story can be begun with the migration into Tennessee from Pennsylvania of John Swan (b. 1758, d. Tenn. 1801) in 1800–1801. John Swan and his wife, Margaret, had five children: William Harvey (d. 1806); Samuel (d. approximately 1818); John, Jr.; Isaac; and Catherine (who married James Swan, of whom nothing further is known). The senior Swans settled on land in Knox County west of Knoxville, bordering on Sinking Creek, in what became the Eleventh District of the county. There is evidence that at least William and John, Jr., came to Tennessee after their parents, buying portions of the land from their father. We conclude that William fathered six children: three in Pennsylvania (William H., Jr., b.1798; Martha, b.1796; Jane, b.1794) and three in Tennessee (Moses M.; Hannah G.; John McC.). William H., Jr., became a prosperous lawyer (with holdings of $44,000 in 1850 and over $100,000 at his death) and with his wife, Hannah Wells, lived in Knoxville with their child, Marcus Lafayette, and William's two sisters, Jane and Martha. Marcus was born in 1827 and thus was twenty-one at the time of the first publication of *The Harp of Columbia.*

An extraordinary coincidence leads to a notion of an influence on the authors of *The Harp of Columbia*. The title page of Ananias Davisson's *Supplement to Kentucky Harmony* (1825) lists as one of the agents favored to sell the book the firm of Crosier & Barton, Knoxville. The will of Hannah W. Swan (as noted above, the wife of William H., Jr., and mother of Marcus) reveals her maiden name to be Crozier, and further investigation shows that the Croziers (the spelling in Davisson's book is an error) and Bartons not only were associated in business, but were personally related—John Crozier married Hannah Swan. Furthermore, John Crozier, Jr., was the editor of *The Times* of Knoxville in 1839. It is not strange, therefore, that the Swans were encouraged to compile a songbook because the Crozier family was involved in the sale of such previous books.

Another person who could have shared authorship of *The Harp of Columbia* would be William Harvey Swan (b. 1816, d. 1892), probably the son of Samuel mentioned above and therefore a cousin of Marcus. William H., Jr., and William Harvey were associated in real estate transactions, and the latter held various appointed and elected positions in county government. Adding to the dilemma is the description of himself by the author of the preface (W.H. Swan alone) as a teacher, understanding the need for easy principles of music; this fact throws no light on authorship because one man was an attorney and the other a farmer and political appointee. Two circumstances, however, point toward William H., Jr. (Marcus's father) as co-author. First, he was far wealthier than his nephew; thus he could have financially backed the publication and its preparation and given it more leisure time. Second, he died between the dates of *The Harp* (last edition, 1855) and *The New Harp* (first edition, 1867) perhaps accounting for his elimination as co-author of the latter.

The relative roles of W.H. Swan and M.L. Swan in the compilation of *The Harp* are not as previously thought; it has been assumed (by George Pullen Jackson among others) that the leading role belonged to Marcus. The preface of the fourth edition of *The Harp of Columbia*, 1852, states: "The author has composed a large number of new tunes, variously turned, that the different tastes might be suited; and selected from other works a choice variety." As noted above, the preface, written in the singular, is signed by W.H. Swan alone; in fact, then, it was W.H. Swan and not Marcus who was the primary composer and compiler. In the same volume the "Introductory Remarks" are by both authors.

On the back cover, conversely, there is an advertisement for the book, together with a plea for agents to sell the volume. The text includes: "Applications for agencies, with recommendations, can be addressed to M.L. Swan, Knoxville, Tennessee." It would thus appear that Marcus might have been the publisher and managing editor, while William H., Jr., was the composer.

It is little wonder, then, that the changes made by M.L. Swan in the production of *The New Harp of Columbia* were mostly substitutions and that few new compositions appeared.

The Harp of Columbia must have been a rapid success, for the original edition of 1848 had become the "seventh edition" (probably just a series of reprints) of 5,000 copies by 1855. For Marcus, already from a well-to-do family, the proceeds may have provided him with the means to meet and court his future wife, whose family was also reputedly wealthy. According to Jackson, Marcus's marriage to Mary Morrison on September 15, 1853, found him in Bellefonte, Alabama, and the introduction to the postwar *New Harp of Columbia* was written there. Jackson states that he was apparently buried there too, without a gravestone in a private cemetery.

Evidence presented by Jackson would have it that the combined fortunes of Marcus and Mary were lost in the Civil War, during which Marcus (who by then was in his early thirties) served an inactive role (because of rheumatism) with the Confederate Army. Nevertheless, his will left $75,000 to his heirs, who, together with the executor, promptly squandered the estate. Jackson indicates that after the war Marcus turned to singing-school teaching in northeastern Alabama and eastern Tennessee, but no good record of this—or of his being in any other profession—exists, except in the 1850 census where he is listed as "author music."

Marcus is reported by Jackson to have died in 1869 of typhoid fever, at age thirty-two. Census data list his age in 1869 as forty-two, not thirty-two, which therefore opens the question of the year of his death as well. No information has been unearthed to ascertain which date is correct, but a death date of 1869 would have meant only four years after the Civil War and only two years after the appearance of *The New Harp of Columbia.* Also, if his fortunes had been leveled in the war, the time remaining to him would have been short to amass $75,000 as his residual estate.

The 1848 *Harp of Columbia* was "Stereotyped by L. Johnson and Co., Philadelphia," but the 1852 (fourth) edition was "Published and for sale by the authors, Knoxville, Tenn. Printed at the Register Office." *The Register* was a Knoxville newspaper of the day. The 1855 (seventh) edition was "published by M.L. Swan [although still authored by both Swans], and for sale by merchants generally in east Tennessee." By 1867, M.L. Swan was in Bellefonte, Alabama, and *The New Harp of Columbia* was produced by the printing house of the Methodist Episcopal Church of Tennessee in Nashville, and all subsequent reprints through 1921 bear the same publishing house name.

That many songs in *The New Harp of Columbia* are to be found in preceding books leads to conjecture on the books available to the Swans from which to choose their selection. Surely one source was *Southern Harmony* by Walker (various editions from 1835 through 1847), for fully one-third of all songs in *The New Harp* not composed by the Swans are also found in *Southern Harmony*, almost invariably in the same key signature and with the same poetry. Another set of books presumably in their hands were *Kentucky Harmony* and *Supplement to Kentucky Harmony*, both by Davisson, for the books were sold by Crozier & Barton. In fact, if Crozier & Barton were general booksellers, many such songbooks must have been available to the Swans. Caldwell's *Union Harmony* and Jackson's *Knoxville Harmony* are also frequently cited.

In the preface to *The New Harp*, M.L. Swan stated: "Between fifty and one hundred tunes, selected and original, will be found in this that are not in the old Harp. Such tunes as are seldom used have been discarded, and their places filled by others of superior merit. No alterations whatever have been made in the tunes retained from the old book." Several observations can be made about this report. First, in the far majority of substitutions, a full-page tune (two "braces") has been replaced by two tunes, each consisting of a single "brace." Marcus eliminated some tunes by "Swan" (for example, "I Have My Trials," "Persia," "Bower") as well as tunes by others, and many substitutes (too numerous to name, but for example, numbers 20, 21, 23, 34, and 41) were attributed to Lowell Mason. Other substitutes are attributed wholly or in part (counter, harmony, and so on) to M.L. Swan (e.g., numbers 36, 69, 86, 87). Second, when substitutions were made, the page numbers of those retained were carefully preserved. If the present custom of harp singing prevailed at that time, songs were "called" to be sung by number, with everyone able to relate the number, brace, title, tune, and words. If numbers had been altered, the new book would have been much less useful to groups whose members already owned *The Harp of Columbia*. Third, although it is claimed that no alterations whatever were made to tunes retained from *The Harp*, a glance at the very first tune ("Old Hundred") reveals very different harmony in 1867 from that in 1848. Fourth, as usual, lyrics were repeated with different tunes to take advantage of meters in common. For example, the lyrics of numbers 12 and 44 are identical, as is the case with 28 and 66, 58 and 158, 90 and 131, and 17, 93, and 112. Most of these (i.e., 12, 17, 28, 58, and 66) and several others were holdovers from the 1848 *Harp*, not substitutions made later. Comparative data on *The Harp* and *The New Harp* are shown in Table 1.

Of *The New Harp of Columbia*, several reprints were issued over the years. The earliest we have examined are dated 1905, 1907, 1909, 1912, and 1919, are bound in white boards, and show no names on the title page other than the author and publisher. Indeed, the printing imperfections of the 1867 *New Harp of Columbia* may be found faithfully reproduced in all later reprints (along with others added along the line as the plates were marred through repeated handling). In fact, some imperfections found in the 1848 *Harp of Columbia* are also to be found in the 1867 *New Harp*, so perhaps some of the 1848 plates were in continual use since the first edition. Several reprints were issued after 1921, all bearing the same date. One "1921" reprint is bound in boards and bears the name L.D. Schultz of Knoxville as "special agent." Another reprint (deep-red pebbled cloth binding) bears the name of A.A. Hicks, "editor." Still another is bound in brown cloth, with the cover type style changed. The latest reprint (maroon buckram) was produced by Phil Tabor in Chattanooga around 1968.

The 1905, 1907, 1909, 1912, and 1919 reprints of *The New Harp of Columbia* bear an interesting advertisement on the back covers. Several books are named, most having been printed in both "round note" and "character note" editions, and a couple ("New Life" and "The Emerald") additionally without notes, in either paper or board covers. The "character notes" are depicted, and they are not those used in *The New Harp of Columbia* but those in the style of *Christian Harmony*. Incidentally, *The New Harp* was priced at $7.20 per dozen from 1905 through 1919.

Despite their immense popularity in their day, singing-school books are rare in private hands today, and only a bit less so in libraries. For example, the Library of Congress houses only a 1921 reprint of *The New Harp of Columbia*, and none of the original *Harp*. George Pullen Jackson, the foremost writer on the subject and a collector of such books, owned no copy of *The Harp of Columbia* and saw only one copy of the 1855 edition, then in the hands of the Swan family. He owned only one copy of the 1921 reprint of *The New Harp*. The McClung Collection of the Knoxville-Knox County Public Library is blessed with an 1848 *Harp of Columbia*, an 1867 *New Harp of Columbia*, and several 1921 reprints.

The popularity of singing-school books was immense, as circumstantial facts attest. In the preface (and erstwhile advertisement) to the *Harp of the South*, I.B. Woodbury, admittedly one of the more popular compilers of such books, said of two of his former works that *The Dulcimer* had sold 125,000 copies in two years and *Carmina Sacra* had sold 300,000 copies. On the back cover of the older reprints of *The New Harp of Columbia*, the publishers advertised some fourteen other song books and claimed that "A MILLION or more of our people have used them, and with UNIFORM SATISFACTION. SALES INCREASING EVERY DAY." *The Harp of Columbia* itself went from the original edition of 1848 to the seventh "edition" of 1855 with its printing of 5,000 copies.

The shape notes used in *The Harp of Columbia* and its sequel are unique to these books. In the past several decades, hymnals using seven-note solmization have almost universally employed the system pioneered by J.B. Aiken in *Christian Minstrel*. As in most systems, the shapes for mi, fa, sol, and la are identical, originating from the four-note system. This left do, re, and si to the discretion of the author or compiler, and the Swans adopted shapes for these syllables not used elsewhere. Parenthetically, another system was invented by the Reverend William B. Gillham, "Pastor of the First C.P. Church in Columbia, Tenn.," and used in *The Aeolian Lyricist*. If, as expected, the "C.P." stands for "Colored People's," this book joins *The Colored People's Sacred Harp* as particularly for the South's black population.

But all these words about the books and the Swan family give only half the story of the tradition in East Tennessee. The people who sing are more vital to this tradition than the composers of the songs, and the setting for the singing is at least as intriguing as the book being sung from. The broad valley between the Cumberland Plateau and the Great Smokies is dissected by a file of roughly parallel ridges running to the northeast. The entire valley, from central Pennsylvania to Alabama has acted as a topographical flume for settlers who, seeking their own parcel of land, compulsively moved southwestward before the expanding population descending from the northeast. Scots, Irish, English, and Germans occupied the narrow bottomlands of the mountain creeks and ascended the narrow paths into the draws and streamlet drainages of the southern highlands of East Tennessee. The trek down the Shenandoah Valley through Greene and Sevier counties to Blount County had already begun by 1800, and the Swan family came shortly thereafter. Graves at Myer's Cemetery in Blount County start in 1801 and those in Headrick's Cemetery in Sevier County in 1809.

Immigration into East Tennessee was from two directions, however, since another route passed over the mountains from North Carolina. Whether harp singing took place in western North Carolina before the migration is not known; it is, however, found there today—the same tradition but from a different book, *Christian Harmony*. This migration came a bit later than the first and the new settlers were integrated into the extant social structure.

Horace Kephart, in the 1910s, unable to find literature describing the area and its people, came to live alone among the mountain people and to write a poignant but matter-of-fact documentary on their life and times. He spoke of the reclusive mountaineers as different from their more gregarious, ever so slightly more cosmopolitan neighbors who settled the stream bottomlands and flood plains. It was almost surely these latter who, simply because they enjoyed togetherness, must have responded to the convening of a singing school at a local church. Strong family ties were the rule, adding to the attraction of singing schools and their successors, "harp sings."

Today the scene of harp singing has changed little. The Greene County Convention ceased in the late 1930s, but annual sings are held in Anderson, Blount, Knox, Morgan, Roane, and Sevier counties, and occasionally in Greene and Jefferson counties as well (see Table 2 for the schedule of traditional East Tennessee harp sings).

Wear's Valley, stretching eight miles between Townsend (Blount County) and Pigeon Forge (Sevier County), is nestled among the same mountains from which the Great Smoky Mountains National Park takes its name. Until a few years ago, entering the valley brought a sense that time was standing still, a reminder of the more patient, earth-based pace that once characterized life in the southern mountains. Times have changed. The two-lane road that so long was sufficient is now being widened near Pigeon Forge to accommodate the ever-increasing numbers of tourists who drive through the valley and those who have built vacation homes there. One of the few remaining traditions that have eroded little in the last century is harp singing.

Located alongside the winding road through the valley, barely within the Sevier County line, is a small, clapboard church known as Headrick's Chapel. Looking somewhat out of place, it stands stalwartly, forcing the road to bend around it. Except for the sound of an occasional car, the rural setting admits little evidence of the late twentieth century, which may account, in part, for the popularity of this particular harp sing. It is commonly held among the regular harp singers that the Headrick's Chapel sing, convened each year on the fourth Sunday in September, is one of the best in Tennessee. The physical structure of the chapel itself contributes a resonance which threatens to carry the sound of singing throughout the valley. There is no carpeting, no accoustical ceiling, no air conditioning. Except for its foundation the chapel is entirely of wood, built in 1902, with a plainness not often seen these days, even in these parts. It is quite small, seating no more than 150, but on the day of the harp sing that limit is pushed as folding chairs are set up to accommodate the overflow crowd. In Headrick's Chapel one can imagine that with only a few changes, mostly in costume, the sing could as easily be in 1878 as in 1978. This sing epitomizes the tradition in East Tennessee.

Headrick's Chapel has been the scene of two series of "sings." The first series started early, perhaps around 1910, and ended in obscurity, its founder and dates unknown. The second series was actually started at the Primitive Baptist Church just outside Wear's Valley near Townsend by an Adams in the 1920s. That church was built as a Union Church—that is, without denomination—but was occupied exclusively by the Primitive Baptists over the years. In 1968, when the congregation split over a matter of doctrine, the more conservative group left. By agreement, this group took up meeting one Sunday a month at Headrick's Chapel. Because the leaders of the annual sing at the Primitive Baptist Church were part of the departing group, the sing emigrated with them to the chapel. Charles Clabough and Otha Henry still act as hosts, as they have since the sing moved.

Of course, singing in the valley has been going on longer than the folks still there. Shape notes were already popular before the Swans introduced their books. But some present-day singers are living links to the past. In 1977, for instance, at least four people over eighty years of age led songs in the afternoon sing, and there was a small host of leaders over seventy. Since the start of the singing at Wear's Valley Baptist Church, the first Sunday in October 1923, Burl Adams, as responsible as any for the perpetuation of harp singing in the Wear's Valley area, has missed only one sing—and that because of a heart attack.

The Headrick's Chapel sing is an all-day affair. Folks begin to gather before eleven in the morning, and singing replaces the regular service. Many of the singers who will attend in the afternoon are at home churches for morning worship, and the morning sing cannot match in number, volume, or tone the afternoon celebration. The pews are not full, and those seated behind the first few rows keep a respectful silence, participating only by their presence.

The actual arrangement of the singers comes directly from the tradition of the singing school. The benches or seats constitute a square, with each part occupying a side. In churches, the lead section (in this area singing the third line) usually sits in the front pews facing the altar, so that the song leader faces both the congregation and the lead section simultaneously. In front and to the left of the leads are the basses, the only group traditionally exclusively male. Opposite the leads and facing them are the altos, usually but not always female. To the right of the lead section are the tenors, singing the top line. In Headrick's Chapel the basses look out at the hillside opposite the chapel, and the tenors glimpse the mountains to the southeast. The altos view the cemetery, a further reminder of the frailty of life, a common allusion in the words of many of the harp songs.

An interesting anachronism may be found between the parts sung and the original intention of Marcus Swan. In the preface to *The New Harp of Columbia*, Swan states: "In some books the Air is termed the Treble. It can make no difference which it is called, Treble or Tenor, so it is understood. Teachers can direct their class in this area as they may prefer." Then again in Lesson VI, the following account of the parts appears:

Upper Staff, Treble, ladies who can sing high.

Next below, Alto or Counter, ladies who can sing low.

Next below, Tenor, men who can sing high.
Lowest Staff, Bass, men who can sing low.

Again, "There is no distinction in the sounds of the Tenor, Alto, and Treble, unless the Alto is represented by the F, or Bass Clef. Then it bears the same connection to the Tenor and Treble that the Bass does."

The clearest directive indicates that the ladies were to sing the top staff, and men the third. In practice, both men and women sing the third staff, which in this area is known as the Lead. But more noticeable, the top staff is dominated by male voices, with only very low female voices occasionally joining in this line, which is called Tenor or Treble indiscriminately. This would seem a violation of Swan's directives, but it developed before the memory of any living singer.

Although a sing is hosted by a congregation, a single leader is almost always acknowledged. Sometimes that person is leader both in fact and title, as when he is also the pastor or music director of the congregation itself. At other sings, however, the overall leader remains passive, abdicating actual responsibility to another. This is the situation when the Knox County Old Harp Singers travel to a nearby parish and Bates Elliott, the president, acts as leader. The major responsibility of the leader is to select song leaders, usually progressing around the square through the parts, sometimes cajoling against claims of roughness of throat. Both men and women lead, and leaders often have traditional favorites which they have led for years. Frequently, certain tunes are sung in memory of deceased family members or singers who loved those particular hymns. Songs are called by number, not by tune title or first line, and traditionally number 107, "Holy Manna" opens the sing with the words "Brethren, we have met to worship, And adore the Lord our God."

The initial pitch is gained either accurately—by sounding a tuning fork (rarely) or by a pitchpipe (most frequently)—or inaccurately by guess when a sounding instrument is unavailable. At Headrick's Chapel, a tuning fork was used for some years, until its owner, Frank Carter, died; then a pitchpipe was substituted. Once the primary pitch is found, the harmony pitches, if any, are enjoined by the singers, the leader, or both. Frequently the pitch must be altered for voices grown lower with age. It is this blatant and prolonged searching for the sound that marks the singing of East Tennessee as so informal and unique. The leader then orders, "Let's sound that chord," and with a sweep of the hand the whole chorus sustains their pitches. "Now sing the sounds," and the solmized tune is sung through in syllables, including all repeats. Hardly missing a beat, the leader may exhort, "And now the poetry," and the song is sung again. Everyone knows how many, and which, verses are to be sung except for songs sung infrequently or led by a new leader (see Table 3 for songs sung).

It is almost as though the morning sing points the way to dinner on the ground. There is nearly audible relief when, as noonday approaches, a break is suggested so the tables can be unfolded and loaded with the covered dishes. Dinner is outdoors in good weather, up the center aisle in bad. It is a time not only for nourishment but for fellowship, for renewing acquaintances with those not seen for as long as a year, or for meeting visitors and singers who have come to the sing from places far from Wear's Valley. The visitors often include singers from other areas and other traditions who have come long distances simply because they enjoy singing shape notes regardless of the notation, the book, or the location. Dinner is announced as intended for an hour, but it always runs over by half again that period, much to the credit of the food and the camaraderie.

There are no restrictions on songs to be sung. Often songs are repeated in the morning and afternoon, and occasionally a song will be repeated more often, especially when the number of leaders is very small. Inaccuracies of tempo and gross retards often mark the singing, but these are accepted unabashedly, having become part of the tradition long before most people can remember. Frequently, some testimony is offered between songs, and this usually meets with silent tolerance or some low verbal expression of impatience if it drags out over a few words. To sing is not to preach. Such testimony takes two general forms. One is a minisermon or exhortation to "mind the words" or "listen to the message" inherent in the song. Until recently a second commentary was common, on the fragility of the custom through attrition of the class, but the infusion of younger singers in recent years has changed that message to thankfulness that the tradition will continue. Infrequently a singer or listener will be "seized by the spirit" and shouts or moans are accompanied by a dance-like step in the aisle, a behavior often attributed to "the pentacostals." All in all, the atmosphere is very informal, the songs are sung more slowly, the background buzz is louder, and the testimony is much more frequent than at sings farther south, throughout Georgia and Alabama for example, where leaders are preregistered, songs are sung much faster, and very little testimony is tolerated.

In the last few years, as mentioned above, part of the testimony has dwelt on the apparent resurrection of popularity of the tradition. Indeed, in many of the sings now, especially ones as popular as those at Headrick's Chapel, fully a third of the singers are under forty, a welcome phenomenon for the older practitioners who feared so long for the life of the tradition. With the recent revival of interest in folk and rural culture, many singers have come to harp sings out of sociological curiosity, but some have found much more. Even to those for whom the religious message is not preeminent, a kind of spiritual calm comes from singing these old songs—a sense of historical continuity, a sense of sharing a meaningful tradition with those long dead. For the older singers, who learned shaped notes from their parents, grandparents, or singing-school teachers, the sing brings memories of days and folks gone by. After a particularly good sing, like that in Headrick's Chapel, there is a sense of having "created something good" by raising voices in song.

Time, not enthusiasm, limits the sing, although voices are hoarse before the conclusion. By tradition, the last song is number 95, "Parting Hand," with only the poetry sung. A few announcements on future sings or other special services are followed by a closing prayer, and the singers disband. In the early fall, parting may be for only a week, but a bit later the recess may last for several months. In the spring, one conversational topic to be relied on is the informal count of those who have survived the winter. Although advanced age might account for such concerns, in some places where sings are held it has not been long since survival was truly at stake during the relatively long winter months.

Many who began their harp singing in Wear's Valley or other local places have taken the tradition with them as they moved about. Harp singing groups recently have sprung up all over eastern North America, from Toronto to Washington to Florida, and a small group in California uses *The New Harp of Columbia*. Books vary with the location, as does the style of singing, but these groups are based on historical and folklore interests. Conversely, authentic continuous traditions are also very alive. For instance, *The Original Sacred Harp* is undoubtedly the most widely used book, particularly popular in Georgia, Alabama, and other Deep South states; *Christian Harmony* is sung from in western North Carolina; and the Mennonites of the Shenandoah Valley of Virginia sing from *Harmonia Sacra*. In all these locales, the traditions are long and deep, and the foundations religious.

To the memories of the East Tennessee singers—of the families Adams, Cardwell, Carter, Clabough, Dunn, Elliot, Garner, Headrick, Henry, Pate, Teffeteller, Wheeler, Whitehead, and others—and to the sounds which softly comfort the ears we dedicate this book.

Table 1. COMPARATIVE DATA: *The Harp of Columbia* (1848) AND *The New Harp of Columbia* (1867)

Number	Title	
	The Harp of Columbia	*The New Harp of Columbia*
18	"Reed" as author	"Leed" as author
20	"Fairfell," Hitchcock	"Uxbridge," L. Mason, and "Hebron," L. Mason
21	"Consolation," Dean	"Rockingham," L. Mason, and "Mendon"
22	"Detroit," Bradshaw	"Missionary Chant" and "Orford"
23	"Salem," Boville	"Danvers," L. Mason, and "Duke Street," J. Hatton
34	"New Salem," Lewis	"Anvern," arr. L. Mason, and "Migdol," L. Mason
36	"Middlebrook," Jackson	"Watts," M.L. Swan, and "Upton"
41	"Sweet Rivers," More	"Sudbury" and "Nashville," arr. L. Mason
52	"Evening Shade"	"Ballerma" and "Henry," S.B. Pond
53	"Redeeming Love," Caldwell	"Warwick," Stanley, and "Dundee"
58	"Emerald Gates," Davisson	"Lanesboro" and "Woodstock," D. Dutton, Jr.
59	"New Durham," Austin	"Marlow" and "Arlington"

Number	Title: *The Harp of Columbia*	Title: *The New Harp of Columbia*
62	"Florida," Whetmore	"Peterboro" and "Ono"
63	"New Market," Caldwell	"Naomi" and "Azmon"
64	"I Have My Trials," Swan	"Zerah" and "Fountain," L. Mason
69	"Christmas," Woods	"Return," M.L. Swan, and "Middleton," M.L. Swan
72	"Messiah," Carrell	"My Mother's Bible," arr. M.L. Swan, and "Chimes"
73	"Crucifixion," Davisson	"Oh, Sing to Me of Heaven" and "Belleville"
74	"Davisson's Retirement," Davisson	"Never Part Again"
76	"Persia," Swan	"Ariel," L. Mason
80	"Indian Philosopher"	"Laban" and "Shawmut"
81	"Few Happy Matches," Crane	"Shirland," Stanley, and "Golden Hill"
82	"Exultation," Humphreys	"Bealoth"
86	"Bower," Swan	"Tabor," M.L. Swan
87	"Confidence," Jackson	"Hightower," M.L. Swan, and "A Home in Heaven," arr. M.L. Swan
96	"David's Victory"	"Haddam," L. Mason, and "Wilmot"
97	"Africa" and "Athens"	"Temple," M.L. Swan, and "Heritage," M.L. Swan
104	"Pilgrim's Lot"	"Mount Vernon," L. Mason, and "Tamworth," Lockhart
108	"Star in the East," Jackson	"Waynesville" and "Harwell"
114	"Tennessee"	"Zion" and "Richmond"
125	"Cumberland"	"Thou Art Passing Away" and "New Haven"
126	"Tranquility," Caldwell	"Lucas"
127	"Jalinda," Caldwell	"The Rock," M.L. Swan
144	"Salutation"	"Rowley"
154	"Solitude in the Grove"	"Yarmouth"
162	"David's Lamentation," Billings	"Merdin"
168	"Lena"	"When Shall We Meet Again?" alto by M.L. Swan
184	"Down Derry," "The Church Bell," "Morning Bell," "Welcome," and "Sabbath" (all rounds)	"Watchman! Tell Us of the Night," L. Mason

Table 2. Schedule of Traditional Harp Sings in East Tennessee

Date	Church	County
Easter	Tuckaleechee Methodist (afternoon)	Blount
4th Sunday in April	Three-in-one Methodist	Jefferson
1st Sunday in May	Jonesville	Roane
2nd Sunday in May	Mt. Carmel Presbyterian	Morgan
3rd Sunday in May	Dumplin Baptist	Jefferson
2nd Sunday in July	Gethsemane Baptist	Blount
3rd Sunday in July	Free Liberty Primitive Baptist	Claiborne
5th Sunday in July	New Salem (afternoon)	Sevier
1st Sunday in August	Hillvale Baptist	Anderson
2nd Sunday in August	Calvary Baptist	Sevier
2nd Sunday in September	Conners Heights Baptist (afternoon)	Sevier
3rd Sunday in September	Spring Hill Baptist	Anderson
4th Sunday in September	Headrick's Chapel	Sevier
1st Sunday in October	Wears Valley Baptist	Sevier
4th Sunday in October	Maryville College (afternoon)	Blount

Table 3. Tunes Led at Headrick's Chapel in 1976

Leader	Tune and Number
Burl Adams	Humility 112
	Christian Contemplation 48
Burl Adams & Mrs. Alred	Edom 146
	Western Mount Pleasant 206
Burl Adams & John W. Dunn	Ocean 159
Burl Adams & Nan Taylor	Wondrous Love 143
	Whitestown 180
Mrs. Alred	Long Ago 183
Willie Cardwell	Holy Army 119
	Morality 89
	Parting Hand 95
Charles Clabough	Importunity 60
	North Salem 110
	Zion 114
John Wright Dunn	Leander 61
Bates Elliott	Holy Manna 107
	Clinton 66
Will Garner	Idumea 44
	Morning Trumpet 99
	Paradise 68
Will Garner & Mrs. Alred	Leander 61
Otha Henry	Morning Trumpet 99
	Long Ago 183
Mr. King	Ninety-fifth 35
Mr. King	Christian Contemplation 48
	Pleasant Hill 43
Tommy Long	Holy Manna 107
Billy Joe Mann	Whitestown 180
Mr. Nolan	Sion's Security 30
Arthur Ogle	Mount Olivet 51
	Heavenly Armour 56
	Hightower 87
Granville Pate	Heavenly Armour 56
Ron Petersen	Coronation 117
	Boylston 181
	Old Hundred 11
Nan Taylor	Mear 14
	Boylston 181
Tom Taylor	Importunity 60
Bruce Wheeler	Paradise 68
	Northfield 115
	Saint's Adieu 124
Russell Whitehead	Anticipation 75

THE

New Harp of Columbia:

A SYSTEM OF MUSICAL NOTATION,

WITH A NOTE FOR EACH SOUND, AND A SHAPE FOR EACH NOTE;

CONTAINING A VARIETY OF MOST EXCELLENT

PSALM AND HYMN TUNES, ODES AND ANTHEMS,

HAPPILY ADAPTED TO

CHURCH SERVICE, SINGING-SCHOOLS AND SOCIETIES.

ORIGINAL AND SELECTED.

By M. L. SWAN.

Nashville, Tenn.
Dallas, Tex.; Richmond, Va.
Publishing House of the M. E. Church, South.
Smith & Lamar, Publishing Agents.
1919

PREFACE.

In this, the New Harp of Columbia, the same system of Notation is adhered to as in the old Harp.

The "Elements of Music" are arranged in a different form, and somewhat extended. They are written as short as possible, and but little space is taken up with practical exercises. In many books the Elementary Principles, or Rudiments, by the introduction of many exercises for practice, are swelled to from twenty to thirty pages, and yet contain no more important directions than are found in the few pages of this work. The new beginner, in looking at the many pages of rules, may suppose that all of this long list is something obliged to be learned, and hence is disheartened, and often deterred from an effort to learn. Then let the practical part be obtained in singing tunes anywhere through the book, by which an interest is kept up in the mind of the learner.

Between fifty and one hundred tunes, selected and original, will be found in this that are not in the old Harp. Such tunes as are seldom used have been discarded, and their places filled by others of superior merit. No alterations whatever have been made in the tunes retained from the old book.

A lesson on the transposition of the keys will be found, and all the newly inserted tunes are written with the signs of transposition. Teachers who feel it important to give instructions in this lesson can question their classes as to what signatures (*sharps* or *flats*) would be placed to those tunes having none, and thus advance them as fast as by any other means.

The objection to the system of *round* notes is the constant exertion necessary to read the music with facility and certainty, even by good singers and those of much practice.

A very popular error exists in the minds of many, who are not strangers altogether to music, in regard to transposition, or the characters called *flats* and *sharps*. Many suppose that they affect the music: when the truth is, they serve no purpose but as signs of the key, and without which music in *round* notes would be a sealed book. The stereotyped argument in favor of *round* notes, "that before you can sing you must know the principles," is true; but it is no more true than that they must be understood to sing *shaped* notes. Think of a man attempting to sing a tune, in any kind of notes, that he never heard, without knowing the time, the relative length of the notes, the key, the sounds of the scale, tones and semitones, &c.!

The English alphabet is composed of twenty-six sounds, for each of which there is a distinct character or shape representing it, called a letter. We might, possibly, have learned to read with these all of the same *shape*, but we could not have learned any more correctly than we have done.

Music, then, has seven natural sounds, for each of which, in this work, there is a character, or *shape*, called a note, from which any one can sing much more readily, and as correctly as if they were all the same *shape*.

The use of the system of *four notes* has generally, very willingly, and reasonably, given way to this.

Not expecting nor desiring to entirely supersede all other books, the "Elements of Music" in this are made sufficiently comprehensive to enable any one who understands them to sing from others.

The parts are arranged as will be seen in Lesson VI. In some books the Air is termed the Treble. It can make no difference which it is called, Treble or Tenor, so it is understood. Teachers can direct their class in this as they may prefer. See the definition by Webster.

As the Air is the leading part, and as the female voice is superior, I would assign that part mainly to females, and the Treble (as here called) to men whose voices are high. Thus I present the book to the public.

M. L. Swan

Bellefonte, Ala., 1867.

ELEMENTS OF VOCAL MUSIC.

LESSON I.

BRACE, CLEFS, STAFF, AND BARS.

MUSIC is written on five parallel lines and the spaces between, which is called a Staff.

In Vocal Music there are mostly four parts: Bass, Tenor, Alto, and Treble. These parts are included by a Brace at the beginning, represented by characters called Clefs, and are entitled to a note, or sound, for each degree, or line and space, and are divided into measures by perpendicular lines, called Bars, as in the example below.

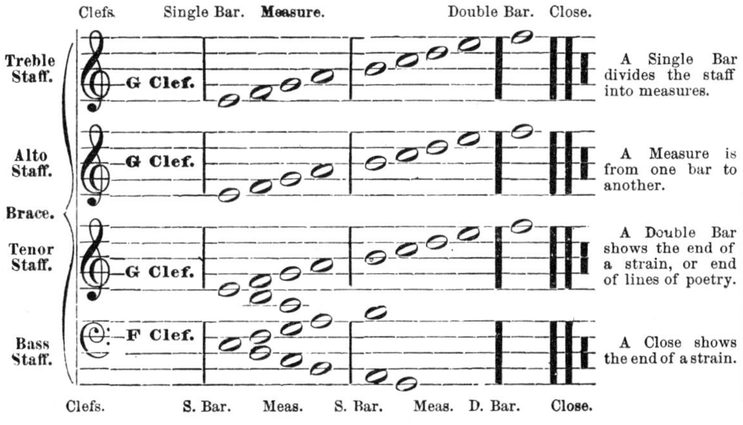

G Clef always stands on the Tenor and Treble, and generally on the Alto; giving the same line or space in each of these parts the same sound. Thus, the notes or characters on the Tenor, Alto, and Treble staffs, as in the above example, have the same sound on a corresponding degree.

F Clef always stands on the Bass staff, and places it one sixth below the other three parts; thus making the third space in the Bass to have the same sound as the first line of the other parts. When the Alto is represented by the F Clef, it is sounded like the Bass.

In counting the degrees of the staff, count from the lowest line upward. When notes transcend the staff, either above or below, short lines are used, called Leger Lines, or Added Lines.

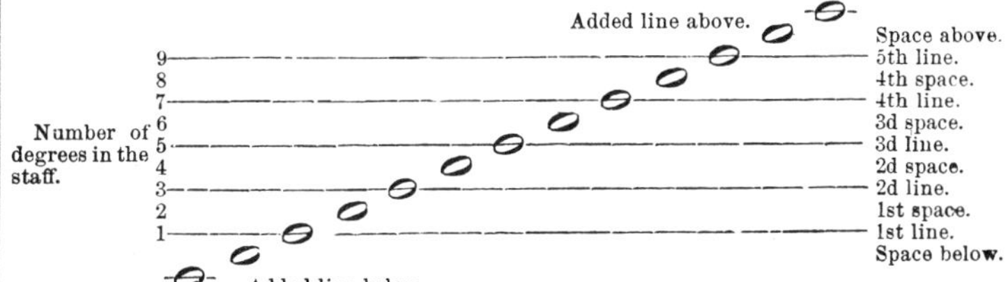

The staff having nine degrees does not show that there are nine distinct sounds, as will be seen hereafter

LESSON II.

NOTES AND RESTS.

Notes of different names and different lengths are used to convey musical sounds,—either high or low, from their place on the staff, or long or short, from forms representing a relative length.

In this work, seven notes of different shapes and names are used to represent the seven natural sounds of music, which are shaped and called thus:—

Names of Syllables.	Do.	Ra.	Mi.	Fa.	Sol.	La.	Si.	Do.
Pronounced.	Do.	Ray.	Mee.	Faw.	Sole.	Law.	See.	

In the above scale, the 8th note is the same sound as the 1st; that is, the same character of sound, but a higher pitch.

RELATIVE LENGTH OF NOTES.

A Whole Note is white without a stem; also called a Semibreve.

A Half Note is white with a stem; also called a Minim.

A Quarter Note is black with a stem; also called Crotchet.

An Eighth Note is black with a hook to the stem; also called Quaver.

A Sixteenth Note is black with two hooks to the stem; called Semi-quaver.

A Thirty-Second Note is black with three hooks to the stem; called Demi-semi-quaver.

Each of these notes has a rest of equal length to itself.

Whole Rest. Half Rest. Quarter Rest. Eighth Rest. Sixteenth Rest. Thirty-Second Rest.

A Repeat—or points in the spaces of the staff—directs a return from the first double bar, or close, and to sing that strain again.

1 2

The figures 1 and 2 show that the note under 1 is sung before repeating, and that under 2 in repeating.

1 2

If two notes are connected by a slur, the one under the figure 1 is sung before repeating, and both in repeating.

The Slur shows the number of notes sung to one syllable of the words.

Two or more notes having their stems joined are also sung to one syllable of the words.

A Dot, or point, at the right hand of a note or rest, adds one-half more length to the note.

3

The figure 3 over or under three notes indicates that they are sung one-third quicker than the regular time of such notes.

A Hold, or Pause, over a note or rest, adds to that note or rest about one-fourth of its proper time.

D. C.

D. C., or Da Capo, at the apparent end of a tune, shows that the tune is concluded with the first strain, or any designated strain

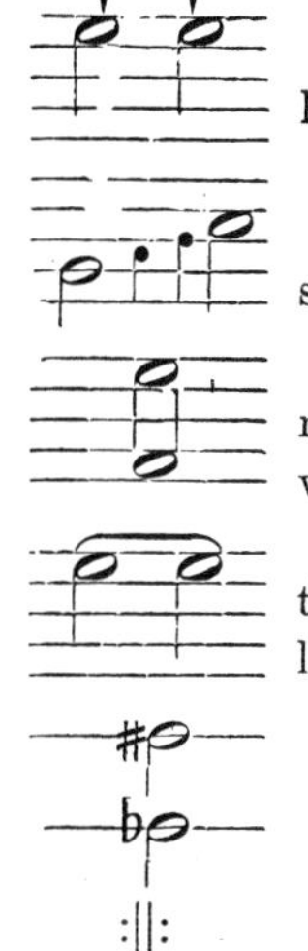

Staccato marks show that the notes over which they are placed are to be sung short and distinct.

Grace Notes guide the voice to the succeeding note, with slight stress,—being barely sounded.

Choosing Notes are placed one over the other:—either may be sung, or one voice may sound one, and another voice the other.

When two or more notes of the same sound are slurred, the first, only, is named, and the sound continued on the length of the others.

A Sharp before a note elevates that note half a tone.

A Flat before a note depresses that note half a tone.

A Prisa denotes a repetition of preceding words.

LESSON III.

VARIETIES OF TIME.

There are three distinct kinds of Time, or movement: Double, Even, or Common; Triple, or Uneven; and Sextuple, or Compound; and each has consistent varieties, which are designated by two figures in the staff, at the beginning of all tunes.

DOUBLE, EVEN, OR COMMON TIME.

2 over 2 is the representation of the first variety, or mode, of this time; sung in about three seconds to each measure, two beats, accented on both parts of the measure when filled by half-notes, and when filled by fourths, on the first and third parts of these.

4 over 4 represents the second variety of this time (or it may be called Quadruple time); sung in about two seconds and a half to the measure, four beats, and accented on the first and third parts of the measure.

2 over 4 is the third variety; sung in about one and a half seconds to the measure, two beats, and accented on the first part of the measure.

TRIPLE OR UNEVEN TIME.

3 over 2 represents the first variety of this time; sung in about three seconds to a measure, three beats, full accent on the first and partial on the second part of the measure.

3 over 4 marks the second variety of this time; sung in about two seconds to a measure, beat and accented as the first.

3 over 8 is the third variety; sung in about one second, beats and accent like the first and second.

SEXTUPLE OR COMPOUND TIME.

6 over 4 represents the first variety of this kind of time; sung in about two and a half seconds to the measure, two beats, and accented on the first and fourth parts of the measure.

6 over 8 is the second variety; sung in about one and a half seconds to the measure, same beats and accent as the first.

The upper figure shows how many parts the measure is divided into, and the lower figure the value or length of these parts: $\frac{2}{2}$ shows that two half-notes fill a measure, $\frac{3}{2}$ that three half-notes, or $\frac{6}{4}$ that six fourth-notes, or their equivalent, fill a measure.

Beating Time is a motion of the hand to regulate the time all the way through the tune; by which every measure, and the notes of each measure, are apt to be made equal, in proportion to their value.

In beating two beats, perform them down and up; three beats, down, left, and up; and for four beats, down, left, right, and up.

In Sextuple, or Compound time, six beats, down, down, left, right, up, up, would be a complete and proper keeping of the time; but it may be kept very properly, and perhaps with more ease, to beat down on the first part, rest the hand on the second and third, up on the fourth, and rest on the fifth and sixth.

LESSON IV.

OF THE KEYS.

There are two keys: the Major, or greater key, and the Minor, or lesser key. In all properly arranged tunes the last note in the Bass is the key-note. If that note is Do, it is 1 of the scale, and is the representative and foundation of the Major key. If it is La, the tune is a Minor key, and that note is 1 of that scale. In the seven sounds, natural with the

MAJOR KEY.

		8
	si	7
Tone.		
	la	6
Tone.		
	sol	5
Tone.		
	fa	4
Semitone.		
	mi	3
Tone.		
	ra	2
Tone		
	do	1

MINOR KEY.

		8
	sol	7
Tone.		
	fa	6
Semitone.		
	mi	5
Tone.		
	ra	4
Tone.		
	do	3
Semitone.		
	si	2
Tone.		
	la	1

voice, there are five tones, and one semitone, or half-tone, in the Major key; while there are but four whole tones, and two semitones, in the Minor key. The semitones always occur between *Mi* and *Fa*, and *Si* and *Do*. See example.

Thus it is seen that the Major key is greater than the Minor by one half-tone. In each of the above examples there is a lack of one note to complete the Octave, or eighth sound. This would be Do in the Major, and La in the Minor key. Each of these sounds would be the same as the first, only on a higher pitch, and would be the last of that Octave, or the first of another going on higher. The vibration of the human voice, in making this eighth sound, is discovered to correspond so exactly with the first, that a similarity is seen in these two sounds, the 1st and 8th, not to be found in any other two of the Octave.

This, together with the singular natural difference between the male and female voices, justifies the opinion that there are but seven sounds in music. The female voice is naturally eight degrees more acute, or higher, than the male voice, and thus when 1 of the scale is sounded by the male voice, that of the female, in imitating it, makes exactly the pitch of the male voice for the 8th sound, and so on as far as the voices can reach, either high or low; the female voice an 8th, or an Octave higher, and yet the same sound.

The note on the next degree of the staff, either above or below any given note, is called a Second, the next a Third, &c. In counting these degrees, or intervals, as sometimes called, the first and last notes are always counted with those intervening; as from *Do* to *Sol*, ascending the scale, is a fifth, and in descending, a fourth.

A Major 3d is three sounds without a semitone; a Minor 3d is three sounds with a semitone.

Some authors insist that there is but one key, but the majority of writers adopt the two keys; although it must be admitted that the distinction of sounds in the two is slight.

In the Major scale, Do is 1, Mi is 3, and Sol is 5; while in the Minor we take La as 1; then Do is 3, and Mi 5, of that scale, which brings the semitones lower in this scale than in the Major key.

When the key is changed in a tune, the key-note to which it is changed takes the same sound as the other had, if occupying the same degree of the staff.

The key is rarely changed, except in Anthems.

LESSON V.

MUSICAL LETTERS, AND TRANSPOSITION OF THE KEYS.*

The different sounds of the Natural, or Diatonic Scale, are said to be represented by the first seven letters of the alphabet, A, B, C, D, E, F, and G, and each line and space of the staff is named from one of these letters, as in the example below:—

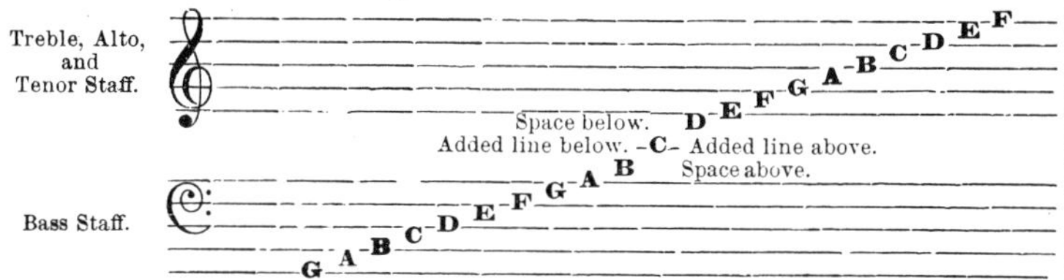

It thus appears that the first line of the Bass Staff is called G, and the other degrees go on with the letters in regular order to the added line above (or middle line), and then into the Tenor, Alto, and Treble Staffs, E being the first line of these staffs, etc.

* For remarks on this lesson, see the Preface.

If the Alto is represented by the F, or Bass Clef, as it sometimes is, the letters then stand on it as on the Bass.

Transposition is removing the key from one letter, or place, upon the staff to another, either higher or lower.

The key takes its name from the letter on which it stands: as, for example, when Do is on C it is called the key of C, and is said to be the Natural key.

When no signatures, (♯) sharps or (♭) flats, are found at the beginning of the tune, immediately after the Clefs, Do is on C, and the Relative Minor key, La, is on A

The Relative Minor to any Major key is found a sixth above, or a third below.

When Do, or the key-note, stands on other letters of the staff, one or more of the characters called (♯) sharps or (♭) flats are placed on certain letters of the staff, at the beginning of the tune, as a sign of the key.

One	♯	is the signature of	G.	One	♭	is the signature of	F.
Two	♯♯	" " "	D.	Two	♭♭	" " "	B.
Three	♯♯♯	" " "	A.	Three	♭♭♭	" " "	E.
Four	♯♯♯♯	" " "	E.	Four	♭♭♭♭	" " "	A.

Or, as in the next example, which shows the letters of the staff, upon which these signatures are placed for each key.

THE KEYS BY SHARPS

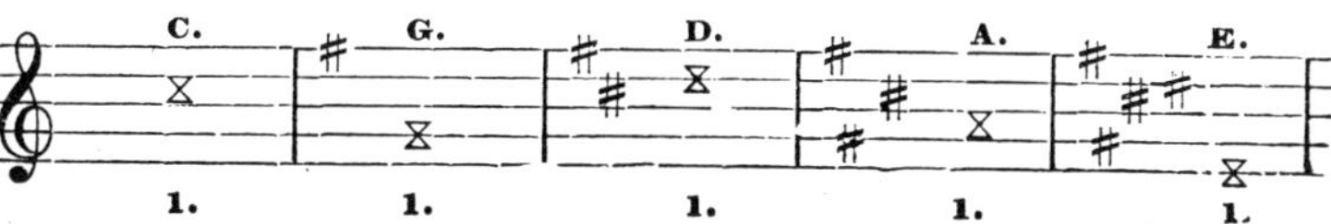

THE KEYS BY FLATS

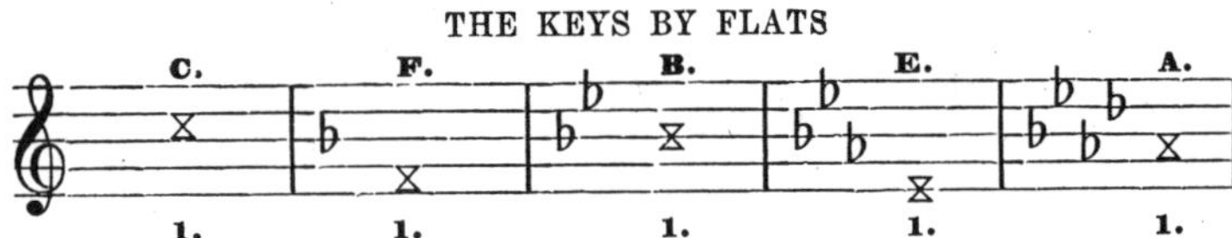

The above are the keys of the several letters, and are pitched high or low, as they stand high or low on the staff.

To get the proper pitch of a tune, in any of the keys, by the voice, sound the key-note, and pass from that to the lowest note in the Bass, and also to the highest note in the Tenor or Treble. If both of these are made with ease, the proper pitch is supposed to be very nearly, if not exactly, ascertained. If the result is not satisfactory, the effort is continued until satisfactory.

LESSON VI.

MUSIC IN PARTS.

A Part in music appears to the eye as any number of notes on any one staff. The Treble is one Part, the Bass is another Part, &c.

Music is composed of one, two, three, four, and sometimes more parts.

When in one part, it is called Melody; in two or more parts, it is said to be in Harmony; and these parts are so composed that all will harmonize when sung together.

Four parts are as many as are used in ordinary church music. The parts, most generally, in this country, have been arranged in the following order:*—

Upper Staff, Treble, ladies who can sing high.

Next below, Alto or Counter, ladies who can sing low.

Next below, Tenor, men who can sing high.

Lowest Staff, Bass, men who can sing low.

Below is a scale showing the connection of the parts, or which degrees of the Bass and the other parts have the same sound, &c.

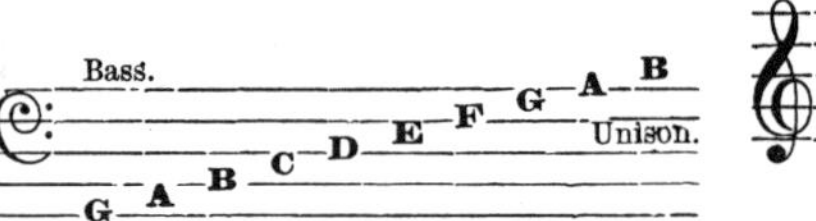

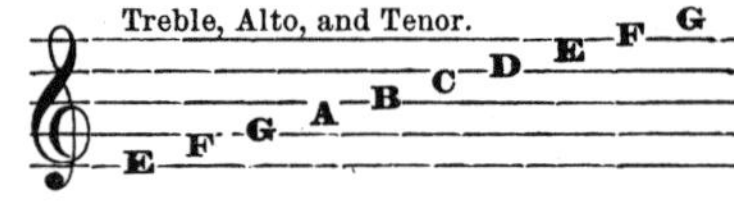

The above scale contains fifteen sounds, or two Octaves; which is about the compass of ordinary voices.

There is no distinction in the sounds of the Tenor, Alto, and Treble, unless the Alto is represented by the F, or Bass Clef. Then it bears the same connection to the Tenor and Treble that the Bass does

THE CHORDS.

The combination of the sounds 1, 3, 5, 8, or Do, Mi, Sol, Do, is the most pleasing and agreeable form of harmony.

Let these sounds be made together by the four parts, one part sounding Do, another Mi, another Sol, another Do (8), and observe how agreeable the Chord.

It is termed the Common Chord.

The 6th is classed among the Concords.

The 2d, 4th, and 7th are reckoned as Discords, but the 4th is used in composition, and is a reasonably good chord.

The 2d and 7th are to be avoided, as being particularly harsh and disagreeable to the ear.

* See remarks in the Preface.

SCALE OF CHORDS, WITH THEIR OCTAVES.

	Concords.				Discords.		
Single Chords.	1	3	5	6	2	4	7
Their Octaves.	8	10	12	13	9	11	14
	15	17	19	20	16	18	21

Two sounds of the same pitch are called a Unison.

When any sound is succeeded by the sound on the first degree of the staff, either above or below, the interval is called a Second; if by the sound on the second degree, the interval is called a Third, &c.

LESSON VII.

CHROMATIC SCALE.

It will be remembered that the natural succession of Tones and Semitones in the Octave forms what is called the Diatonic Scale.

Another Scale is formed by dividing all the Tones of the Diatonic Scale into half-tones, thus forming an entire scale of half-tones.

This is called the Chromatic Scale.

This scale is required but little in ordinary plain music, and is not usually much studied or practised.

OF PERFORMANCE.

To sing in good taste and with the greatest effect, the sounds should be varied,—sometimes singing louder, and sometimes softer, according to the character and sentiment of the words.

One strain, or even one measure, of a tune may be sung loud, and another soft, as the meaning or expression of the words may direct.

In some books, terms are used to denote these distinctions.

Let all singers exercise their own good sense, and vary the performance according to the spirit of the song; study the meaning and sense of every song they sing, and enter into the spirit of the same, never indulging in a careless, lifeless performance.

Let every word, in singing, be spoken or pronounced as distinctly as in speaking; so that not only the sounds of the music are heard, but the song is comprehended, and an effect produced that would not be from sounds alone.

Enter into the emotions expressed by the poetry, and let the sounds come from the heart with an energy, a meaning, and a soul.

And now that the important principles of Vocal Music are explained in the foregoing lessons, on this and the next page will be found exercises of the scale and the intervals, which should be practised until every sound becomes entirely familiar, remembering that all tunes are formed from these sounds.

MAJOR SCALE.

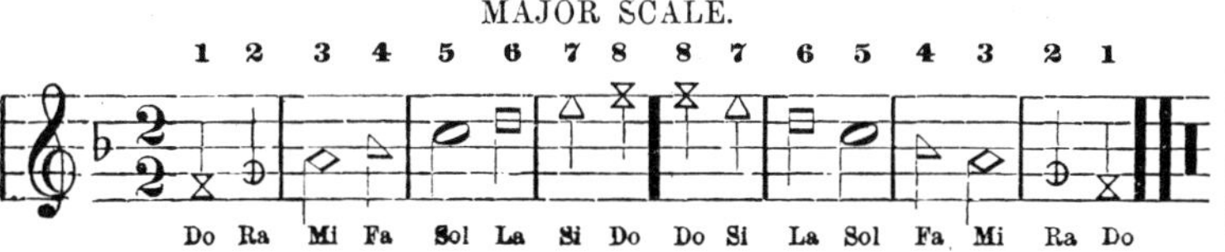

MINOR SCALE.

NOTE.—The small letters under notes, above, show the beats: d, down; l, left; r, right; u, up.

THE

NEW HARP OF COLUMBIA.

PART I.

CONTAINING TUNES USED IN CHURCH SERVICE.

OLD HUNDRED. L. M.

M. LUTHER.

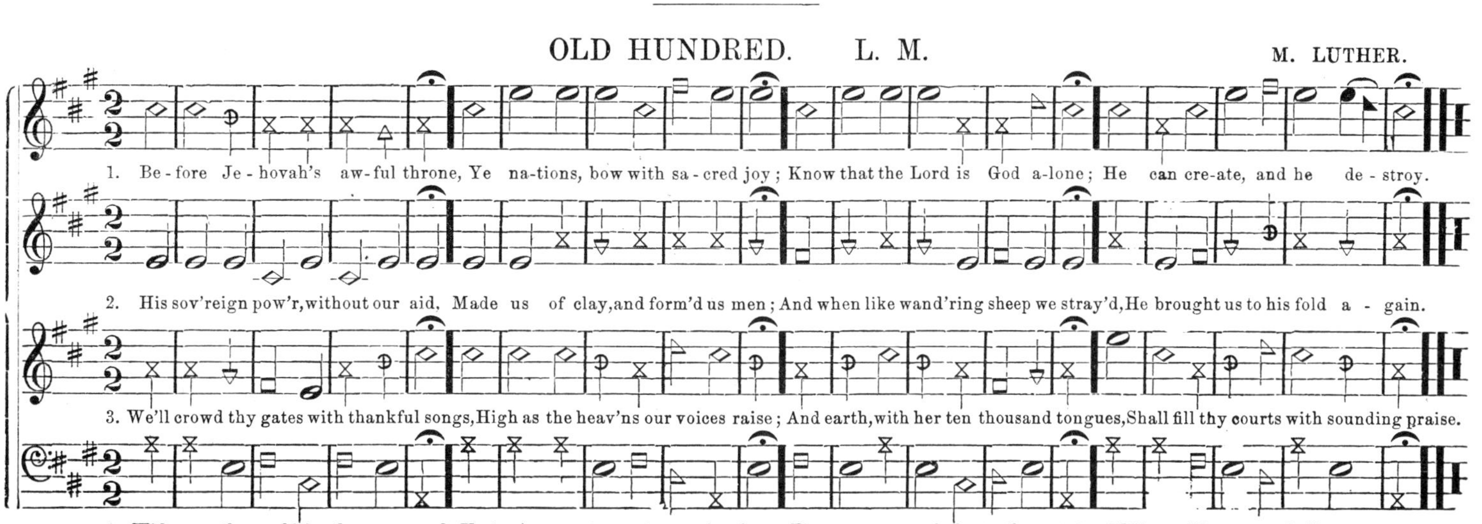

ALBION. S. M.

BOYD

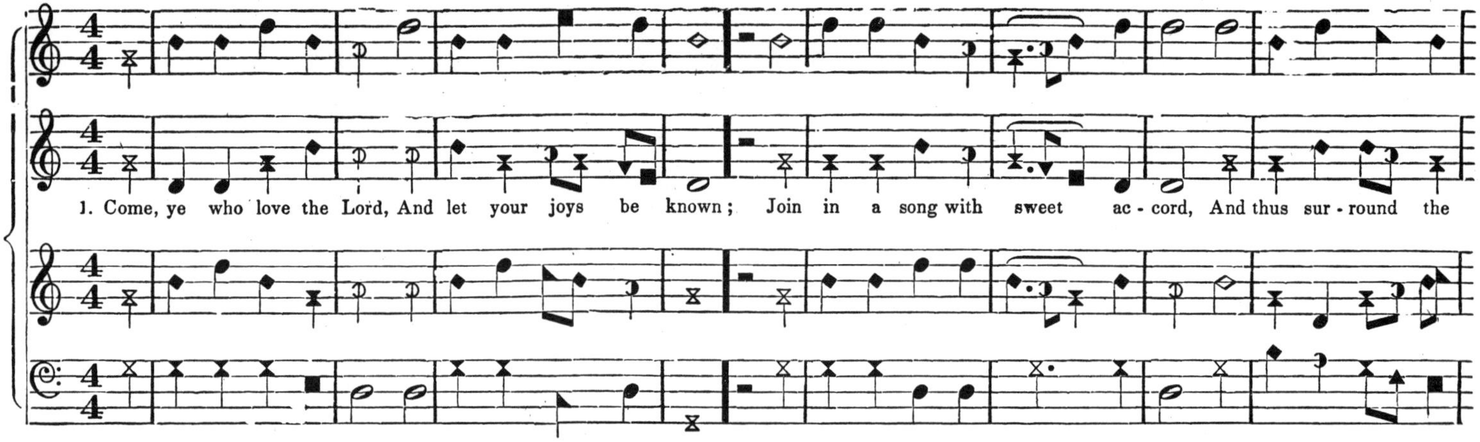

1. Come, ye who love the Lord, And let your joys be known; Join in a song with sweet ac - cord, And thus sur - round the

throne, And thus sur - round the throne.

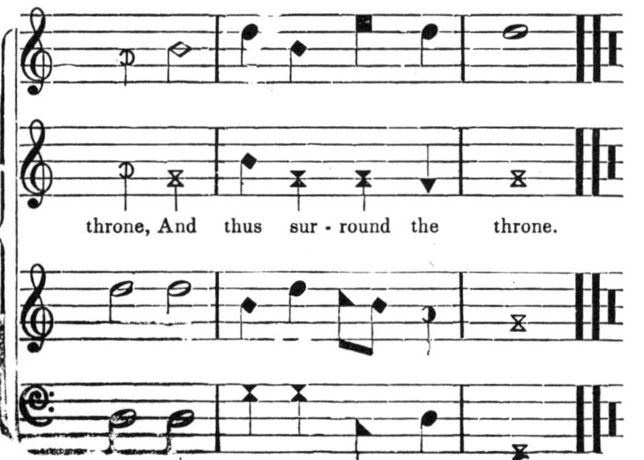

2.

Let those refuse to sing,
Who never knew our God;
But servants of the heavenly King
Should speak their joys abroad.

3.

The men of grace have found
Glory begun below;
Celestial fruits on earthly ground,
From faith and hope may grow.

4.

The hill of Zion yields
A thousand sacred sweets,
Before we reach the heavenly fields
Or walk the golden streets.

5.

Then let our songs abound,
And every tear be dry;
We're marching through Immanuel's ground
To fairer worlds on high.

REFLECTION. C. M.

DAVISSON.

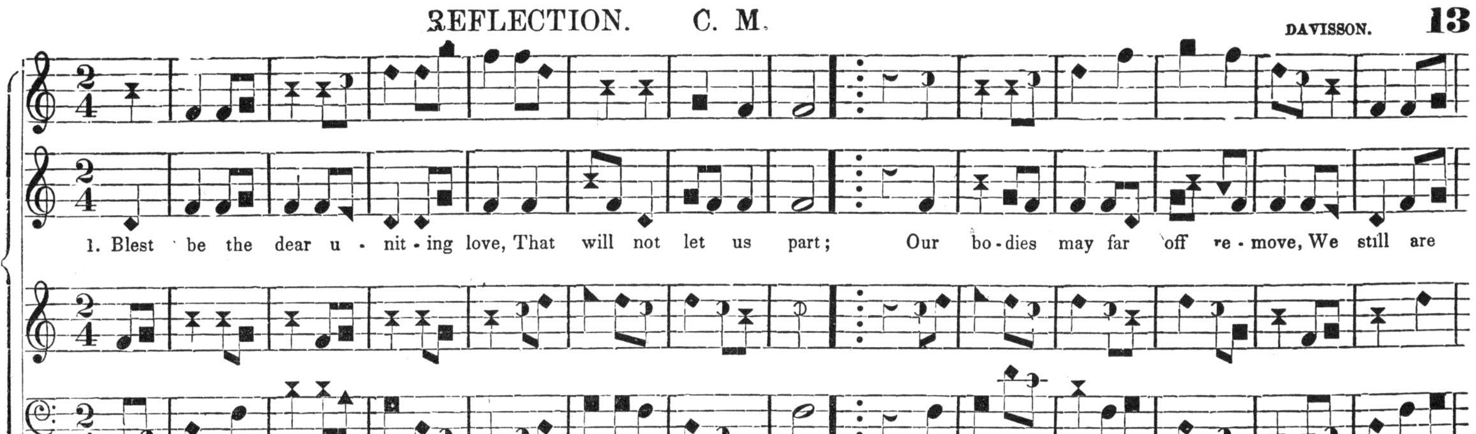

2. Join'd in one spirit to our Head,
Where he appoints we go;
And still in Jesus' footsteps tread,
And show his praise below.

3. O may we ever walk in him,
And nothing know beside,
Nothing desire, nothing esteem,
But Jesus crucified!

4. Closer and closer let us cleave
To his beloved embrace:
Expect his fulness to receive,
And grace to answer grace.

5. Partakers of the Saviour's grace,
The same in mind and heart,
Nor joy, nor grief, nor time, nor place,
Nor life, nor death can part.

6. But let us hasten to the day,
Which shall our flesh restore;
When death shall all be done away,
And bodies part no more.

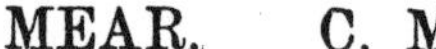

MEAR. C. M.

BROWN.

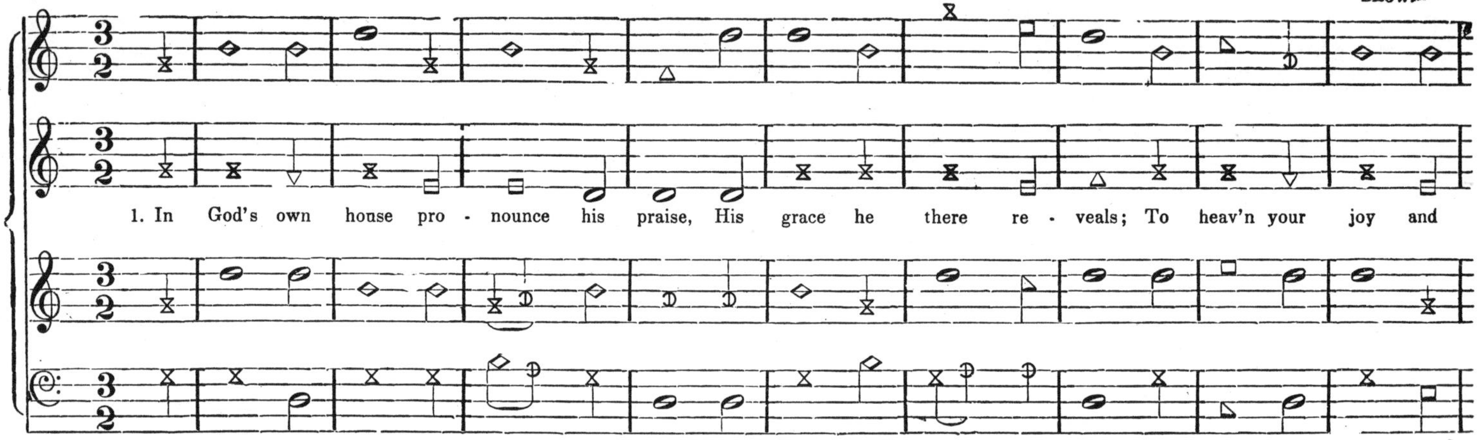

1. In God's own house pro - nounce his praise, His grace he there re - veals; To heav'n your joy and

won - der raise, For there his glo - ry dwells.

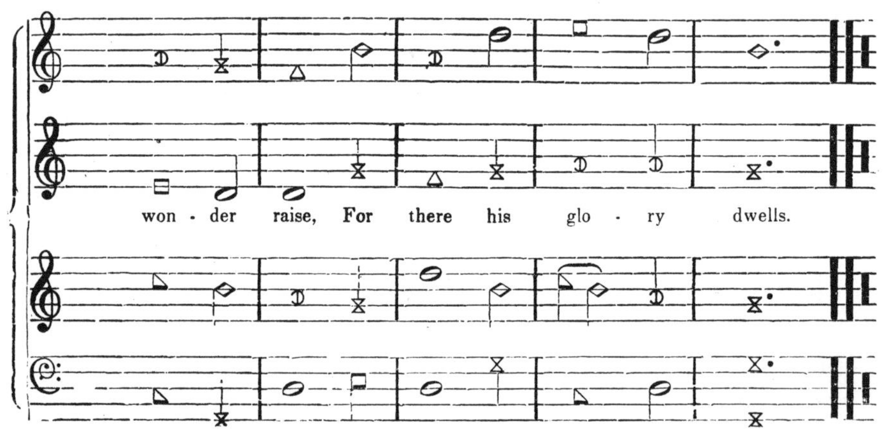

2.

Let all your sacred passions move,
While you rehearse his deeds
But the great work of saving love
Your highest praise exceeds.

3.

All that have motion, life, and breath,
Proclaim your Maker blessed;
Yet, when my voice expires in death,
My soul shall praise him best.

Counter by M. L. Swan.

PROSPECT. L. M

GRAHAM.

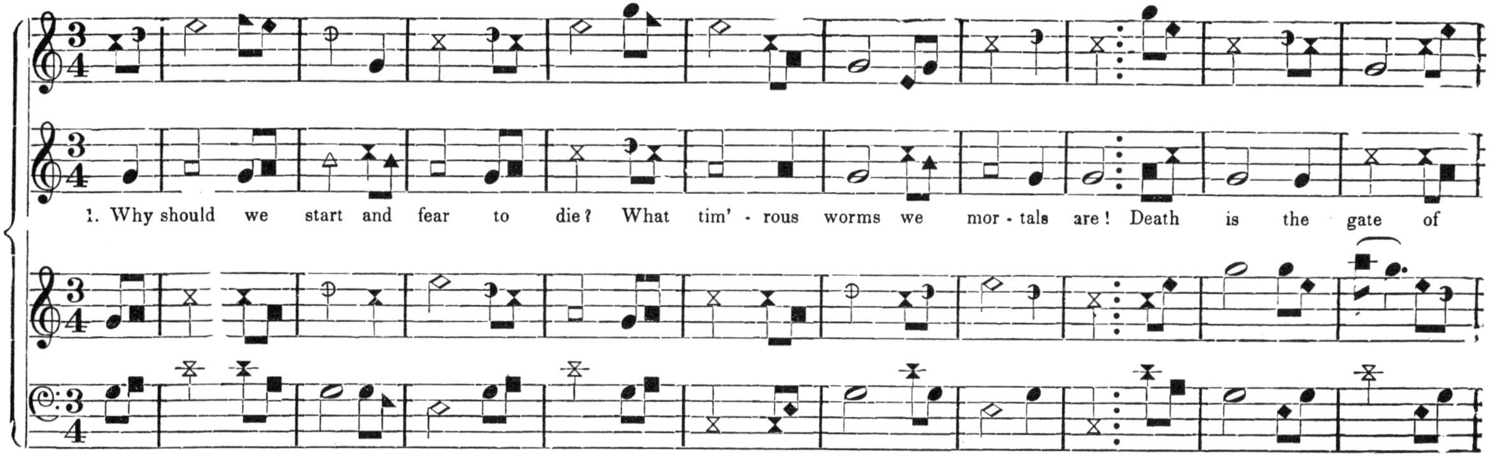

1. Why should we start and fear to die? What tim' - rous worms we mor - tals are! Death is the gate of

end - less joy, And yet we dread to en - ter there.

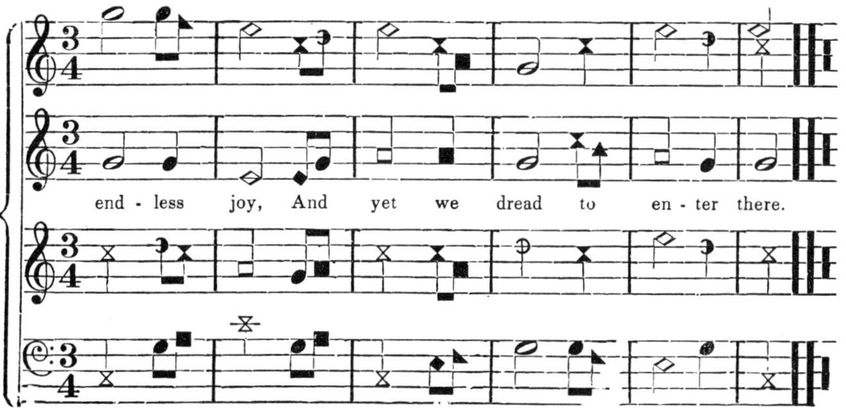

2. The pains, the groans, and dying strife,
Fright our approaching souls away;
Still we shrink back again to life,
Fond of our prison and our clay.

3. Oh! if my Lord would come and meet,
My soul would stretch her wings in haste;
Fly fearless through death's iron gate,
Nor feel the terrors as she passed.

4. Jesus can make a dying bed
Feel soft as downy pillows are,
While on his breast I lean my head,
And breathe my life out sweetly there.

GREENFIELDS.

EDSON.

1. How tedious and tasteless the hours, When Jesus no longer I see;
Sweet prospects, sweet birds, and sweet flow'rs,
Have lost all their sweetness to me:
The midsummer sun shines but dim, But
The fields strive in vain to look gay;

2. His name yields the richest perfume,
And sweeter than music his voice;
His presence disperses my gloom,
And makes all within me rejoice,
I should, were he always thus nigh,
Have nothing to wish or to fear;
No mortal so happy as I,
My summer would last all the year.

3. Content with beholding his face,
My all to his pleasure resigned;
No changes of season or place
Would make any change in my mind.
While blessed with a sense of his love,
A palace a toy would appear;
And prisons would palaces prove,
If Jesus would dwell with me there

4. Dear Lord, if indeed I am thine,
If thou art my sun and my song,
Say, why do I languish and pine?
And why are my winters so long?
O drive these dark clouds from my sky,
Thy soul-cheering presence restore;
Or take me to thee up on high,
Where winter and clouds are no more

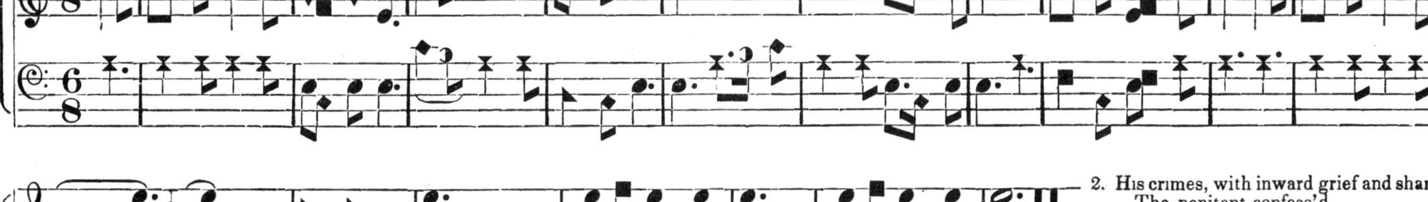

side, . . That languish'd at his side. He pour'd sal - va - tion on a wretch, That languish'd at his side.

2. His crimes, with inward grief and shame,
The penitent confess'd,
Then turn'd his dying eyes to Christ,
And thus his prayer address'd:.

3. "Yet quickly from these scenes of wo,
In triumph thou shalt rise,
Burst through the gloomy shades of death
And shine above the skies."

4. This prayer the dying Jesus heard,
And instantly replies,
"To-day thy parting soul shall be
With me in paradise."

5. Jesus, thou Son and heir of Heaven,
Thou spotless Lamb of God,
I see thee bathed in sweat and tears,
And weltering in thy blood.

6. Amid the glories of that world,
Dear Saviour, think on me,
And in the vict'ries of thy death
Let me a sharer be.

WINDHAM. L. M

LEED.

2. "Deny thyself, and take thy cross,"
Is the Redeemer's great command!
Nature must count her gold but dross,
If she would gain the heavenly land.

3. The fearful soul, that tires and faints,
And walks the ways of God no more,
Is but esteem'd almost a saint,
And makes his own destruction sure.

4. Lord, let not all my hopes be vain.
Create my heart entirely new ;
Which hypocrites could ne'er attain,
Which false apostates never knew.

WELLS. L. M.

HOLDRAD.

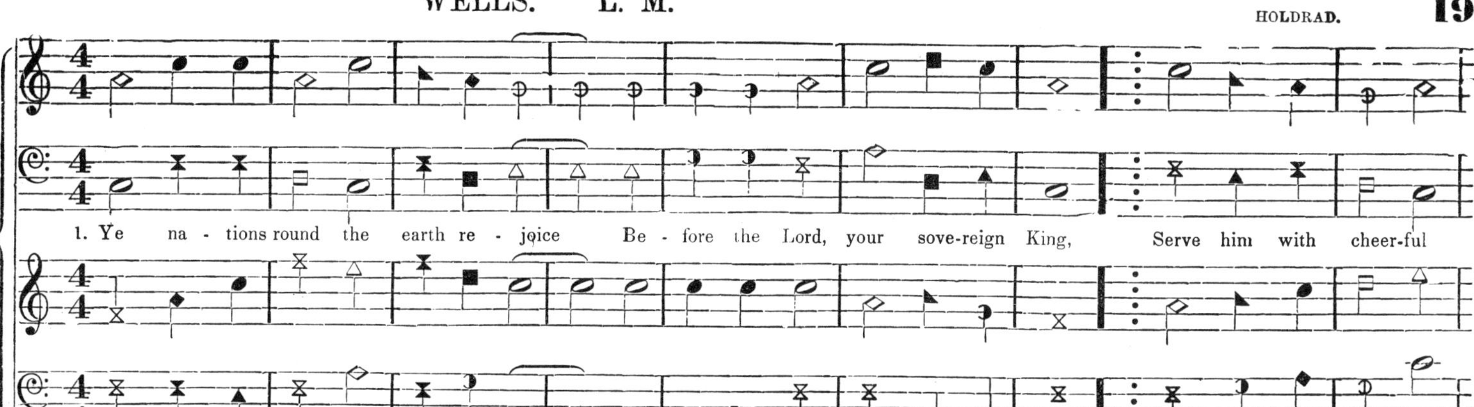

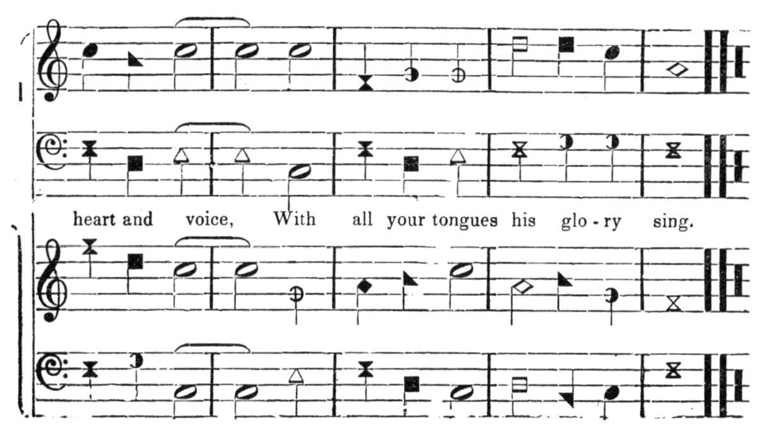

2. The Lord is God, 'tis he alone,
Doth life, and breath, and being give;
We are his work and not our own,
The sheep that on his pasture live.

3. Enter his gates with songs of joy,
With praises to his courts repair,
And make it your divine employ,
To pay your thanks and honors there.

4. The Lord is good, the Lord is kind,
Great is his grace, his mercy sure;
And the whole race of man shall find
His truth from age to age endure.

UXBRIDGE. L. M.

L. MASON.

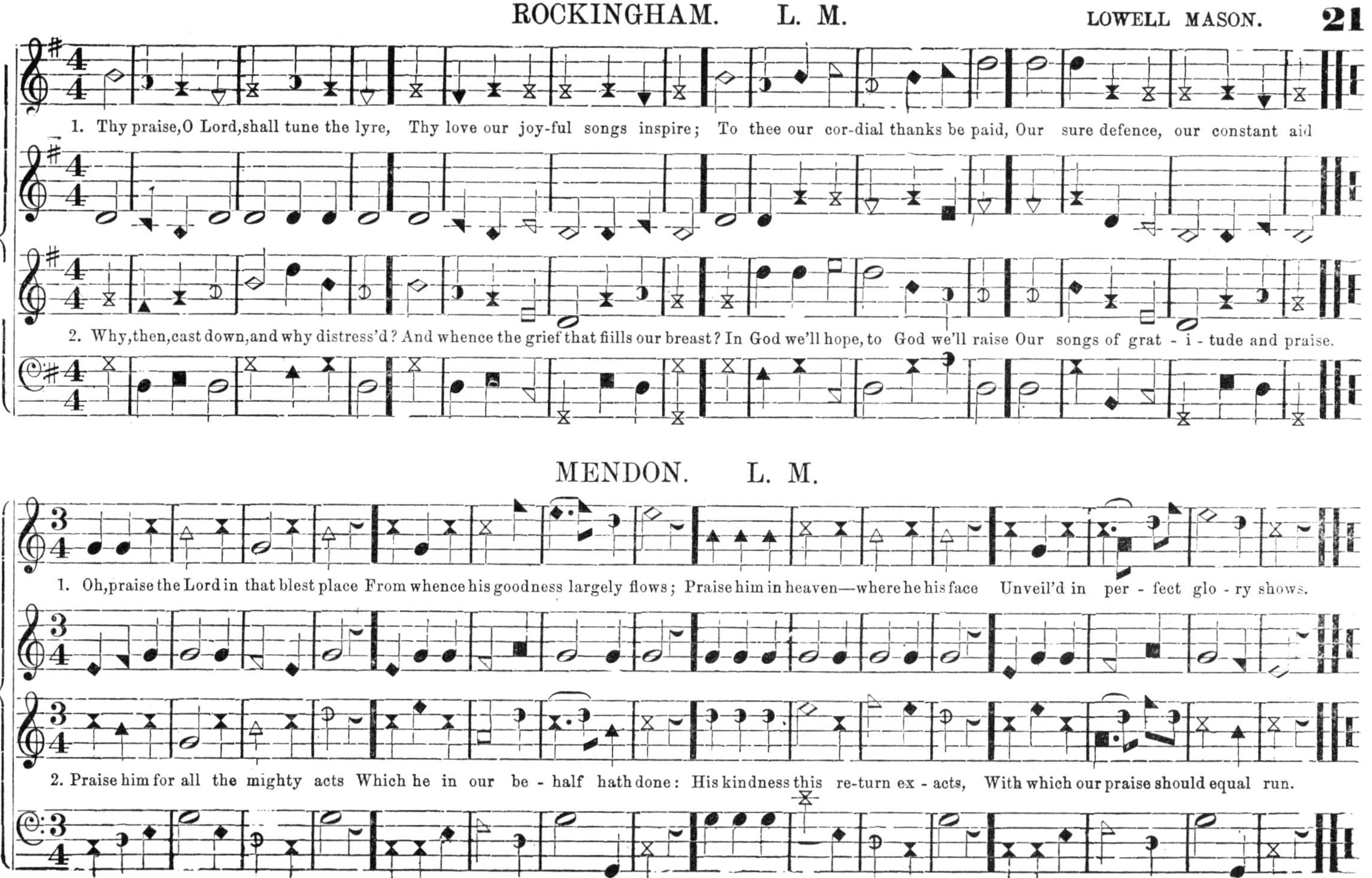
ROCKINGHAM. L. M.
LOWELL MASON.
1. Thy praise, O Lord, shall tune the lyre, Thy love our joy-ful songs inspire; To thee our cor-dial thanks be paid, Our sure defence, our constant aid
2. Why, then, cast down, and why distress'd? And whence the grief that fills our breast? In God we'll hope, to God we'll raise Our songs of grat - i - tude and praise.
MENDON. L. M.
1. Oh, praise the Lord in that blest place From whence his goodness largely flows; Praise him in heaven—where he his face Unveil'd in per - fect glo - ry shows.
2. Praise him for all the mighty acts Which he in our be - half hath done: His kindness this re-turn ex - acts, With which our praise should equal run.

MISSIONARY CHANT. L. M.
1. Ye Christian heroes, go pro-claim Sal - vation in Im-manuel's name; To distant climes the tidings bear, And plant the rose of Sha - ron there.
2. He'll shield you with a wall of fire, With ho - ly zeal your hearts in-spire, Bid raging winds their fu-ry cease, And calm the savage breast to peace.
ORFORD. L. M.
1. How sweet the light of Sabbath eve, How soft the sunbeams ling'ring there! For these blest hours the world I leave, Waft - ed on wings of praise and pray'r.
2. The time how lonely and how still! Peace shines and smiles on all below: The plain, the stream, the wood, the hill, All fair with evening's setting glow.

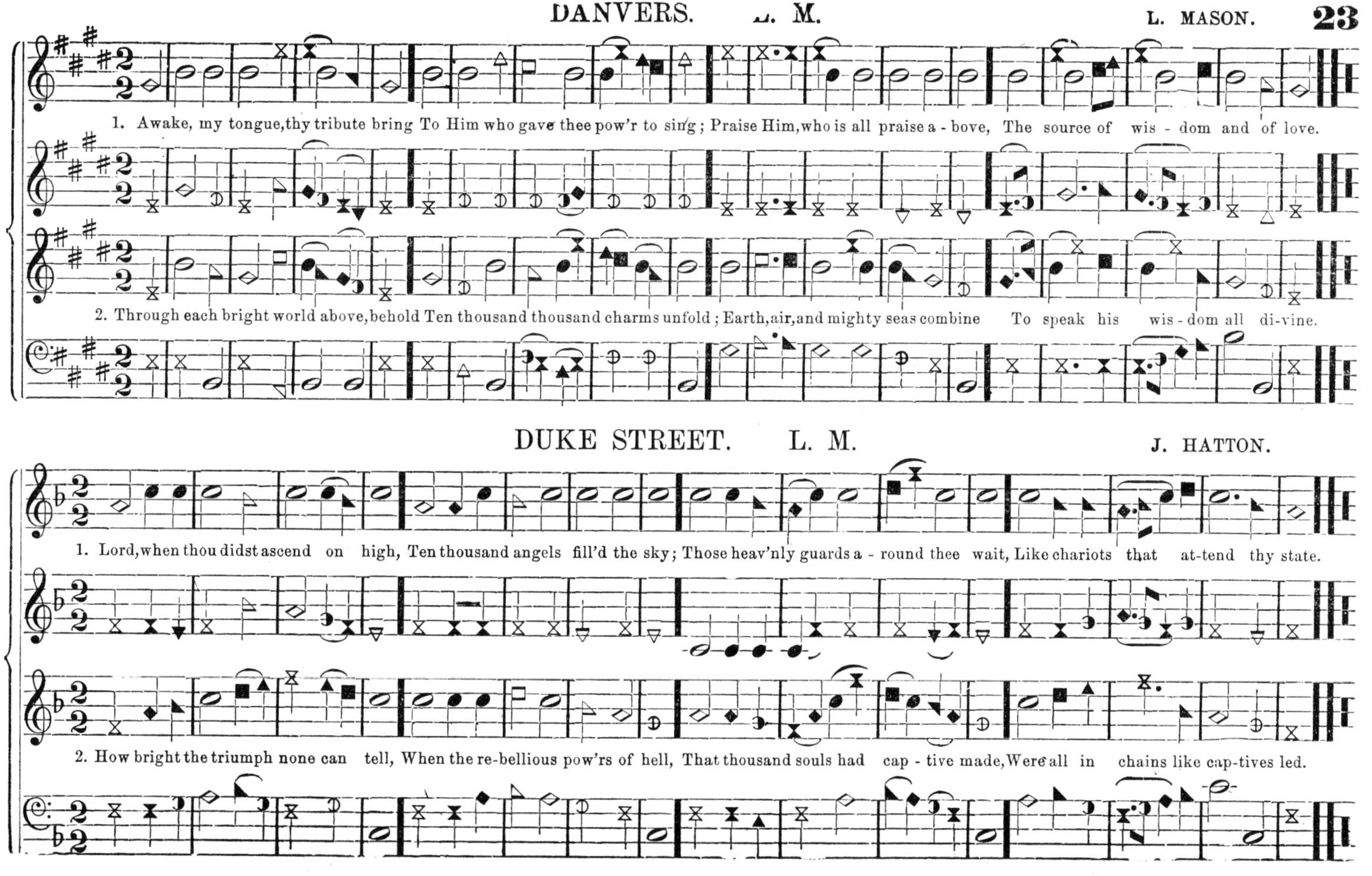
DANVERS. L. M.
L. MASON.
1. Awake, my tongue, thy tribute bring To Him who gave thee pow'r to sing; Praise Him, who is all praise a - bove, The source of wis - dom and of love.
2. Through each bright world above, behold Ten thousand thousand charms unfold; Earth, air, and mighty seas combine To speak his wis - dom all di-vine.
DUKE STREET. L. M.
J. HATTON.
1. Lord, when thou didst ascend on high, Ten thousand angels fill'd the sky; Those heav'nly guards a - round thee wait, Like chariots that at-tend thy state.
2. How bright the triumph none can tell, When the re-bellious pow'rs of hell, That thousand souls had cap - tive made, Were all in chains like cap-tives led.

SALVATION. C. M.

BOYD.

3.

"Prostrate I'll lie before his throne,
And there my guilt confess;
I'll tell him I'm a wretch undone,
Without his sov'reign grace.

4.

"But should the Lord reject my plea,
And disregard my pray'r,
Yet still, like Esther, I will stay,
And perish only there.

5.

"I can but perish if I go—
I am resolved to try;
For if I stay away, I know
I must for ever die.

6.

"But should I die with mercy sought,
When I the King have tried:
I there should die, (delightful thought!)
Where ne'er a sinner died."

NINETY-THIRD. S. M.

CHAPIN.

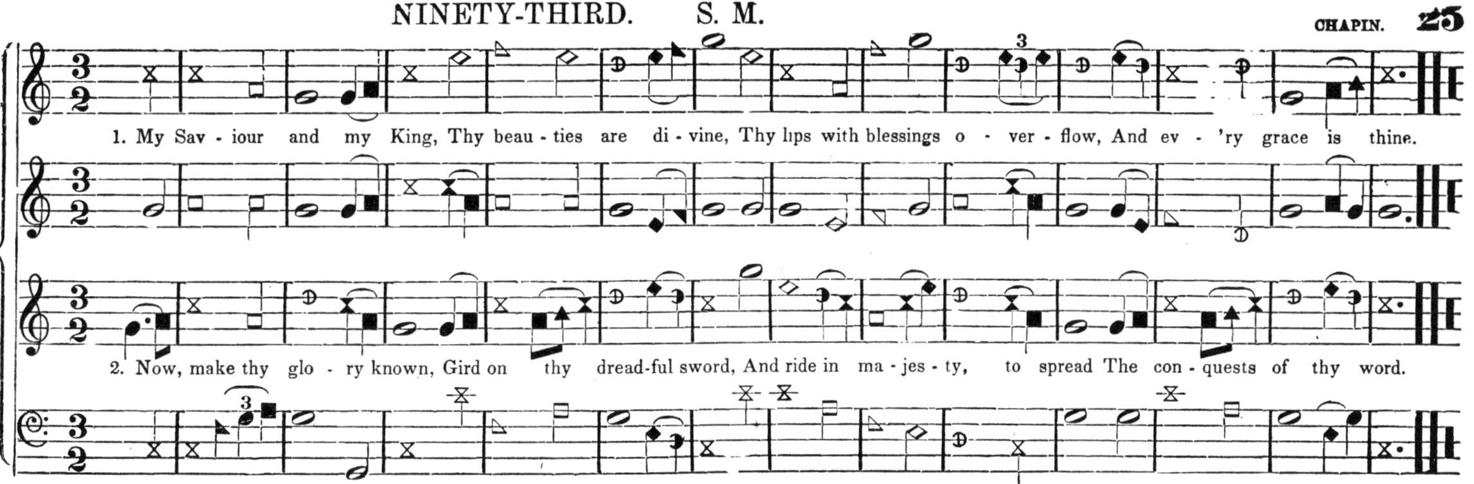

3. Strike through thy stubborn foes,
 Or make their hearts obey,
While justice, meekness, grace, and truth,
 Attend thy glorious way.

4. Thy laws, O God, are right,
 Thy throne shall ever stand;
And thy victorious gospel prove
 A sceptre in thy hand.

5. [Thy Father and thy God
 Hath, without measure, shed
His Spirit, like a grateful oil,
 T'anoint thy sacred head.

6. Behold, at thy right hand,
 The Gentile church is seen,
A beauteous bride, in rich attire,
 And princes guard the queen.]

7. Fair bride, receive his love,
 Forget thy Father's house,
Forsake thy gods, thy idol gods
 And pay the Lord thy vows.

8. O let thy God and King
 Thy sweetest thoughts employ;
Thy children shall his honour sing,
 And taste the heavenly joy.

ERIN. C. M.

SWAN.

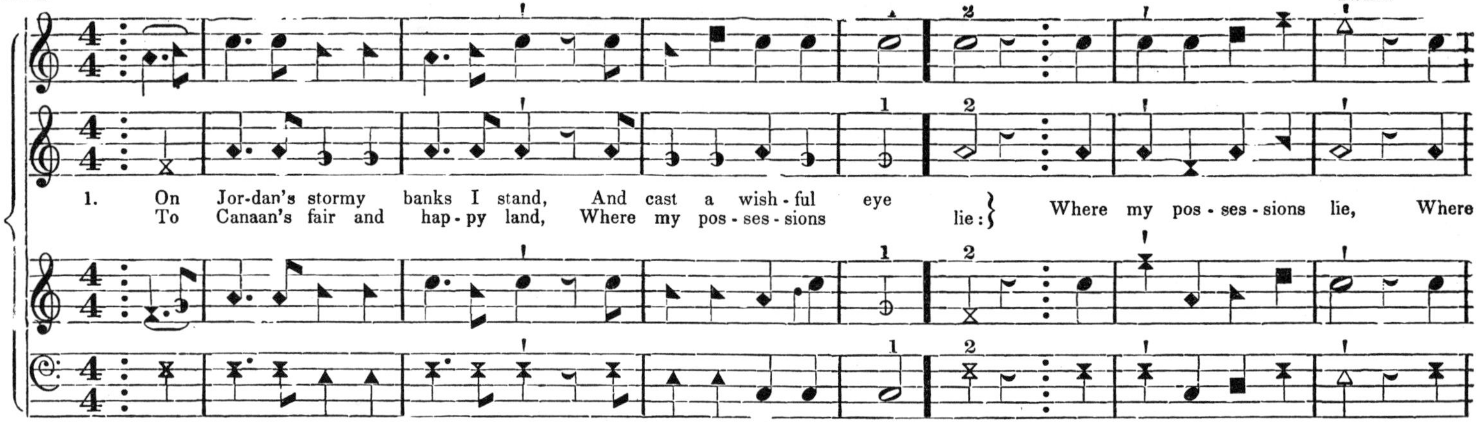

1. On Jor-dan's stormy banks I stand, And cast a wish - ful eye
To Canaan's fair and hap - py land, Where my pos - ses - sions lie: } Where my pos - ses - sions lie, Where

2. Oh! the transporting, rapturous scene
That rises to my sight!
Sweet fields array'd in living green,
And rivers of delight!

3. On all those wide-extended plains
Shines one eternal day;
There God the Son for ever reigns,
And scatters night away.

4. No chilling winds, nor poisonous breath,
Can reach that healthful shore;
Sickness and sorrow, pain and death,
Are felt and feared no more!

5. When shall I reach that happy place
And be for ever blest?
When shall I see my Father's face,
And in his bosom rest?

THEY THAT CONQUER. 7s
SWAN.
Je-sus, Mas-ter, hear me now, While I would re - new my vow, And re-cord thy dy - ing love,—Hear and help me from a - bove.
CHORAL SONG. 7s.
SWAN.
Swell the an - them, raise the song, Prais-es to our God be - long; Saints and angels join to sing, Praise to heaven's al - migh - ty King.

LOVING-KINDNESS. L. M.

1. Awake, my soul, to joy-ful lays, And sing the great Redeemer's praise; He justly claims a song from me; His lov - ing-kind - ness, oh, how free! His loving-kindness, loving-kindness, His

2. He saw me ru - in'd in the fall, Yet loved me not-withstanding all; He saved me from my lost estate: His lov-ing-kindness, oh, how great! His loving-kindness, loving-kindness, His

lov-ing-kindness, oh, how free!

loving-kindness, oh, how great!

MAYSVILLE. L. M. (6 Lines.)

1. { Father of mer-cies, God of love! Oh, hear an humble suppliant's cry; / Bend from thy lofty seat a - bove, Thy throne of glori - ous majes-ty: } Oh, deign to hear my mournful voice, And bid my drooping heart rejoice.

2. { I urge no merits of my own, No worth to claim thy gracious smile; / No! when I bow be - fore thy throne, Dare to converse with God a while, } Thy name, blest Jesus, is my plea, Dearest and sweetest name to me.

CONVOY. 7s.

SWAN.

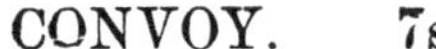

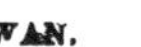

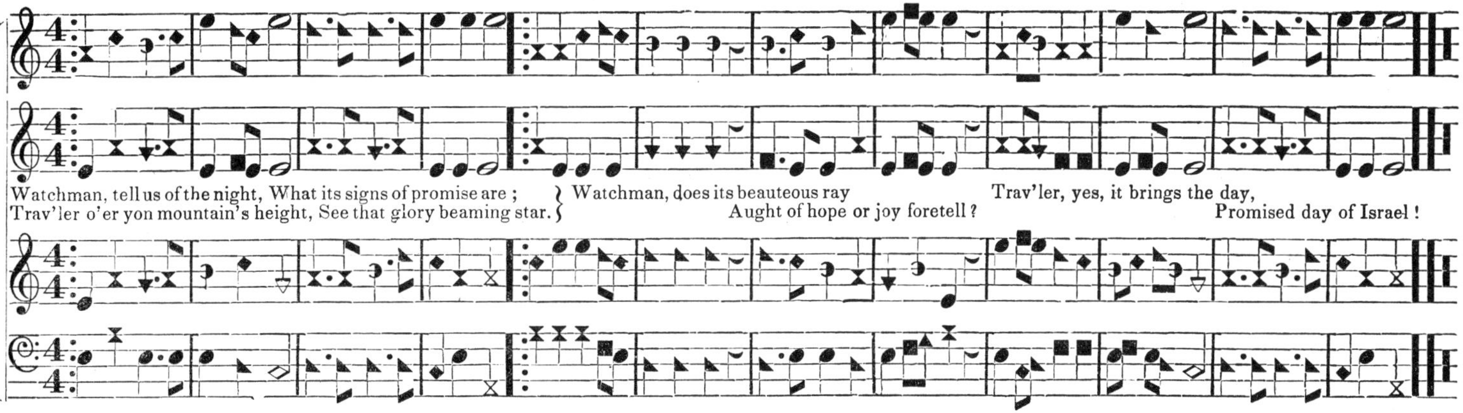

Watchman, tell us of the night, What its signs of promise are ;
Trav'ler o'er yon mountain's height, See that glory beaming star.
Watchman, does its beauteous ray
Aught of hope or joy foretell ?
Trav'ler, yes, it brings the day,
Promised day of Israel !

COME, YE DISCONSOLATE!

SWAN.

Come, ye disconsolate, where'er ye languish,
Come to the mercy-seat, fervently kneel :
Here bring your wounded hearts, here tell your anguish,
Earth has no sorrows that heaven cannot heal.

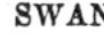

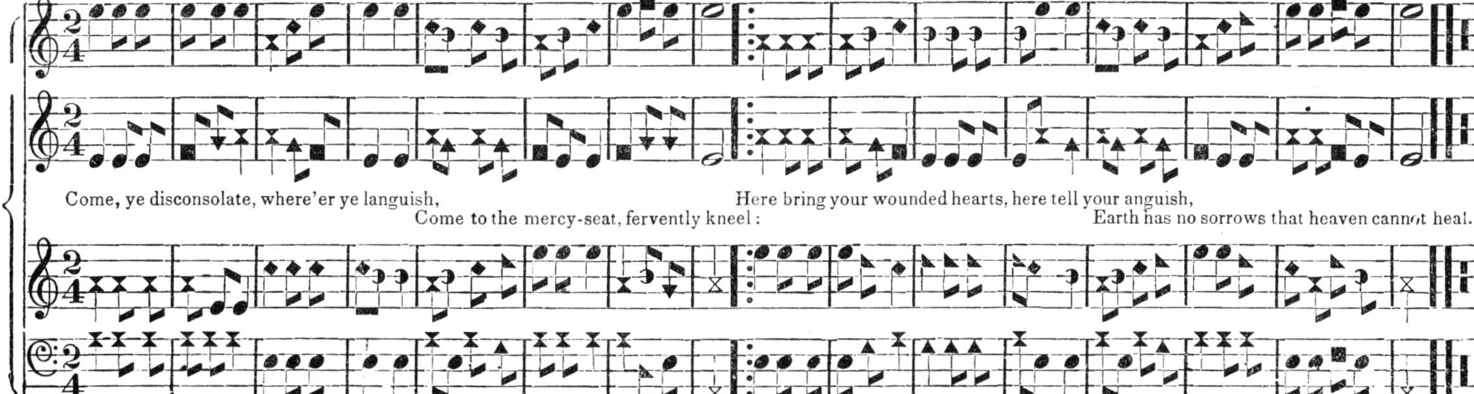

SION'S SECURITY. 8s & 7s

M. L. SWAN.

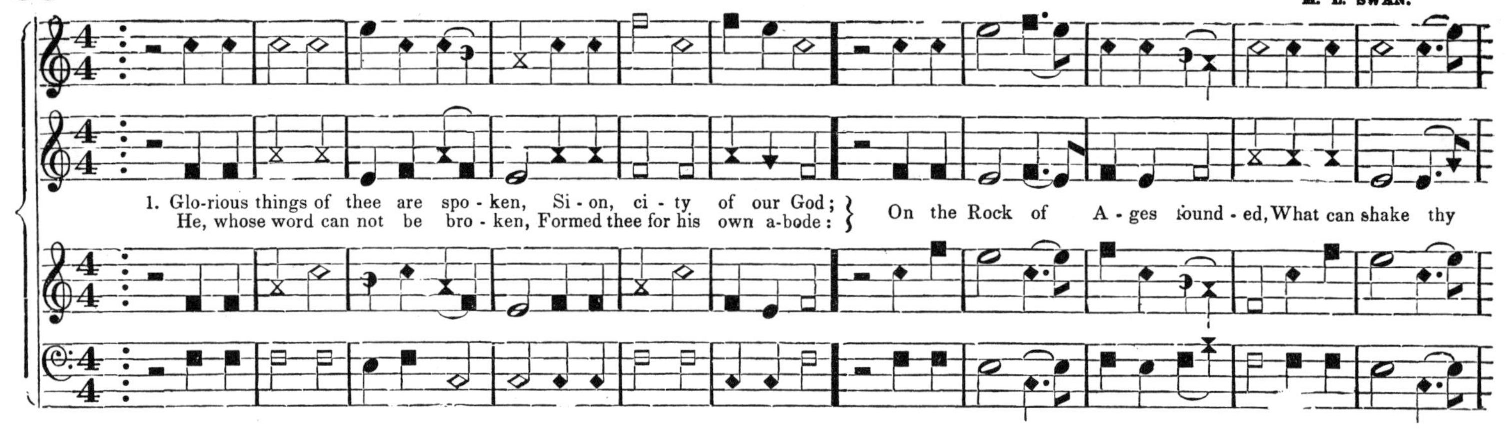

2. See the streams of living waters,
   Springing from eternal love,
Well supply thy sons and daughters,
   And all fear of want remove;
Who can faint while such a river
   Ever flows their thirst t' assuage?
Grace which, like the Lord, the giver,
   Never fails from age to age.

3. Round each habitation hovering,
   See the cloud and fire appear,
For a glory and a covering,
   Showing that the Lord is near,
Thus deriving from their banner,
   Light by night, and shade by day;
Safe they feed upon the manna,
   Which He gives them when they pray.

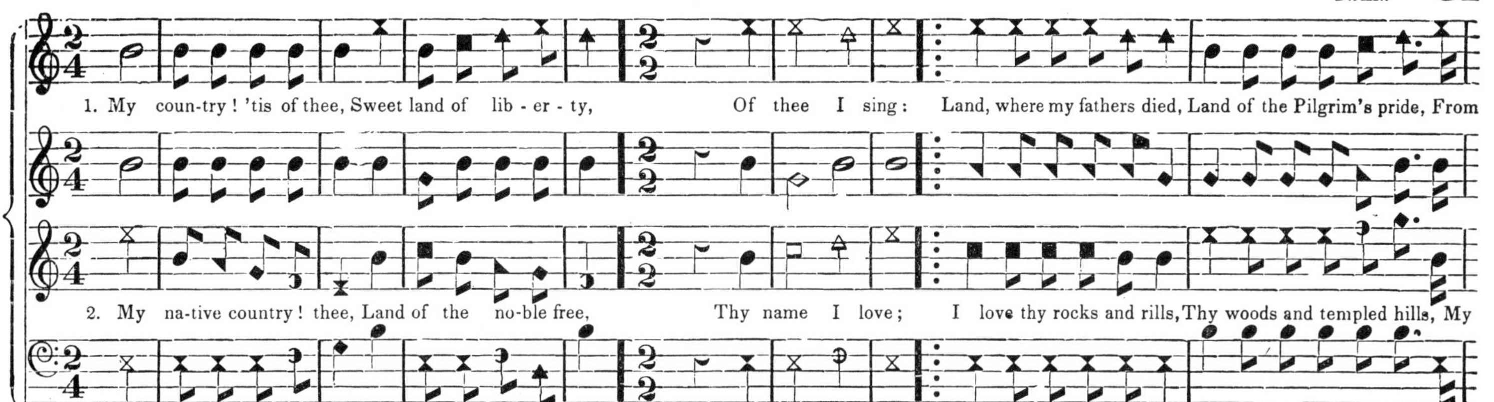

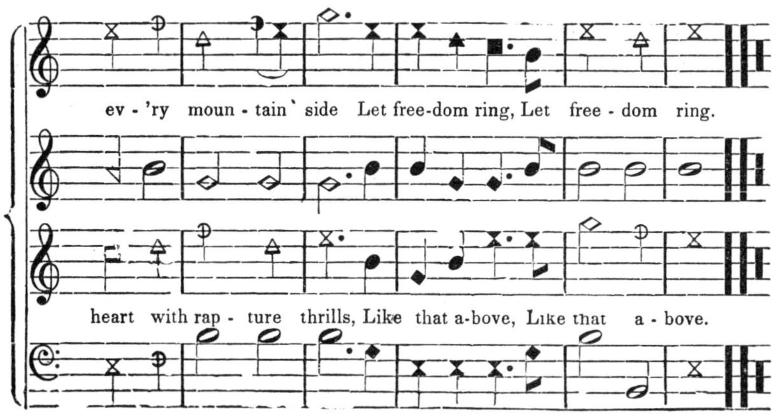

3. Let music swell the breeze,
And ring from all the trees,
Sweet freedom's song,
Let mortal tongues awake,
Let all that breathe partake
Let rocks their silence break,
The sound prolong.

4. Our fathers' God! to thee,
Author of liberty,
To thee we sing;
Long may our land be bright,
With freedom's holy light,
Protect us by thy might,
Great God, our king.

FAREWELL. C. M.

W. ATCHLEY.

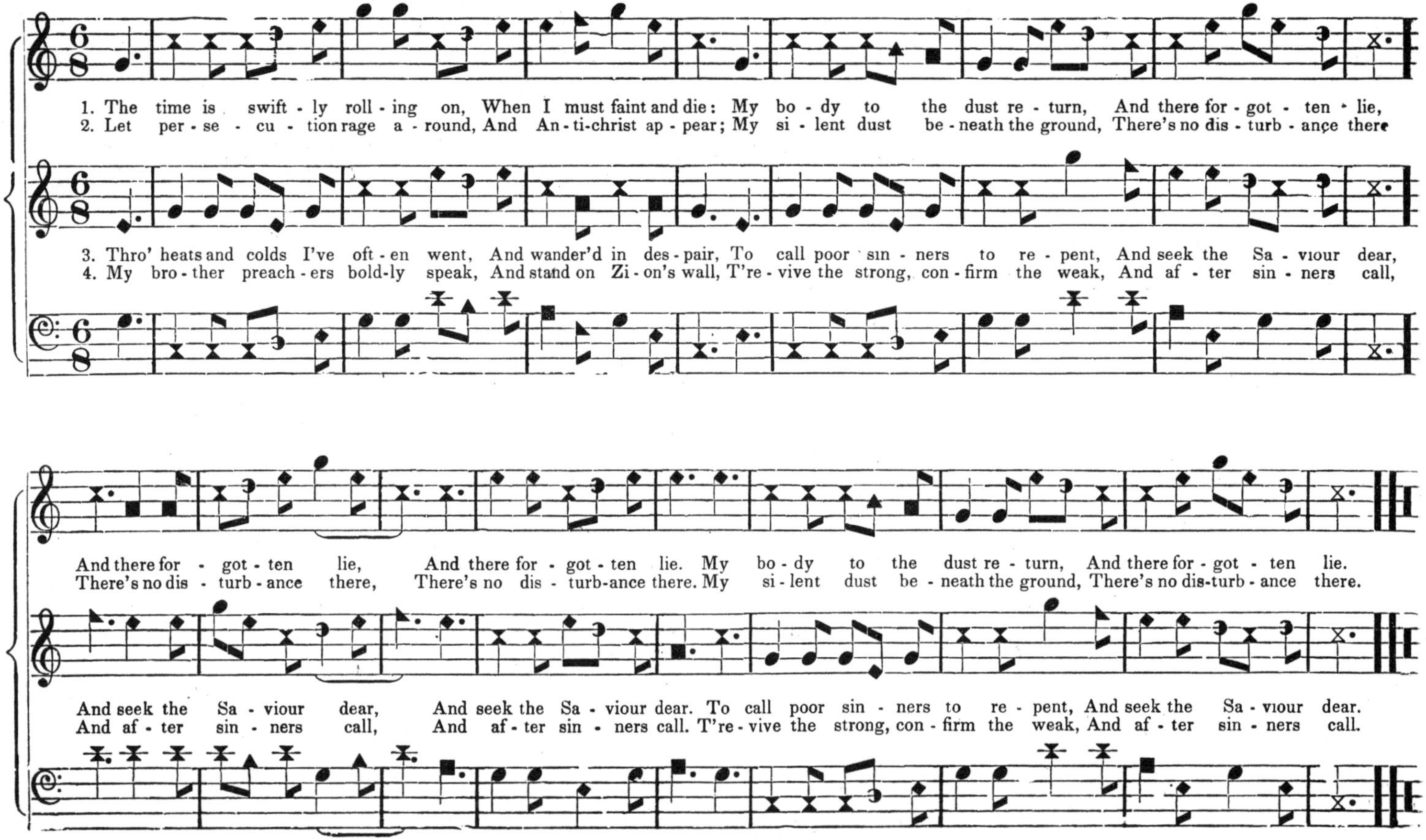

1. The time is swift - ly roll - ing on, When I must faint and die: My bo - dy to the dust re - turn, And there for - got - ten - lie,
2. Let per - se - cu - tion rage a - round, And An - ti-christ ap - pear; My si - lent dust be - neath the ground, There's no dis - turb - ance there

3. Thro' heats and colds I've oft - en went, And wander'd in des - pair, To call poor sin - ners to re - pent, And seek the Sa - viour dear,
4. My bro - ther preach - ers bold - ly speak, And stand on Zi - on's wall, T're - vive the strong, con - firm the weak, And af - ter sin - ners call,

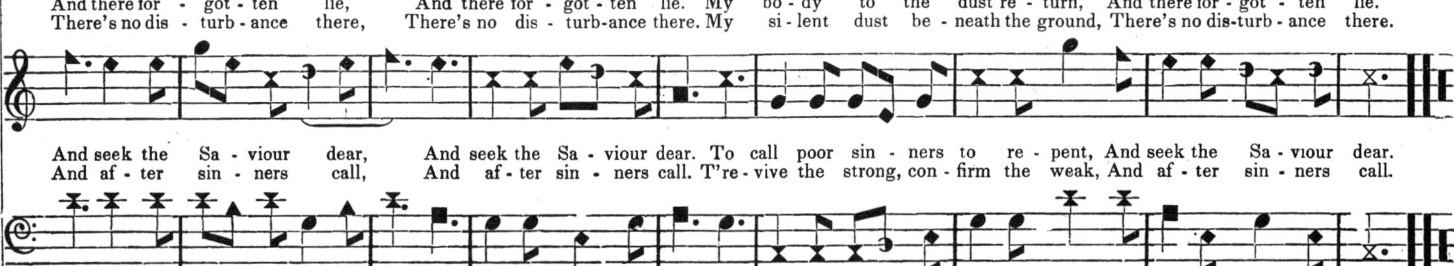

EBENEZER. C. M.

SWAN.

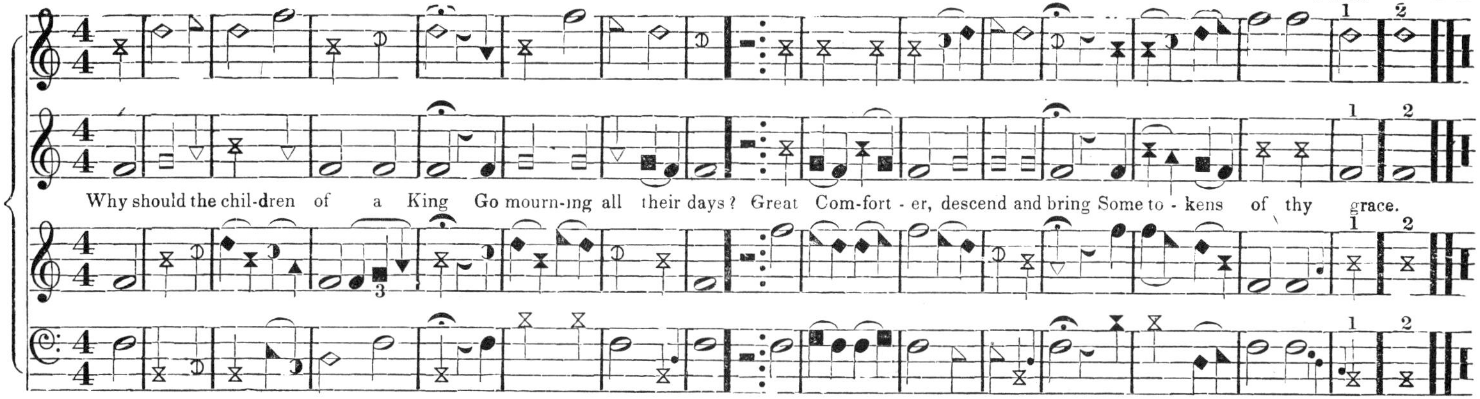

Why should the chil-dren of a King Go mourn-ing all their days? Great Com-fort-er, descend and bring Some to-kens of thy grace.

HOLSTON. C. M.

SWAN.

O for a thou-sand tongues to sing My dear Re-deem-er's praise; The glo-ries of my God and King, The tri-umphs of his grace.

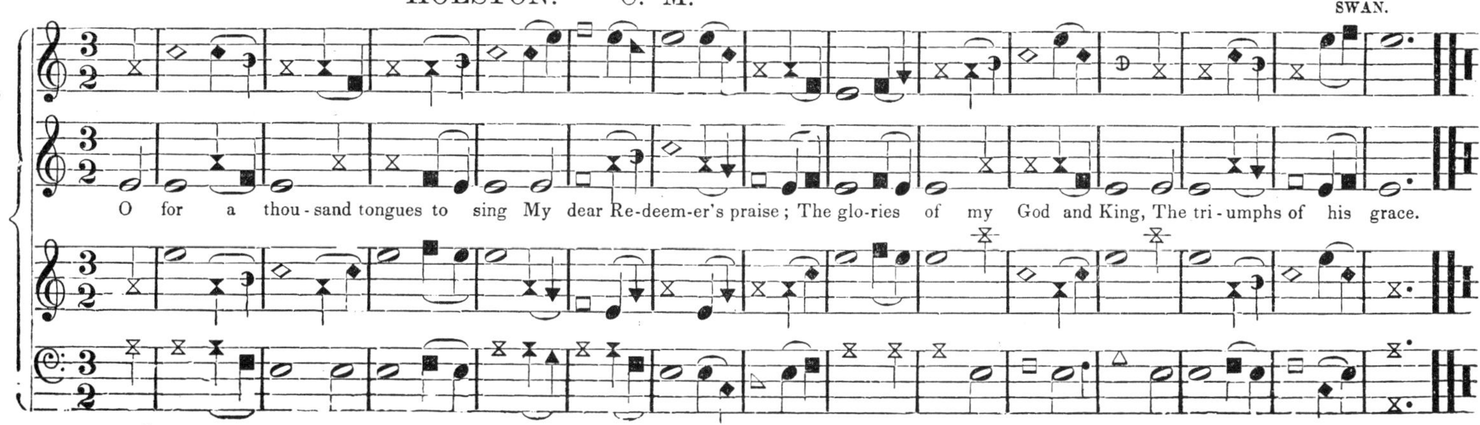

ANVERN. L. M.
Arranged from the German by L. MASON.
1. Tri-umphant Zi - on, lift thy head From dust and darkness and the dead! Tho'humbled long,a-wake at length,And gird thee with a Saviour's strength,And gird thee with a Saviour's strength.
2. Put all thy beauteous garments on,And let thy ex - cel-lence be known; Deck'd in the robes of righteousness, Thy glories shall the world confess,Thy glories shall the world confess.
MIGDOL. L. M.
L. MASON.
1. Soon may the last glad song a - rise Thro' all the mil - lions of the skies, That song of triumph which re-cords That all the earth is now the Lord's.
2. Let thrones and powers and kingdoms be O - be - dient, migh - ty God, to thee, And o - ver land and stream and main Now wave the scep - tre of thy reign.

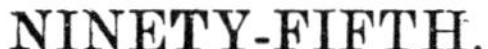

NINETY-FIFTH. C. M.

CHAPIN.

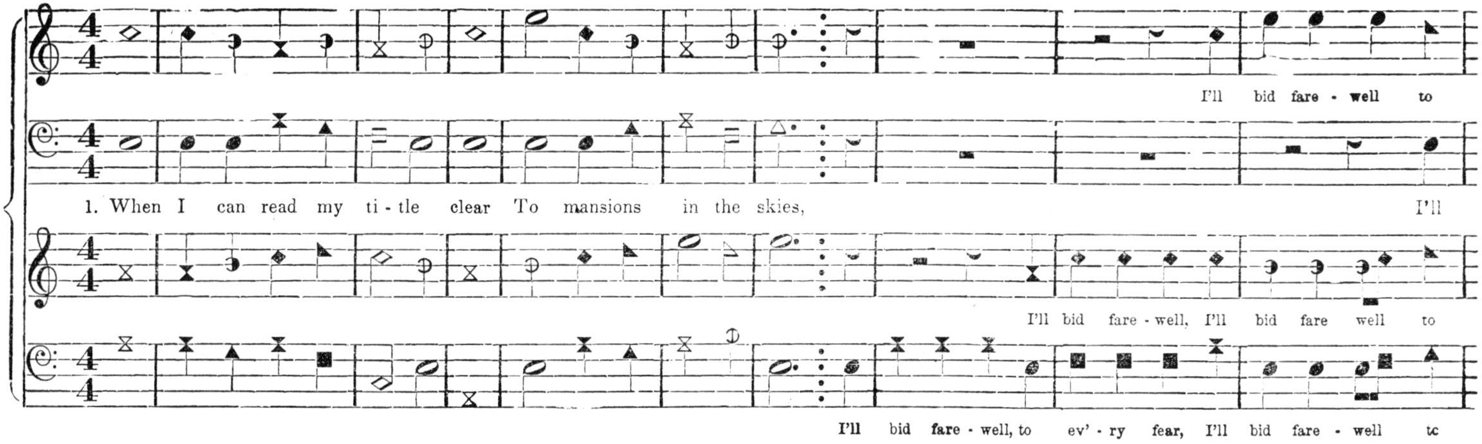

I'll bid fare - well to
1. When I can read my ti - tle clear To mansions in the skies, I'll
I'll bid fare - well, I'll bid fare well to
I'll bid fare - well, to ev' - ry fear, I'll bid fare - well tc

1 2
ev' - ry fear, and wipe . . my weeping eyes.
bid farewell to ev' - ry fear, And wipe my weep-ing eyes.
ev - ry fear, And wipe . . my weeping eyes.
ev' - ry fear, And wipe my weeping eyes

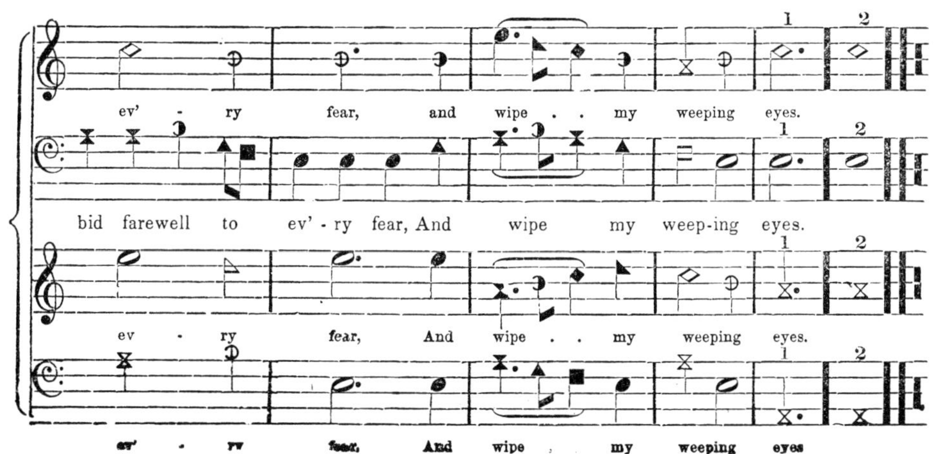

2. Should earth against my soul engage,
   And fiery darts be hurl'd,
Then I can smile at Satan's rage,
   And face a frowning world.

3. Let cares like a wild deluge come,
   And storms of sorrow fall;
May I but safely reach my home,
   My God, my heaven, my all.

4. There shall I bathe my weary soul,
   In seas of heavenly rest,
And not a wave of trouble roll
   Across my peaceful breast.

WATTS. L. M.
M. L. SWAN.
1. With - in thy house, O Lord our God, In glorious ma - jes - ty appear; Make this a place of thine abode, And shed thy choicest blessings here.
2. When we thy mer - cy - seat surround, Thy Spirit, Lord, to us impart; And let thy gospel's joy-ful sound With pow'r divine reach ev'-ry heart.
UPTON. L. M.
1. Bless, O my soul, the liv - ing God; Call home thy thoughts that roam abroad; Let all the pow'rs within me join In work and worship so di - vine.
2. Let ev' - ry land his pow'r con-fess, Let all the earth a - dore his grace; My heart and tongue with rapture join In work and worship so di - vine.

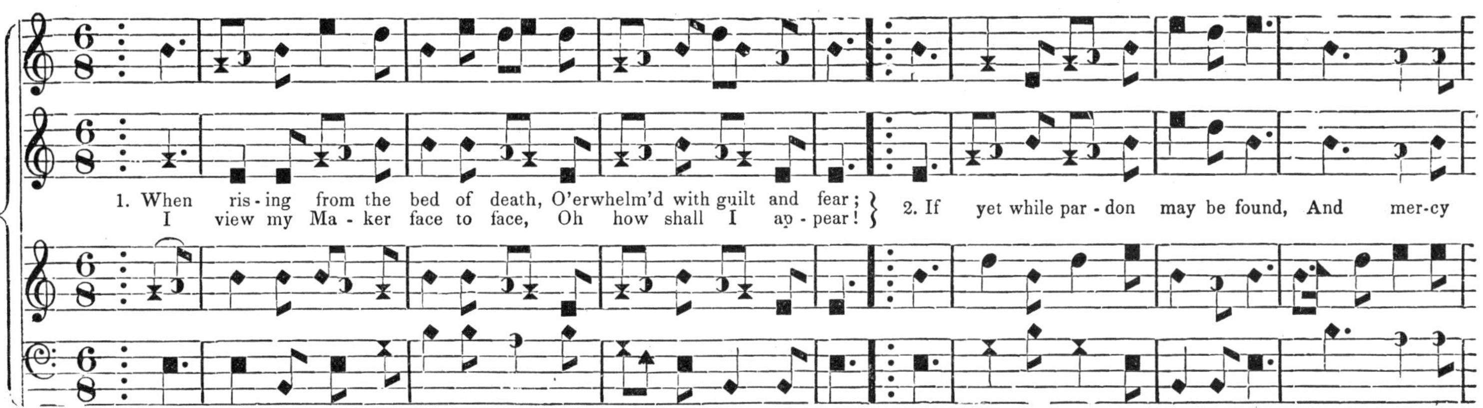

3. When thou, O Lord, shalt stand disclosed
   In majesty severe,
And sit in judgment on my soul,
   Oh how shall I appear!

4. Oh may my broken, contrite heart
   Timely my sins lament,
And early, with repentant tears,
   Eternal wo prevent.

5. Behold the sorrows of my heart,
   Ere yet it be too late:
And hear my Saviour's dying groan,
   To give those sorrows weight.

6. For never shall my soul despair
   Her pardon to secure,
Who knows thine only Son hath died
   To make that pardon sure.

BRADLEY. C. M

SWAN.

2. The little ants for one poor grain
Labour, and tug, and strive,
Yet we who have a heaven t' obtain,
How negligent we live!

3. We for whose sake all nature stands,
And stars their courses move;
We for whose guard the angel bands
Come flying from above;

4. We for whom God the Son came down,
And labour'd for our good,
How careless to secure that crown
He purchased with his blood!

5. Lord, shall we lie so sluggish still?
And never act our parts:
Come, holy Dove, from th' heavenly hill,
And sit and warm our hearts.

6. Then shall our active spirits move,
Upward our souls shall rise:
With hands of faith and wings of love,
We'll fly and take the prize.

CHINA. C. M.
SWAN.
Thee, we adore, E - ter - nal Name, And hum - bly own to thee How fee - ble is our mor - tal frame, What dy - ing worms we be!
ST. MARTINS. C. M.
TANSUR.
U - nite my rov - ing thoughts, u - nite, In si - lence soft and sweet, And thou, my soul, sit gent - ly down, At thy great Sovereign's feet.

2. Should earth against my soul engage,
And hellish darts be hurl'd,
Then I can smile at Satan's rage.
And face a frowning world.

3. Let cares like a wild deluge come
And storms of sorrow fall;
May I but safely reach my home,
My God, my heaven, my all.

4. There shall I bathe my weary soul
In seas of heavenly rest
And not a wave of trouble roll
Across my peaceful breast.

SUDBURY. L. M. 6 Lines.

LENOX. P. M

EDSON.

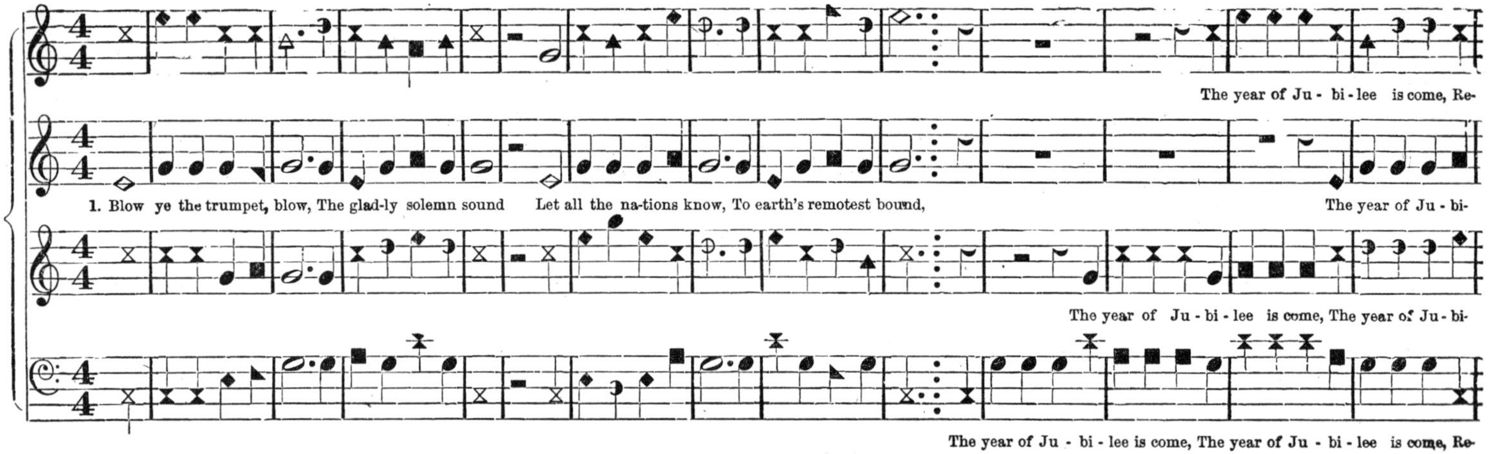

The year of Ju - bi - lee is come, Re-

1. Blow ye the trumpet, blow, The glad-ly solemn sound Let all the na-tions know, To earth's remotest bound, The year of Ju - bi-

The year of Ju - bi - lee is come, The year of Ju - bi-

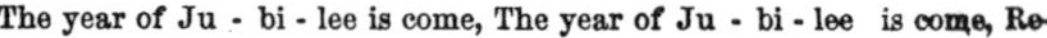

2. Jesus, our great High Priest,
Hath full atonement made;
Ye weary spirits, rest,
Ye mournful souls, be glad;
The year of Jubilee is come,
Return, ye ransom'd sinners, home.

3. Extol the Lamb of God,
The all-atoning Lamb;
Redemption in his blood,
Throughout the world proclaim;
The year of Jubilee is come,
Return, ye ransom'd sinners, home.

4. Ye who have sold for naught
Your heritage above,
Shall have it back unbought,
The gift of Jesus' love;
The year of Jubilee is come,
Return, ye ransom'd sinners, home.

5. The gospel trumpet hear,
The news of heavenly grace;
And, saved from earth, appear
Before your Saviour's face;
The year of Jubilee is come,
Return, ye ransom'd sinners, home

PLEASANT HILL. C. M

NICHOLSON.

1. And let this fee - ble bo-dy fail, And let it faint or die; }
My soul shall quit this mourn-ful vale, And soar to worlds on high; }
Shall join the dis - em - bo - died saints, And

2. In hope of that im - mor - tal crown, I now the cross sus - tain; }
And glad - ly wan - der up and down, And smile at toil and pain: }
I'll suf - fer on my three-score years, Till

3. Oh what hath Jesus bought for me
Before my ravish'd eyes,
Rivers of life divine I see,
And trees of Paradise!
I see a world of spirits bright,
Who taste the pleasures there!
They all are robed in spotless white,
And conquering palms they bear.

4. Oh what are all my sufferings here,
If, Lord, thou count me meet,
With that enraptured host t' appear,
And worship at thy feet!
Give joy or grief, give ease or pain
Take life or friends away:
But let me find them all again
In that eternal day.

IDUMEA. S. M.

DAVISSON.

2. Let those refuse to sing
Who never knew our God;
But servants of the heavenly King
May speak their joys abroad.

3. The God that rules on high,
That all the earth surveys,
That rides upon the stormy sky,
And calms the roaring seas;

4. This awful God is ours,
Our Father and our Love;
He will send down his heavenly powers
To carry us above.

5. There we shall see his face
And never, never sin,
There, from the rivers of his grace,
Drink endless pleasures in:

6. Yea, and before we rise
To that immortal state,
The thoughts of such amazing bliss
Should constant joys create.

7. The men of grace have found
Glory begun below:
Celestial fruit on earthly ground,
From faith and hope may grow;

8. Then let our songs abound,
And every tear be dry:
We're marching through Immanuel's ground,
To fairer worlds on high.

Counter by Swan. KEDRON. L. M DARE.

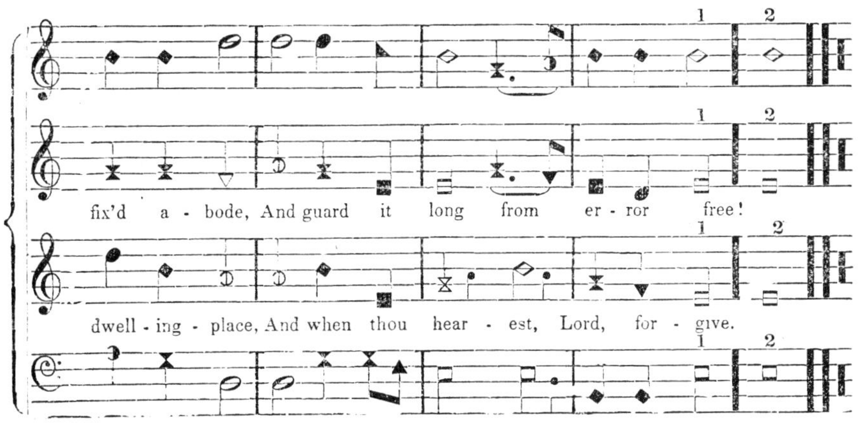

3. Here, when thy messengers proclaim
The blessed gospel of thy Son,
Still by the power of his great name
Be mighty signs and wonders done.

4. When children's voices raise the song,
Hosanna! to their heavenly King,
Let heaven with earth the strain prolong
Hosanna! let the angels sing.

5. But will, indeed, Jehovah deign
Here to abide, no transient guest!
Here will our great Redeemer reign,
And here the Holy Spirit rest?

6. Thy glory never hence depart,
Yet choose not, Lord, this house alone;
Thy kingdom come to every heart
In every bosom fix thy throne.

CONCORD. P. M.

CALDWELL.

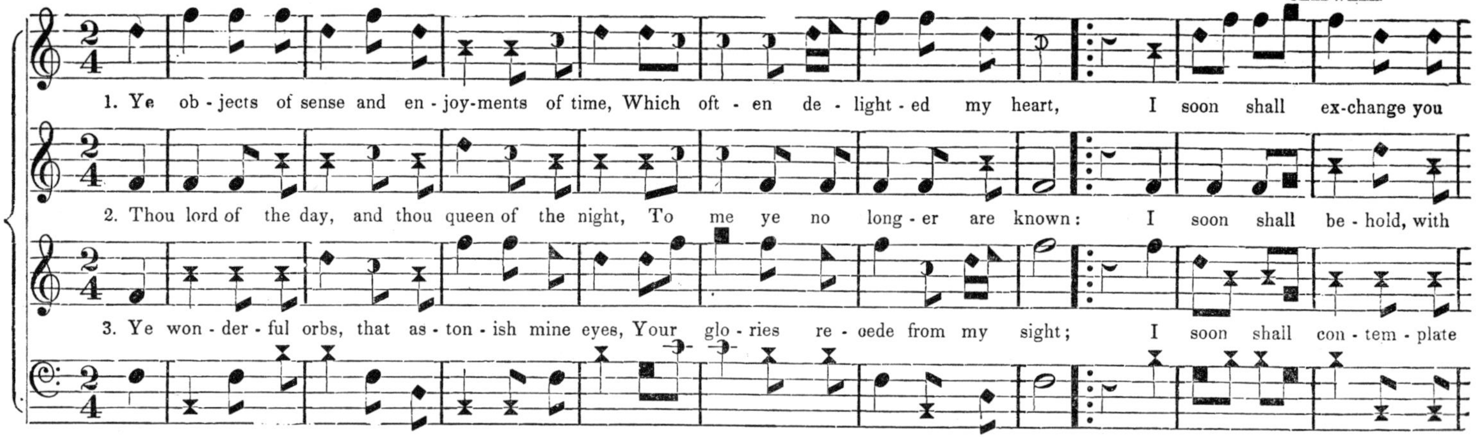

1. Ye ob - jects of sense and en - joy-ments of time, Which oft - en de - light - ed my heart, I soon shall ex-change you
2. Thou lord of the day, and thou queen of the night, To me ye no long - er are known: I soon shall be - hold, with
3. Ye won - der - ful orbs, that as - ton - ish mine eyes, Your glo - ries re - cede from my sight; I soon shall con - tem - plate

for joys more sub - lime, For joys that shall nev - er de - part.
in - creas - ing de - light, A Sun that shall nev - er go down.
more beau - ti - ful skies, And stars more transcend - ent - ly bright.

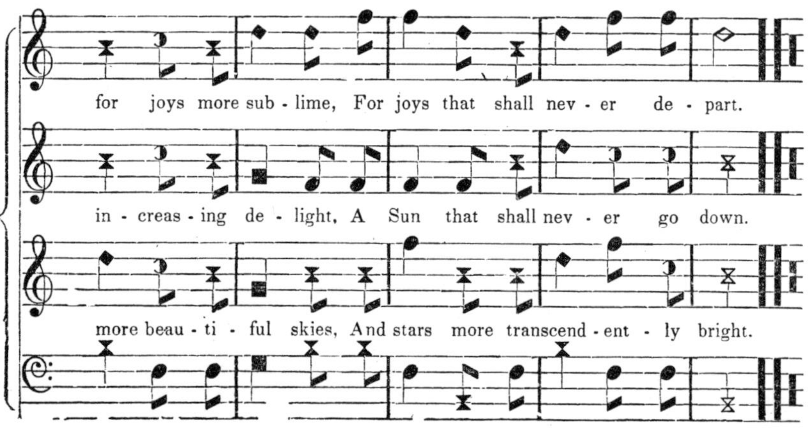

4. Ye mountains and valleys, groves, rivers, and plains,
Thou earth, and thou ocean, adieu;
More permanent regions where righteousness reigns,
Present their bright hills to my view.

5. My loved habitation, and garden, adieu,
No longer my footsteps ye greet;
A mansion celestial stands full in my view,
And paradise welcomes my feet.

6. My weeping relations, my brothers and friends,
Whose souls are entwined with my own,
Adieu for the present, my spirit ascends
Where pleasures immortal are known.

7. My cares and my labours, my sickness and pain,
And sorrows, are now at an end;
The summit of bliss I shall speedily gain,
The height of perfection ascend.

Counter by Swan, and Chorus noted.

THE PROMISED LAND. C. M.

MISS M. DURHAM.

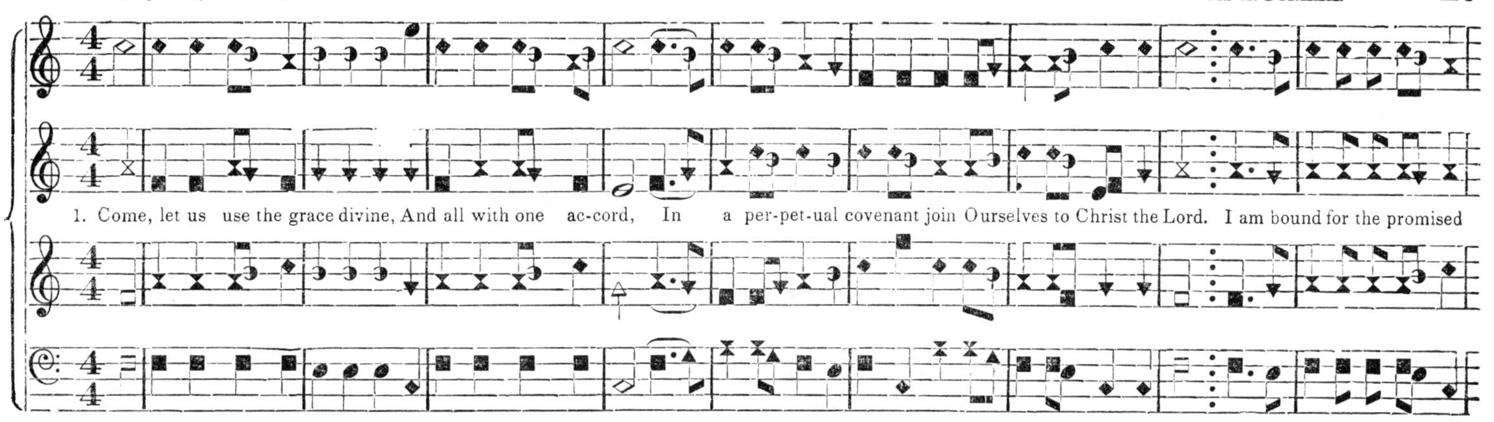

2. Give up ourselves through Jesus' power,
His name to glorify;
And promise in this sacred hour
For God to live and die.
I am bound, &c.

3. The covenant we this moment make,
Be ever kept in mind;
We will no more our God forsake,
Or cast his words behind.

4. We never will throw off his fear,
Who hears our solemn vow,
And if thou art well pleased to hear,
Come down, and meet us now!

5. Thee, Father, Son, and Holy Ghost,
Let all our hearts receive;
Present with the celestial host,
The peaceful answer give.

6. To each the covenant blood apply,
Which takes our sins away;
And register our names on high,
And keep us to that day.

CHRISTIAN CONTEMPLATION. P. M.

CALDWELL.

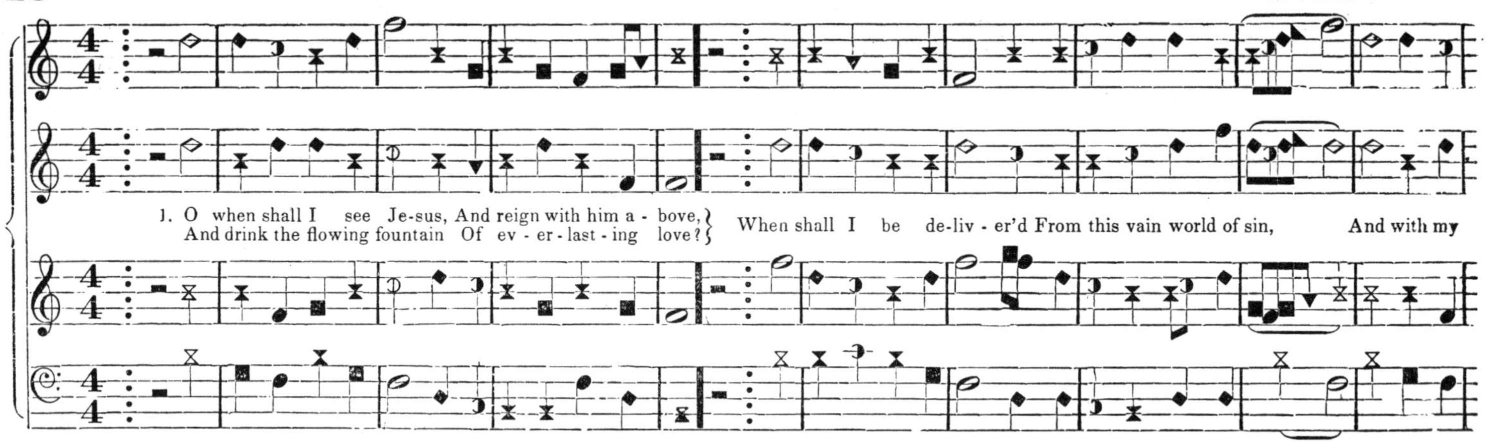

2. But now I am a soldier,
My Captain's gone before,
He's given me my orders,
And tells me not to fear;
And if I hold out faithful,
A crown of life he'll give,
And all his valiant soldiers
Eternal life shall have!

3. Through grace I am determined
To conquer though I die,
And then away to Jesus,
On wings of love I'll fly.
Farewell to sin and sorrow,
I bid you all adieu;
And you, my friends, prove faithful,
And on your way pursue.

4. And if you meet with trials
And troubles on the way,
Cast all your cares on Jesus,
And don't forget to pray.
Gird on the gospel armour,
Of faith, and hope, and love,
And when the combat's ended,
You'll reign with him above.

5. O! do not be discouraged,
For Jesus is your friend;
And if you lack for knowledge,
He'll not forget to lend:
Neither will he upbraid you,
Though oftener you request;
He'll give you grace to conquer,
And take you up to rest.

6. Farewell, my Christian brethren,
I'm going home to God,
To see my blessed Jesus,
Who bought me with his blood;
There I will sit and praise Him,
A crown He's bought for me,
And sing the song of Moses
To all eternity.

LONE PILGRIM. 11s & 8s.

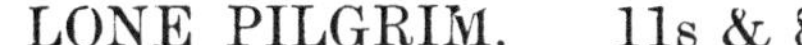

M. L. SWAN.

In songs of sub - lime a - do - ra - tion and praise, Ye pil - grims for Zi - on who press, Break
forth and ex - tol the great An - cient of days, His rich and dis - tin - guish - ing grace.
3
3
3
3

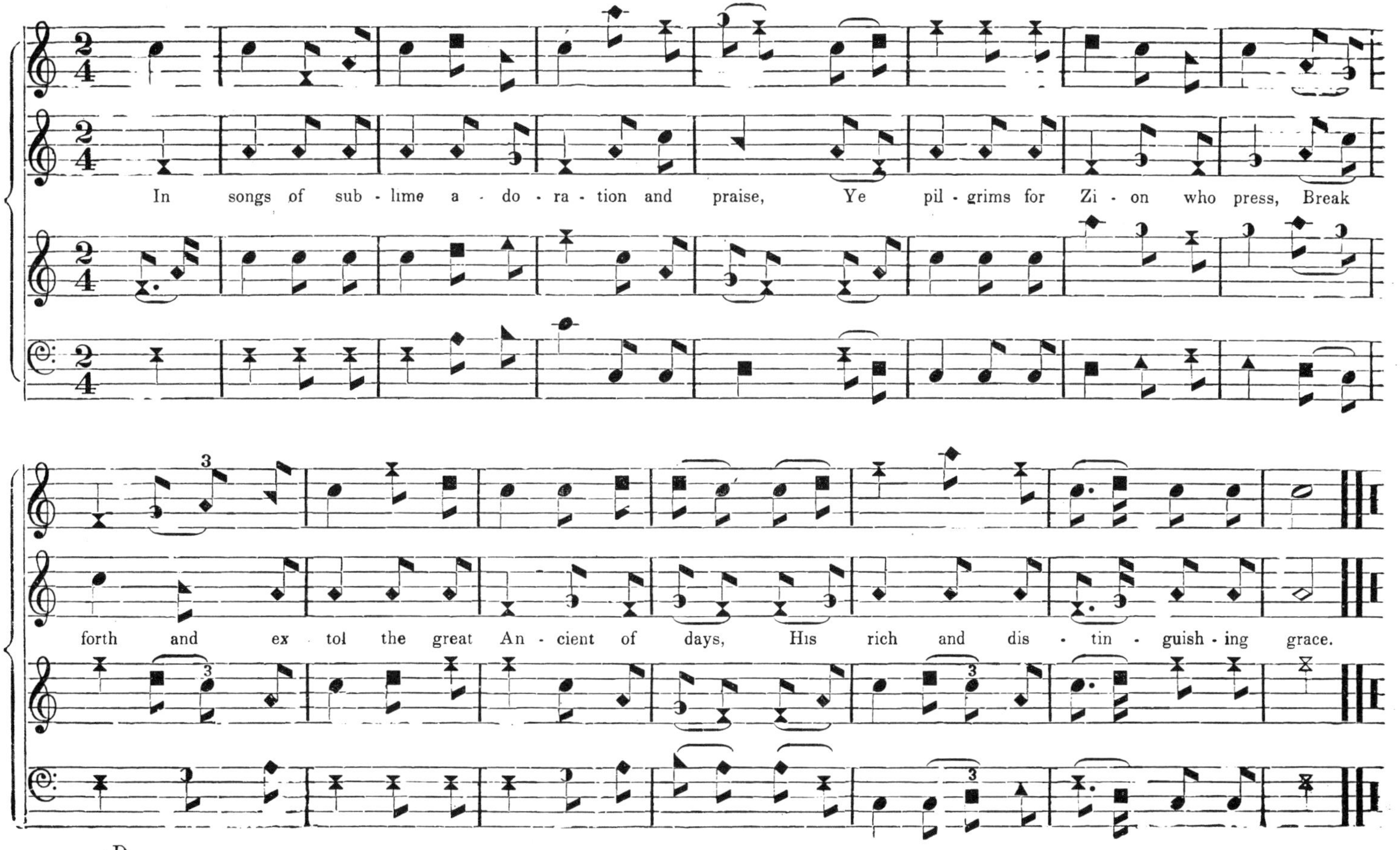

D

BENEVENTO. 8 lines 7s.

WEBBE.

2. Sinners, turn, why will ye die?
God your Saviour asks you why?
He who did your souls retrieve,
Died himself that ye might live,
Will ye let him die in vain,
Crucify your Lord again?
Why, ye rebel sinners, why
Will ye slight his grace and die?

3. Sinners, turn, why will ye die?
God the Spirit asks you why?
Many a time with you he strove,
Wooed you to embrace his love;
Will ye not his grace receive?
Will ye still refuse to live?
Why will ye for ever die?
Oh! ye guilty sinners, why?

MOUNT OLIVET. L. M.

SWAN

New Treble by M. L. Swan.
BALLERMA. C. M.
1. Oh, hap - py is the man who hears In - struc-tion's warn - ing voice; And who ce - les - tial wis - dom makes His ear - ly, on - ly choice.
2. For she has trea-sures great -er far Than east or west un- fold; More pre- cious are her bright re-wards Than gems, or stars of gold.
HENRY. C. M.
S. B. POND.
1. 'Tis by thy strength the mountains stand, God of e - ter - nal pow'r; The sea grows calm at thy com-mand, And tem - pests cease to roar.
2. Thy morning light, and evening shade, Successive com - forts bring; Thy plen-teous fruits make har - vest glad, Thy flow'rs a - dorn the spring.

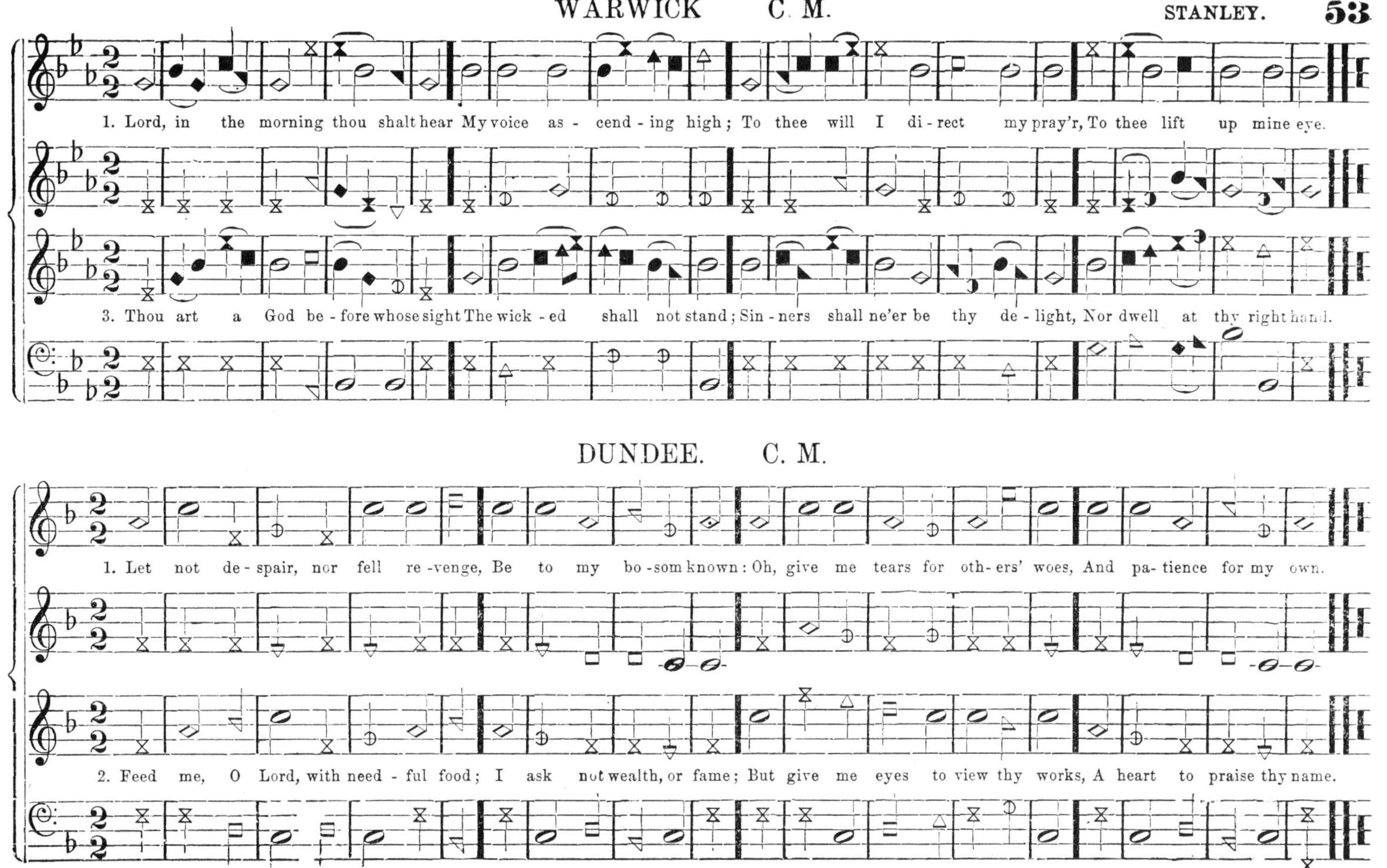
WARWICK C. M.
STANLEY.
1. Lord, in the morning thou shalt hear My voice as - cend - ing high; To thee will I di - rect my pray'r, To thee lift up mine eye.
3. Thou art a God be - fore whose sight The wick - ed shall not stand; Sin - ners shall ne'er be thy de - light, Nor dwell at thy right hand.
DUNDEE. C. M.
1. Let not de - spair, nor fell re - venge, Be to my bo - som known: Oh, give me tears for oth - ers' woes, And pa - tience for my own.
2. Feed me, O Lord, with need - ful food; I ask not wealth, or fame; But give me eyes to view thy works, A heart to praise thy name.

Treble by Caswell.

HOME. 11,11,11,5,11.

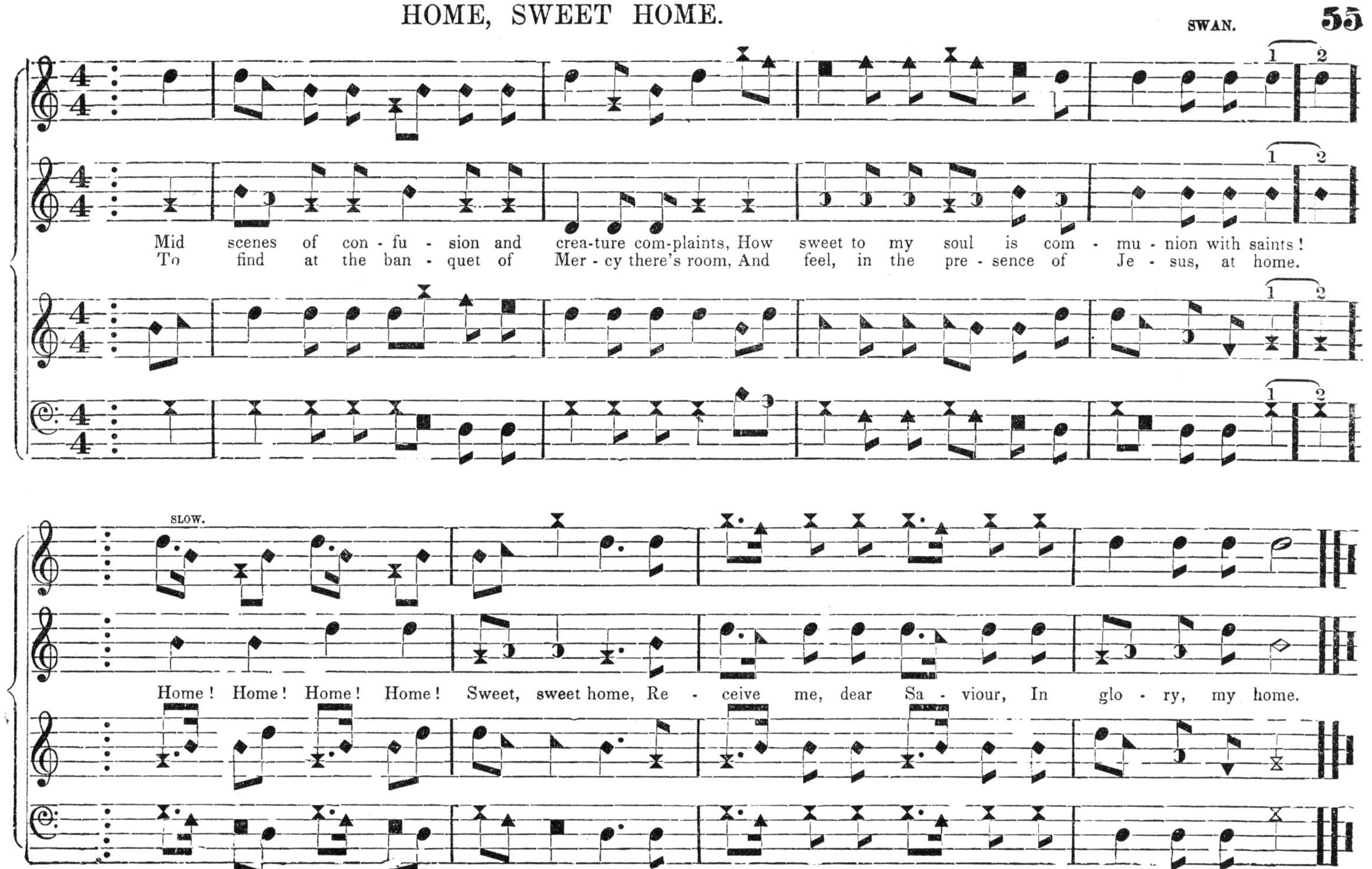
HOME, SWEET HOME.
SWAN.
Mid scenes of con - fu - sion and crea-ture com-plaints, How sweet to my soul is com - mu - nion with saints!
To find at the ban - quet of Mer - cy there's room, And feel, in the pre - sence of Je - sus, at home.
SLOW.
Home! Home! Home! Home! Sweet, sweet home, Re - ceive me, dear Sa - viour, In glo - ry, my home.

HEAVENLY ARMOUR. 8s & 7s.

Wm. Walker.

D. C.
1 2
And if you meet with trou-bles And tri-als on the way,
Then cast your care on Je-sus, And don't for-get to pray.
Gird on the heavenly ar-mour of faith, and hope, and love;
And when the com-bat's end-ed, He'll take you up a-bove.

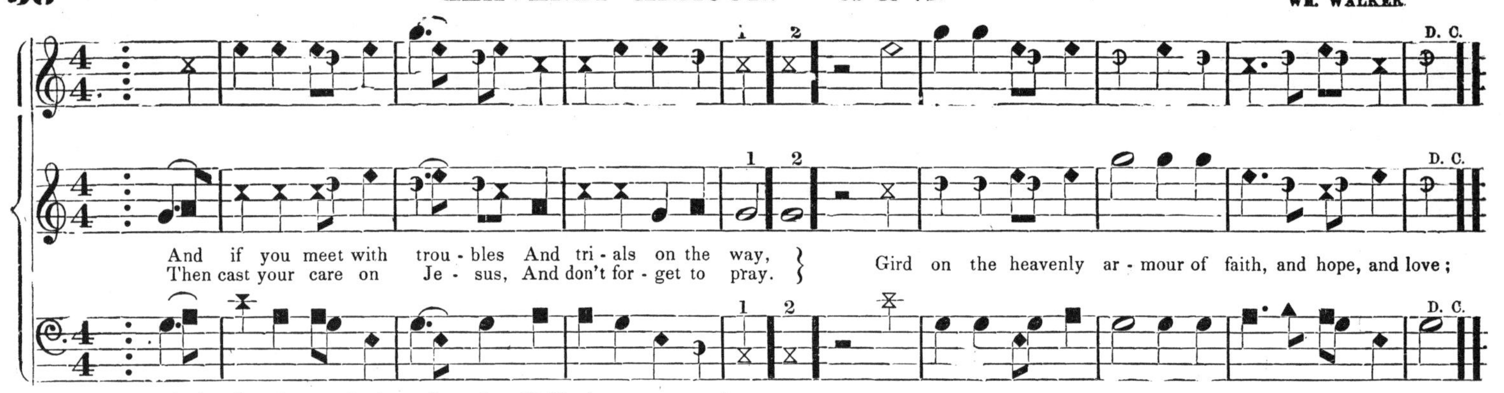

WARRENTON. 8s. & 7s.

CHORUS.
1 2
Come, thou Fount of every blessing,
Tune my heart to sing thy grace;
Streams of mercy, never-ceasing,
Call for songs of loudest praise.
I am bound for the kingdom,
Will you go to glory with me?
Hal-le-lu-jah! praise the Lord!

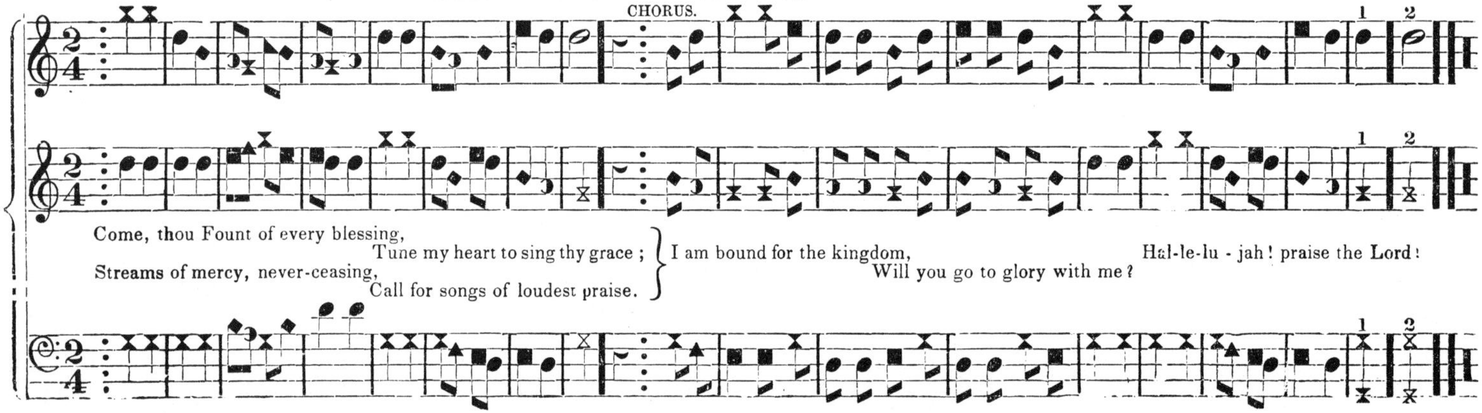

4/4
How firm a foun - da - tion, ye saints of the Lord, Is laid for your faith in his ex - cel lent word! What
more can he say than to you he hath said, You who un - to Je - sus for re - fuge have fled?
1
2

LANESBORO'. C. M.

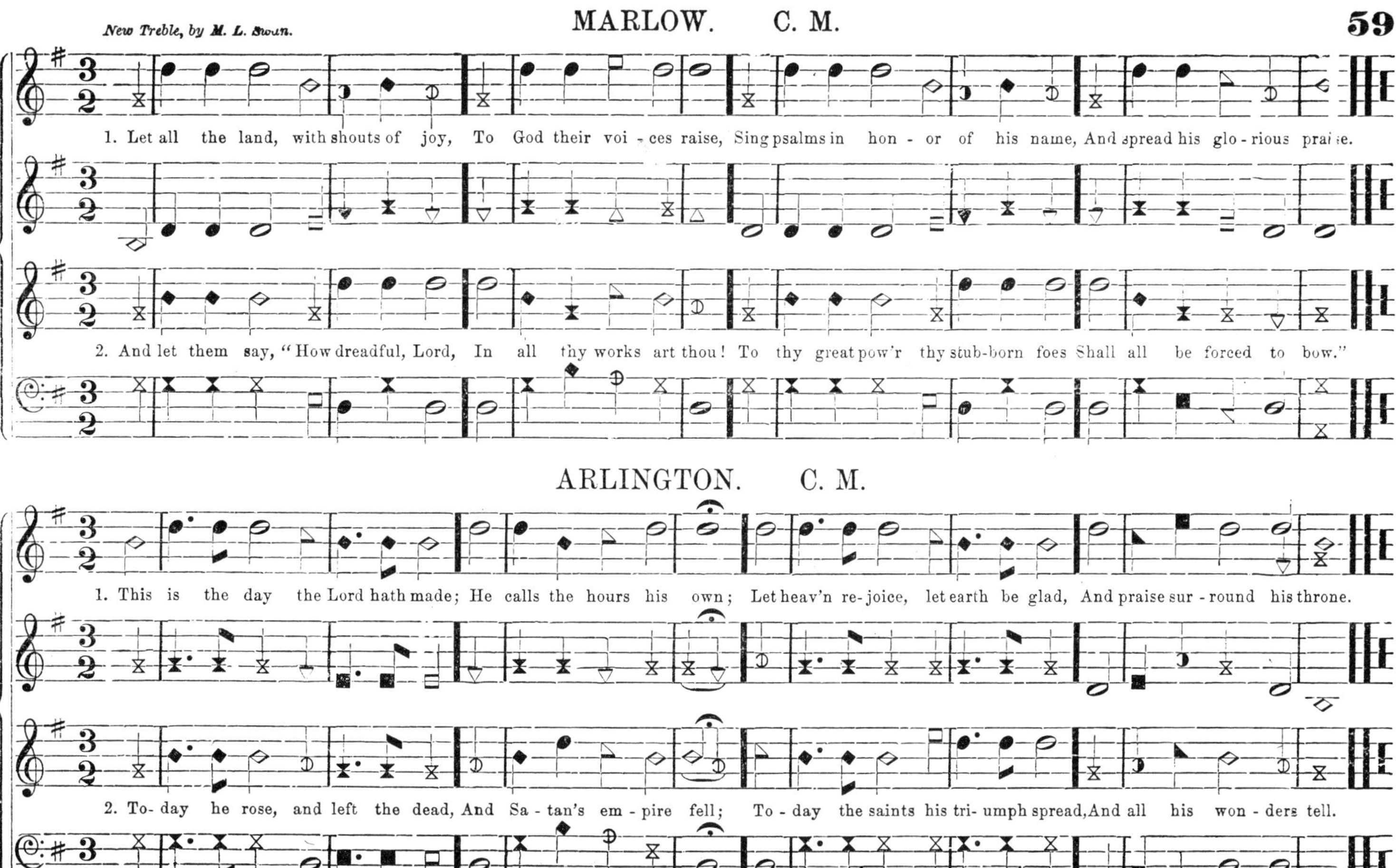
New Treble, by M. L. Swan.
MARLOW. C. M.
1. Let all the land, with shouts of joy, To God their voi - ces raise, Sing psalms in hon - or of his name, And spread his glo - rious praise.
2. And let them say, "How dreadful, Lord, In all thy works art thou! To thy great pow'r thy stub-born foes Shall all be forced to bow."
ARLINGTON. C. M.
1. This is the day the Lord hath made; He calls the hours his own; Let heav'n re-joice, let earth be glad, And praise sur - round his throne.
2. To- day he rose, and left the dead, And Sa - tan's em - pire fell; To - day the saints his tri- umph spread, And all his won - ders tell.

IMPORTUNITY.

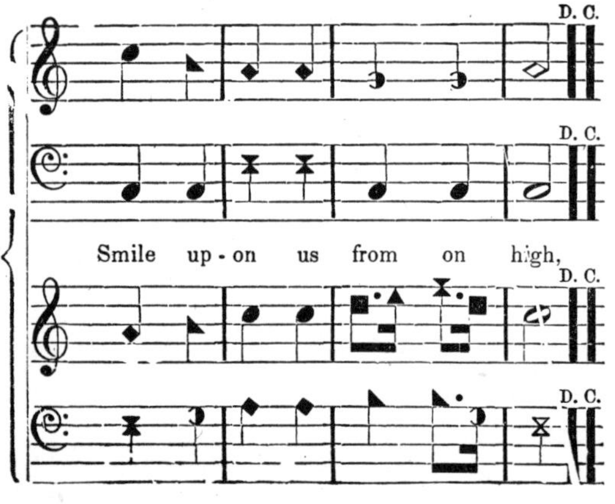

3. Surely once thy garden flourish'd,
Every part look'd gay and green;
Then thy word our spirits nourish'd:
Happy seasons we have seen!

4. But a drought has since succeeded,
And a sad decline we see;
Lord, thy help is greatly needed;
Help can only come from thee.

5. Where are those we counted leaders,
Fill'd with zeal, and love, and truth?
Old professors, tall as cedars,
Bright examples for our youth!

6. Some in whom we once delighted,
We shall meet no more below:
Some, alas! we fear are blighted,
Scarce a single leaf they show

7. Younger plants—the sight how pleasant.
Cover'd thick with blossoms stood·
But they cause us grief at present,
Frosts have nipp'd them in the bud.

8. Dearest Saviour, hasten hither;
Thou canst make them bloom again;
Oh permit them not to wither.
Let not all our hopes be vain!

9. Let our mutual love be fervent,
Make us prevalent in prayers;
Let each one esteem'd thy servant,
Shun the world's bewitching snares.

10. Break the tempter's fatal power,
Turn the stony heart to flesh;
And begin from this good hour
To revive thy work afresh.

LEANDER. C. M

1. It is the Lord—enthroned in light,
Whose claims are all divine;
Who has an undisputed right
To govern me and mine.

2. It is the Lord—should I distrust,
Or contradict his will,
Who cannot do but what is just
And must be righteous still?

3. It is the Lord—who gives me all
My wealth, my friends, my ease,
And, of his bounties, may recall
Whatever part he please.

4. It is the Lord—who can sustain
Beneath the heaviest load,
From whom assistance I obtain
To tread the thorny road.

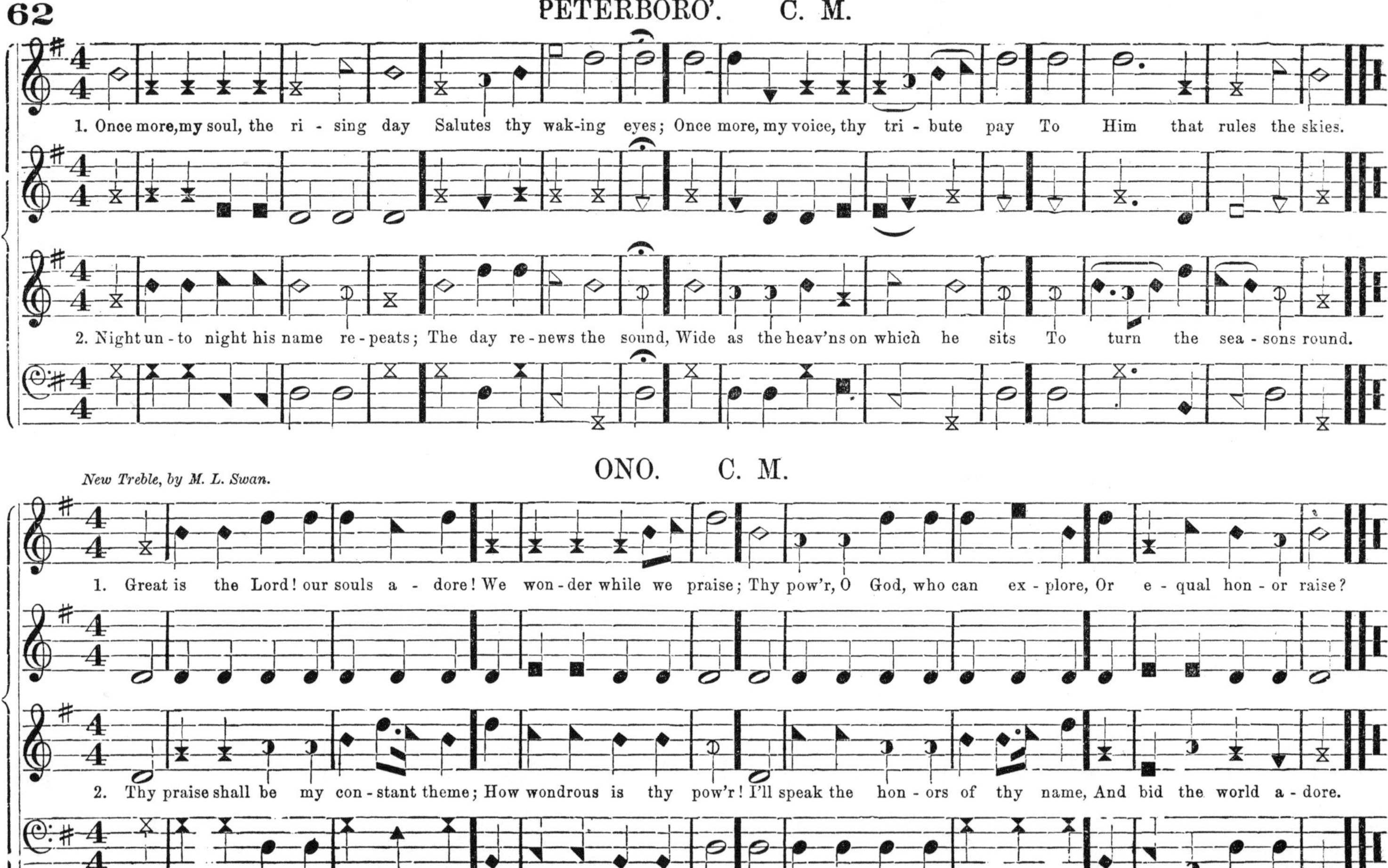
PETERBORO'. C. M.
1. Once more, my soul, the ri - sing day Salutes thy wak-ing eyes; Once more, my voice, thy tri - bute pay To Him that rules the skies.
2. Night un - to night his name re - peats; The day re - news the sound, Wide as the heav'ns on which he sits To turn the sea - sons round.
ONO. C. M.
New Treble, by M. L. Swan.
1. Great is the Lord! our souls a - dore! We won - der while we praise; Thy pow'r, O God, who can ex - plore, Or e - qual hon - or raise?
2. Thy praise shall be my con - stant theme; How wondrous is thy pow'r! I'll speak the hon - ors of thy name, And bid the world a - dore.

NAOMI. C. M.
1. Father, whate'er of earthly bliss Thy sovereign will denies, Ac-cepted at thy throne of grace, Let this pe - ti-tion rise. Hal-le - lu-jah, Hal-le - lu - jah!
2. Give me a calm, a thankful heart, From ev'ry murmur free; The blessing of thy grace impart, And make me live to thee. Hal-le - lu-jah! Halle - lu - jah!
AZMON. C. M.
1. Plunged in a gulf of dark despair, We wretched sinners lay, Without one cheerful beam of hope, Or spark of glimm'ring day. Hallelujah! Hallelujah! Halle-lu - jah!
2. With pitying eyes the Prince of grace Beheld our helpless grief; He saw, and, oh, amazing love! He ran to our relief. Halle - lu-jah! Halle-lu-jah! Halle - lu - jah!

ZERAH. C. M.

1. To us a Child of hope is born, To us a Son is giv'n: Him shall the tribes of earth obey, Him all the hosts of heav'n, Him shall the tribes of earth obey, Him all the hosts of heav'n.
2. His name shall be the Prince of Peace, For evermore adored, The Wonderful, the Counsellor, The great and mighty Lord, The Wonderful, the Counsellor, The great and mighty Lord.
FOUNTAIN. C. M.
L. MASON.
1. There is a foun-tain, fill'd with blood Drawn from Immanuel's veins; And sin-ners, plunged beneath that flood, Lose all their guilty stains, Lose all their guil - ty stains.
2. The dy - ing thief rejoiced to see That fountain, in his day; And there may I, though vile as he, Wash all my sins a - way, Wash all my sins a - way.

TEXAS. 7s.

SWAN.

2 Other refuge have I none
Hangs my helpless soul on thee;
Leave, ah leave me not alone!
Still support and comfort me.
All my trust on thee is stayed,
All my help from thee I bring;
Cover my defenceless head
With the shadow of thy wing.

3. Thou, O Christ, art all I want;
All in all in thee I find;
Raise the fallen, cheer the faint,
Heal the sick and lead the blind:
Just and holy is thy name.
I am all unrighteousness;
Vile and full of sin I am,
Thou art full of truth and grace.

E

CLINTON. L. M.

SWAN.

2. He saw me ruined in the fall,
Yet loved me notwithstanding all,
He saved me from my lost estate,—
His loving-kindness, O how great!

3. Though numerous hosts of mighty foes,
Though earth and hell my way oppose,
He safely leads my soul along,—
His loving-kindness, O how strong!

4. When trouble, like a gloomy cloud,
Has gather'd thick, and thunder'd loud,
He near my soul has always stood,—
His loving-kindness, O how good!

5. Often I feel my sinful heart
Prone from my Saviour to depart
But though I oft have him forgot,
His loving-kindness changes not.

6. Soon shall I pass the gloomy vale.
Soon all my mortal powers must fail;
O! may my last expiring breath
His loving-kindness sing in death.

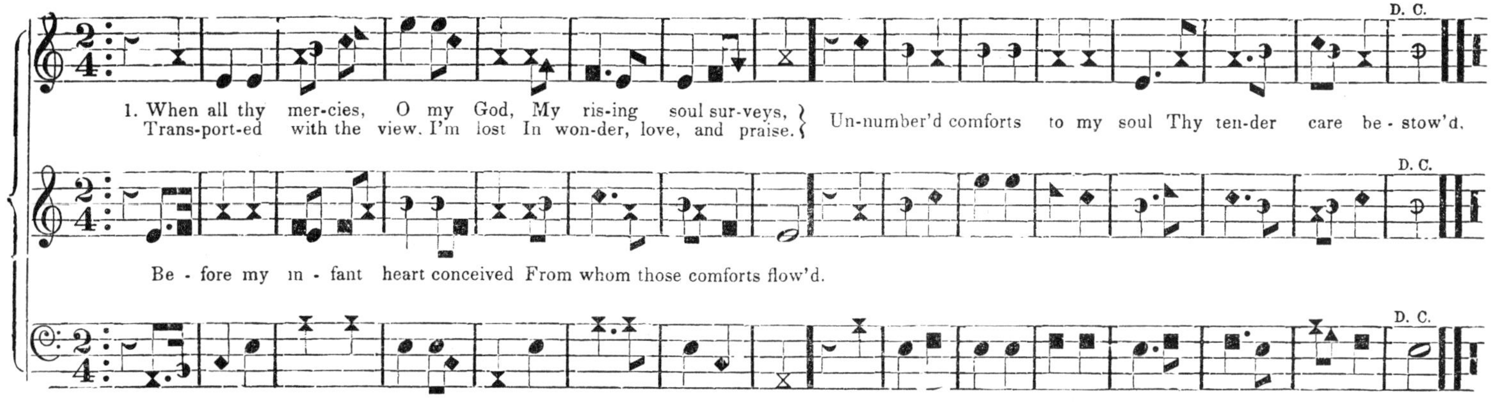

NEW YEAR. S. M.

P. M. ATCHLEY.

PARADISE. L. M.

SWAN.

I know that my Re-deem-er lives, I have a home in glo-ry,
What com-fort this sweet sentence gives, I have a home in glo-ry,
O glo-ry, O glo-ry, There's room enough in Par-a-dise To have a home in glo-ry.

ALBANY. S. M.

M. L. SWAN.

Did Christ o'er sinners weep? And shall our cheeks be dry? Let floods of peniten - tial grief Burst forth from ev'ry eye, Burst forth from ev'ry eye.

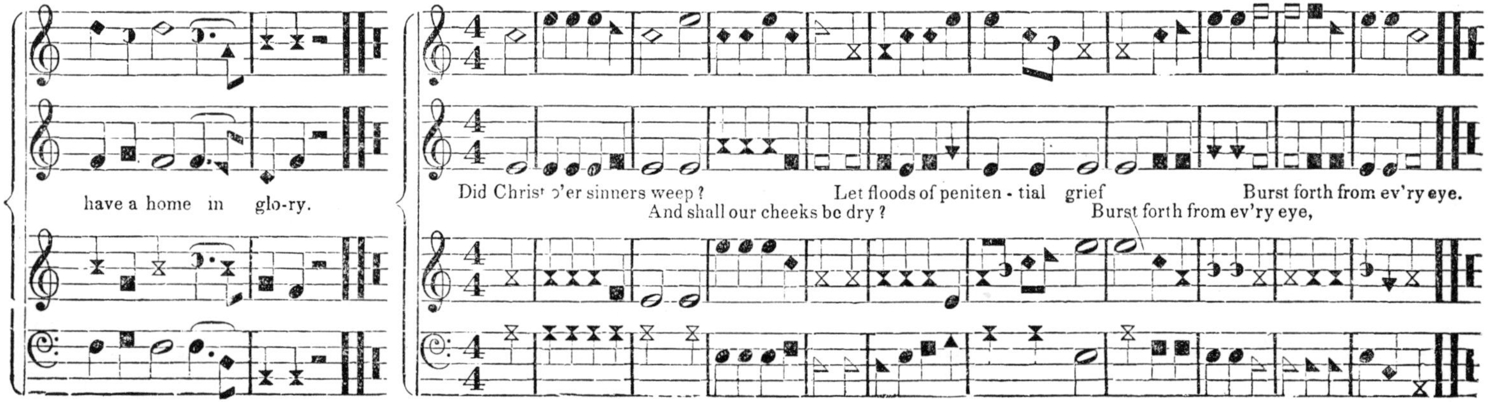

RETURN. C. M.
M. L. SWAN.
1. O thou whose tender mercy hears Contrition's humble sigh,
Whose hand indulgent wipes the tear From sorrow's weeping eye. See, low before thy throne of grace, A wretched wand'rer mourn. Hast thou not bid me seek thy face? Hast thou not said, Return?
3. And shall my guilty fears prevail To drive me from thy feet?
Oh, let not this dear re-fuge fail, This on-ly safe re - treat. Absent from thee, my guide, my light, Without one cheering ray, Through dangers, fears, and gloomy night. How desolate my way!
MIDDLETON. C. M.
Old Tune Harmonized.
M. L. SWAN.
1. Sweet is the mem' - ry of thy grace, My God, my heav'n-ly King! Let age to age thy right-eousness In sounds of glo - ry sing.
2. God reigns on high, but ne'er con-fines His good - ness to the skies; Through the whole earth his bounty shines, And ev' - ry want sup-plies.

BROOKLYN. 11s

SWAN.

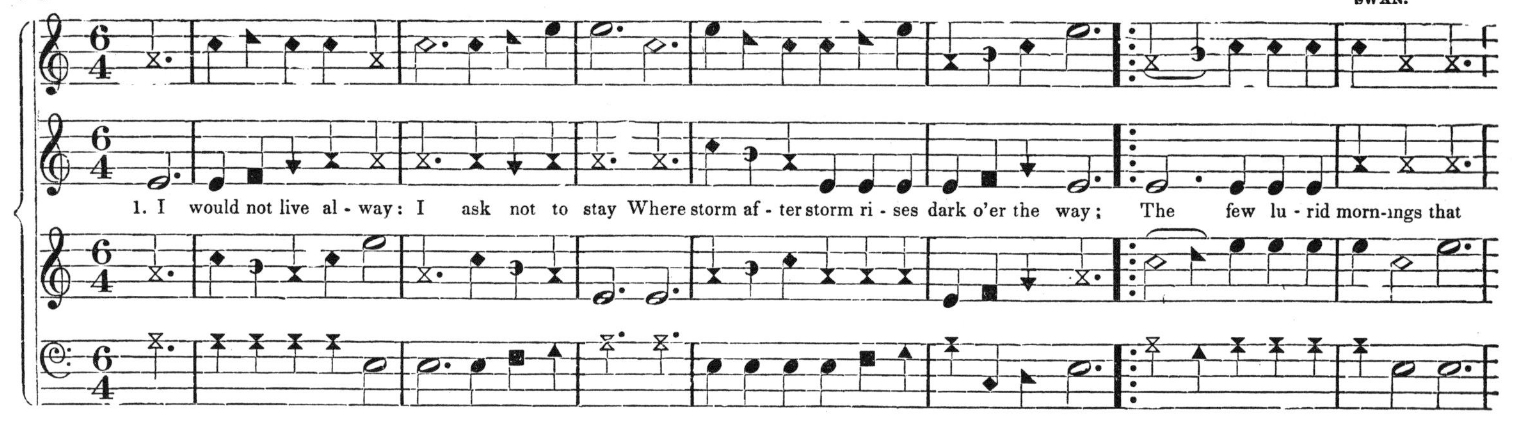

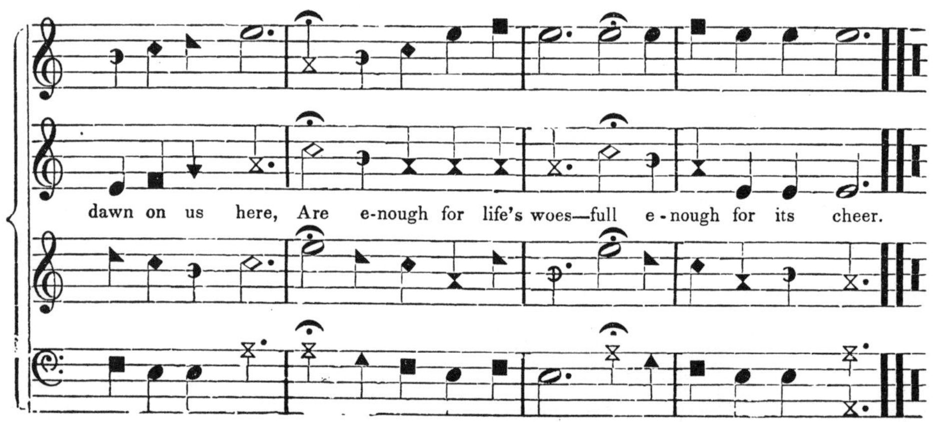

2. I would not live alway: no—welcome the tomb,
Since Jesus hath lain there, I dread not its gloom;
There, sweet be my rest, till he bid me arise,
To hail him in triumph descending the skies.

3. Who, who would live alway, away from his God,
Away from yon heaven, that blissful abode,
Where the rivers of pleasure flow o'er the bright plains,
And the noontide of glory eternally reigns?

4. Where the saints of all ages in harmony meet,
Their Saviour and brethren transported to greet;
While the anthems of rapture unceasingly roll,
And the smile of the Lord is the feast of the soul.

When, in death, I shall calm re-cline, Oh bear my heart to my mis - tress dear,
Tell her it lived on smiles and wine, Of brightest hue while it lin - gered here:
Bid her not shed one tear of sor-row, To

sul - ly a heart so bril - liant and bright, But balmy drops of the red grape bor-row, To bathe the re - lic from morn till night.

"MY MOTHER'S BIBLE." C. M. Double.
Arranged by M. L. Swan.
D. C. 2d strain.
1. This book is all that's left me now; Tears will unbidden start; With falt'ring lip and throbbing brow, I press it to my heart. For ma - ny gen-e - ra-tions past Here is our family tree.
D. C. My mother's hand this Bible clasp'd, She, dying, gave it me.
D. C. 2d strain.
D. C. 2d strain.
2. Ah! well do I remember those Whose names these records bear, Who round the hearth-stone used to close, After the ev'ning prayer, And speak of what these pages said, In tones my heart would thrill:
D. C. Though they are with the silent dead, Here are they living still.
D. C. 2d strain.
CHIMES. C. M.
1. With joy we hail the sa - cred day Which God has call'd his own; With joy the summons we o - bey To wor-ship at his throne. Hal-le - lujah! Halle - lu-jah! Hal-le- lu - jah!
2. Thy cho-sen tem-ple, Lord, how fair, Where will-ing vo-t'ries throng To breathe the humble, fervent pray'r And pour the cho - ral song. Hal - le -lu-jah! Halle - lu-jah! Halle - lu - jah!

OH, SING TO ME OF HEAVEN! S. M.
Harmony by M. L. Swan.
1. Oh, sing to me of heav'n, When I am call'd to die; Sing songs of ho - ly ec - sta - sy, To waft my soul on high.
2. When cold and slug-gish drops Roll off my mar - ble brow, Burst forth in strains of joy - ful - ness; Let heav'n be - gin be - low.
BELLEVILLE. 7s 6s & 8s.
1. Brother, thou art gone to rest; We will not weep for thee; For thou art now where oft on earth Thy spir-it long'd to be, Brother, thy spir - it long'd to be.
2. Brother, thou art gone to rest; Thine is an ear - ly tomb; But Jesus summon'd thee away; Thy Saviour call'd thee home; Brother, thy Saviour call'd thee home.

NEVER PART AGAIN. C. M. & CHORUS

ANTICIPATION. C. M.
M. L. SWAN.
Awake our souls, away our fears! When we get to heaven we will part no more; Fare you well, Oh! fare you well, When we get to heaven we will part no more!
Let ev'ry trembling thought be gone; When we get, &c.
Awake, and run the heavenly race; When we get, &c.
Fare you well, &c.
And put a cheerful courage on; When we get, &c.
LORINDA. 8,6,8,6,8,8,8,6.
SWAN.
D. C.
Sing hal - le - lu - jah, praise the Lord! Sing with a cheer - ful voice; Ne'er cease to sing, thou ran-som'd host,
Ex - alt our God with one ac - cord, And in His name re - joice! To Fa - ther, Son, and Ho - ly Ghost,
Till in the realms of end - less light, Your prais - es shall u - nite.

76
Distinct, and in exact time.
ARIEL. C. P. M.
L. MASON.
1. Oh, could I speak the match - less worth, Oh, could I sound the glo - ries forth, Which in my Sa - viour shine! I'd soar and touch the
2. I'd sing the pre - cious blood he spilt, My ran - som from the dread - ful guilt Of sin, and wrath di - vine; I'd sing his glo - rious
heav'n - ly strings, And vie with Ga - briel, while he sings, In notes al - most di - vine, In notes al - most di - vine.
right - eous - ness, In which all - per - fect, heav'n - ly dress My soul shall ev - er shine, My soul shall ev - er shine.

Treble by Wm. Walker.

J. WILLIAMS.

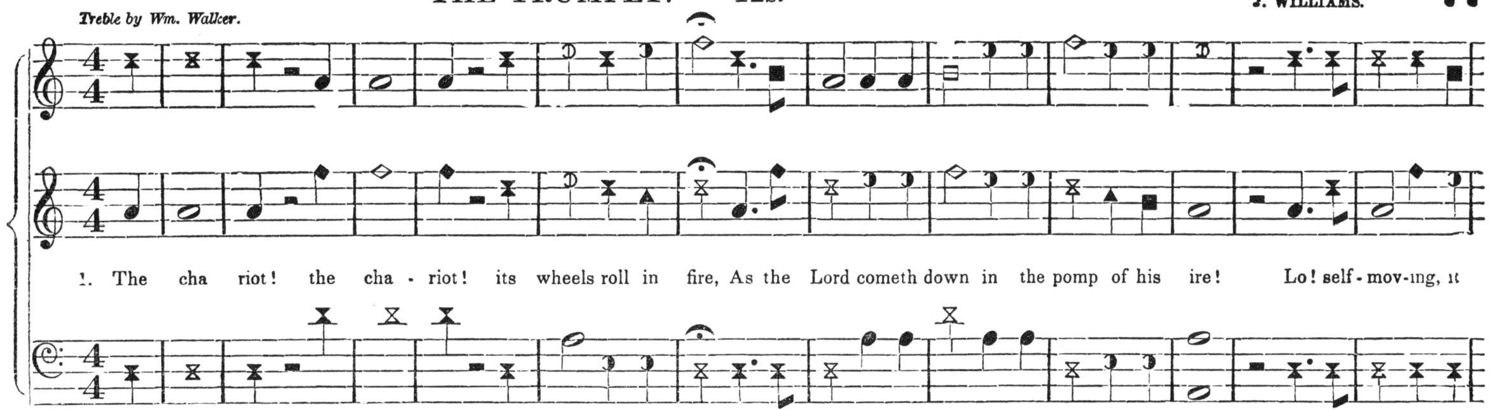

2 The glory! the glory! around him are pour'd
Mighty hosts of the angels that wait on the Lord:
And the glorified saints and the martyrs are there,
And there all who the palm-wreaths of victory wear.

3. The trumpet! the trumpet! the dead have all heard,
Lo! the depths of the stone-cover'd charnel are stirr'd;
From the sea, from the earth, from the south, from the north,
All the vast generations of man are come forth!

4. The judgment! the judgment! the thrones are all set;
There the Lamb and the white-vested elders are met;
There all flesh is at once in the sight of the Lord,
And the doom of eternity hangs on his word.

5. O mercy! O mercy! look down from above,
Great Creator, on us, thy sad children, with love;
When beneath to their darkness the wicked are driv'n,
May our justified souls find a welcome in heav'n!

CRAY RIDGE. 8s & 7s

SWAN.

TRAVELLING TO THE GRAVE. 6,6,6,6,8,6,8,6.

SWAN.

1. Ye sim-ple souls that stray Far from the paths of peace, That un-fre-quent-ed road To life and hap - pi - ness, How long will ye your fol - ly love, And throng the downward road, And hate the wisdom from above, And mock the sons of God? And mock, &c., And mock, &c., And mock, &c.

2. Madness and mi - se - ry, Ye count our lives beneath, And nothing great can see, As glo-rious in our death As born to suf - fer and to grieve, Be-neath your feet we lie, And ut - ter-ly contemn'd we live, And unlamented die, And un - la - ment-ed die, And un - la - ment - ed die, And un - la - ment-ed die.

3. Poor, pensive sojourners, O'erwhelm'd with grief and woes, Perplex'd with needless fears, And pleasure's mortal foes: More irksome than a ga-ping tomb, Our sight ye can-not bear, Wrapt in the me-lan-cho-ly gloom Of fan-ci-ful de-spair, Of fanciful, &c., Of fanciful, &c., Of fanciful, &c.

LABAN. S. M.
1. My soul, be on thy guard; Ten thousand foes a - rise; The hosts of sin are pressing hard To draw thee from the skies.
2. Oh, watch, and fight, and pray; The bat - tle ne'er give o'er; Re - new it bold - ly ev' - ry day, And help di - vine im - plore.
SHAWMUT. S. M.
1. Thy name, al - migh - ty Lord, Shall sound through distant lands; Great is thy grace, and sure thy word; Thy truth for - ev - er stands.
2. Far be thine hon - or spread, And long thy praise en - dure, Till morning light and evening shade Shall be exchanged no more.

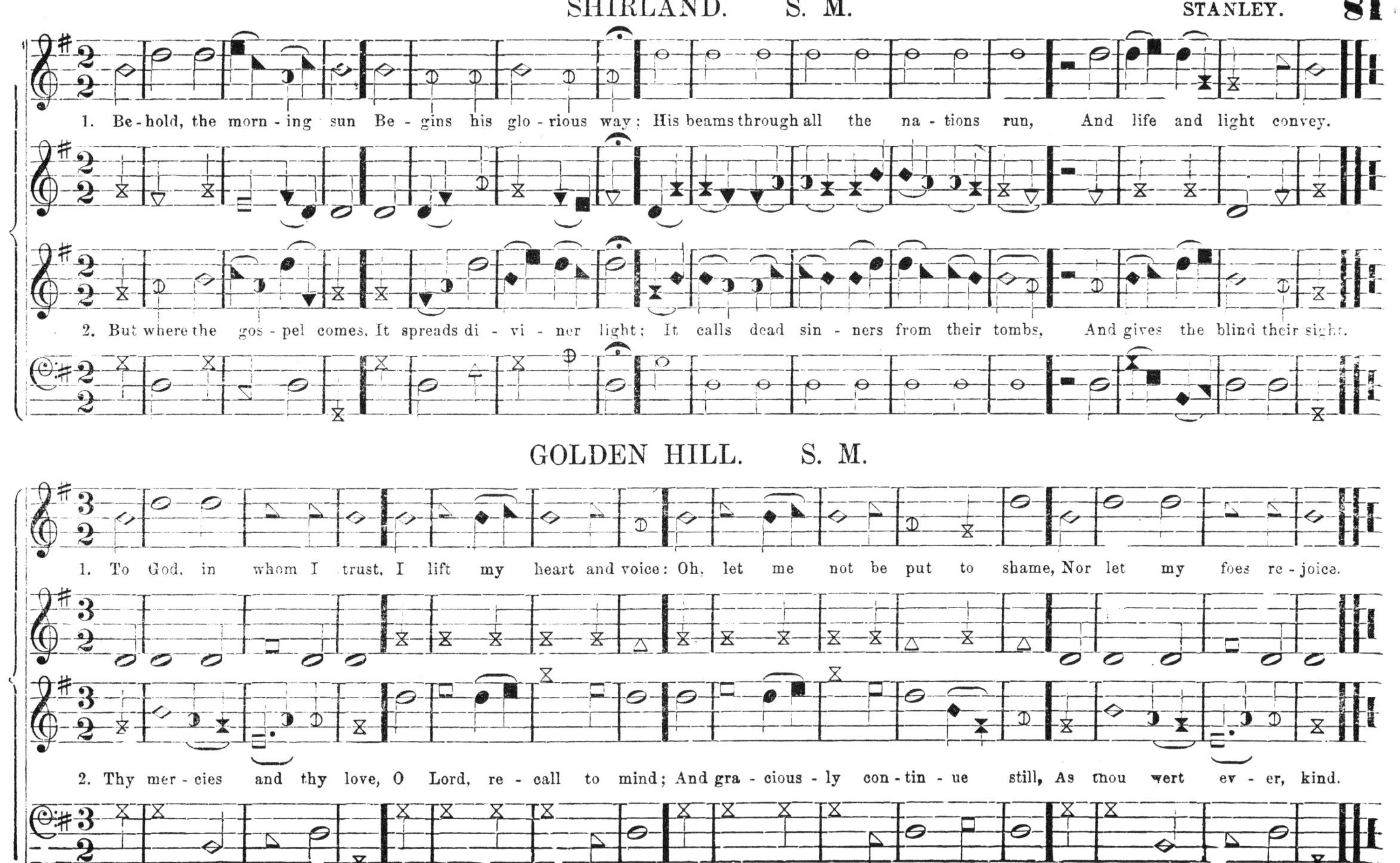

SHIRLAND. S. M.
STANLEY.
1. Be-hold, the morn - ing sun Be - gins his glo - rious way: His beams through all the na - tions run, And life and light convey.
2. But where the gos - pel comes, It spreads di - vi - ner light; It calls dead sin - ners from their tombs, And gives the blind their sight.
GOLDEN HILL. S. M.
1. To God, in whom I trust, I lift my heart and voice: Oh, let me not be put to shame, Nor let my foes re - joice.
2. Thy mer - cies and thy love, O Lord, re - call to mind; And gra - cious - ly con - tin - ue still, As thou wert ev - er, kind.
F

BEALOTH. S. M. (Double.)
1. I love thy king-dom, Lord, The house of thine a - bode, The church our bless'd Re-deem - er saved With his own pre - cious blood.
3. For her my tears shall fall, For her my pray'rs as - cend, To her my cares and toils be given, Till toils and cares shall end.
2. I love thy church, O God; Her walls be - fore thee stand, Dear as the ap - ple of thine eye, And gra - ven on thy hand.
4. Be - yond my high - est joy I prize her heav'n - ly ways, Her sweet com - mu - nion, sol - emn vows, Her hymns of love and praise.

KINGWOOD. 8, 8, 7.
HUMPHREYS
1. My days, my weeks, my months, my years, Fly rap - id as the whirling spheres, Fly rap - id as the whirling spheres Around the stea - dy pole.
2 The grave is near the cra - dle seen, How swift the moments pass be-tween, How swift the mo-ments pass be-tween, And whisper as they fly—
3. My soul, at - tend the so - lemn call; Thine earth-ly tent must short-ly fall, Thine earthly tent must short-ly fall, And thou must take thy flight
Time, like the tide, its mo - tion keeps, And I must launch thro' endless deeps, And I must launch thro' end-less deeps, Where endless a - ges roll.
"Un - think-ing man, re - member this, Tho' fond of sub - lu - na-ry bliss, Tho' fond of sub - lu - na - ry bliss, That you must groan and die."
Be - yond the vast ex - pan-sive blue, To sing a - bove as angels do, To sing a - bove as an - gels do, Or sink in end - less night!

Counter by Swan.

THE MIDNIGHT CRY. 7s & 6s.

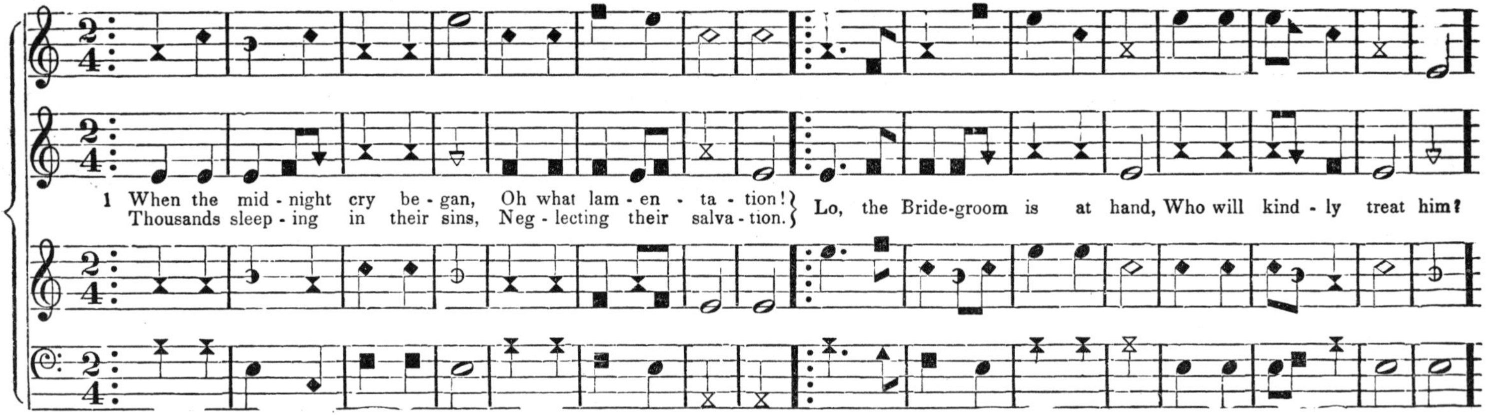

1 When the mid - night cry be - gan, Oh what lam - en - ta - tion!
Thousands sleep - ing in their sins, Neg - lecting their salva - tion.
Lo, the Bride-groom is at hand, Who will kind - ly treat him?

Sure - ly all that wait - ing band Will now go forth to meet him.

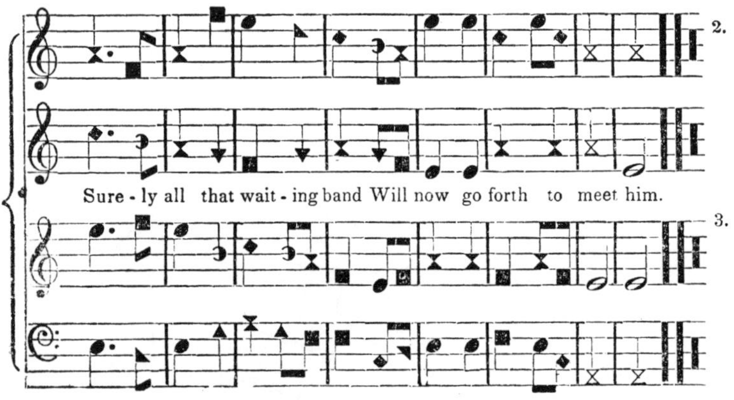

2. Some indeed did wait awhile
   And shone without a rival;
But they spent their seeming oil
   Long since the last revival.
Many souls who thought they'd light,
   Oh, when the scene was closed,
Now against the Bridgroom fight,
   And so they stand opposed.

3. While the wise are passing by,
   With all their lamps prepared,
Give us of your oil, they cry,
   If any can be spared.
Others trimm'd their former snuff,
   Oh, is it not amazing!
Those conclude they've light enough,
   And think their lamps are blazing.

4. Foolish virgins! do you think
   Our Bridegroom's a deceiver?
Then may you pass your lives away,
   And think to sleep for ever;
But we by faith do see his face,
   On whom we have believed:
If there's deception in the case,
   'Tis you that are deceived.

5. And now the door is open wide,
   And Christians are invited,
And virgins wise compass the bride,
   March to the place appointed.
Who do you think is now a guest?
   Yea, listen, carnal lovers,
'Tis those in wedding garments dress'd
   They cease from sin for ever

GREENLAND.

SWAN.

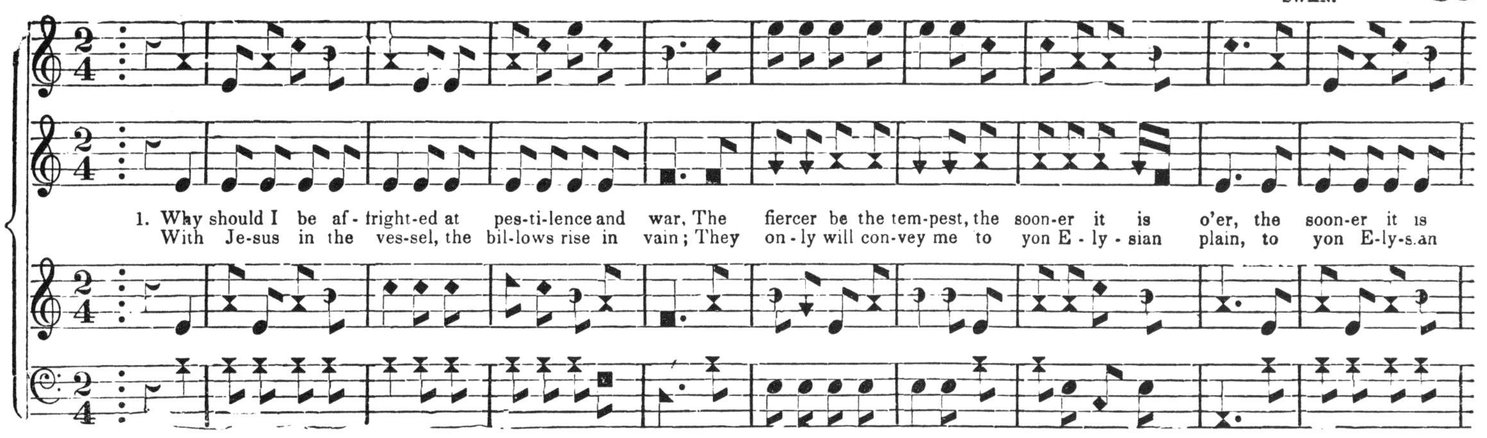

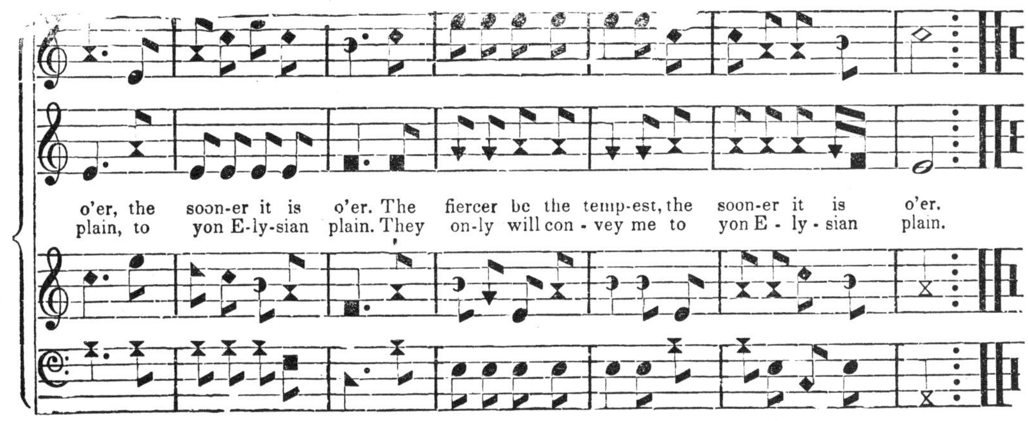

2. This world is full of dangers and foes that press me hard,
But Jesus he has promised that he will be my guard:
Here I shall not be tempted above what I can bear,
When fighting's done, escorted, his kingdom for to share.

3. From him I have my orders, and while I do obey,
I find his Holy Spirit illuminates my way;
The way is so delightful, I wish to travel on
Till I arrive at heaven to receive a starry crown.

TABOR. P. M.
M. L. SWAN.
1. One spark, O God, of heav'n-ly fire A-wakes my heart with warm de-sire To reach the realms a-bove;
2. Oh, could I wing my way in haste, Soon with bright ser-aphs would I feast, And join their sweet em-ploy;
Im-mor-tal glo-ries round me shine, I drink the streams of joy di-vine, And sing re-deem-ing love.
I'd glide a-long the heav'n-ly stream, And join their most ex-alt-ed theme Of ev-er-last-ing joy.

HIGHTOWER. 7s & 6s.
M. L. SWAN.
87
D.C. 2d Strain.
1. Time is winging us a-way To our e-ter-nal home; Life is but a winter's day, A journey to the tomb. Youth and vigor soon will flee, Blooming beauty lose its charms:
D.C. All that's mortal soon shall be En-closed in death's cold arms.
2. Time is winging us a-way To our e-ter-nal home; Life is but a winter's day, A journey to the tomb. But the Christian shall enjoy Health and beauty soon a-bove,
D.C. Far beyond the world's alloy, Se-cure in Je-sus' love.
"A HOME IN HEAVEN." 9s & 10s.
Arranged by M. L. SWAN.
Slow.
1. A home in heav'n! what a joyful thought! As the poor man toils in his weary lot, His heart oppress'd, and with anguish riven, From his home below to a home in heav'n.
2. A home in heav'n! as the suff'rer lies On his bed of pain, and up-lifts his eyes To that bright home, what a joy is given With the blessed thought of a home in heav'n!

Treble by Caldwell

MISSIONARY HYMN. 7s & 6s.

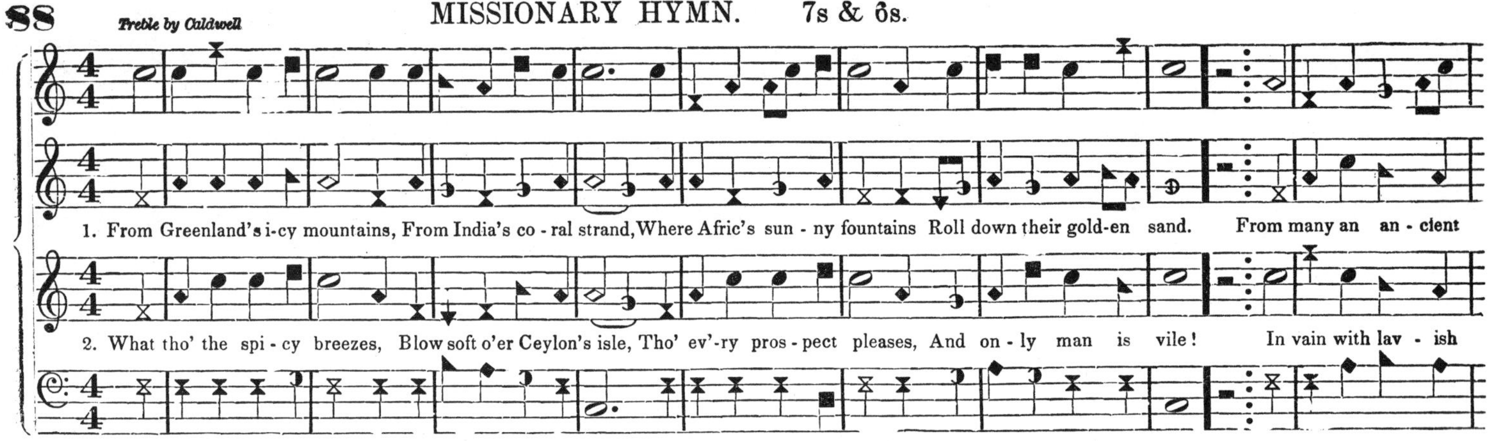

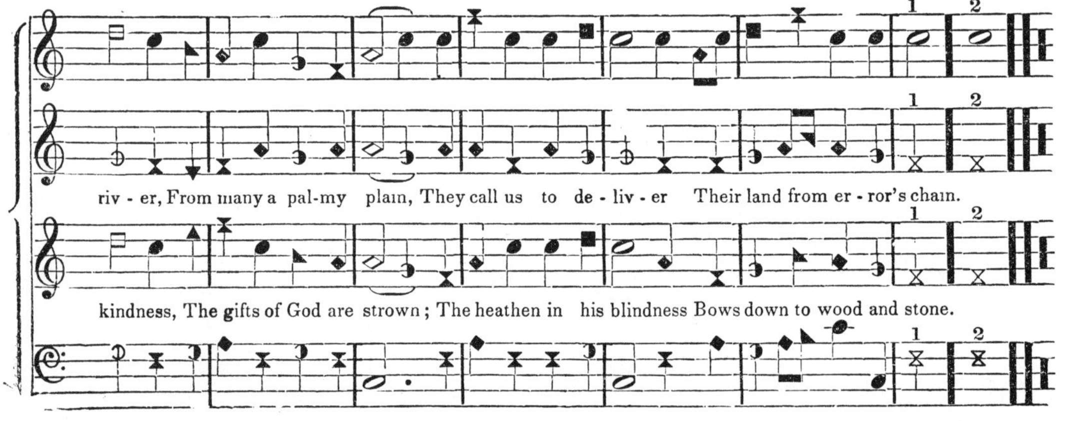

3. Shall we, whose souls are lighted
By wisdom from on high,
Shall we to men benighted
The lamp of life deny?
Salvation! O salvation!
The joyful sound proclaim,
Till earth's remotest nation
Has learned Messiah's name.

4. Waft, waft, ye winds, the story,
And you, ye waters, roll,
Till, like a sea of glory,
It spreads from pole to pole;
Till o'er our ransom'd nature,
The Lamb for sinners slain,
Redeemer, King, Creator,
Returns in bliss to reign.

MORALITY. 10s
WHITE & DAVISSON.
89
While beau - ty and youth are in their full prime, And fol - ly and pas - sion af - fect our whole time, Oh!
let not the phan - tom our wish - es en - gage, Let us live so in youth that we blush not in age.
1
2

ARBOUR. S. M.

SWAN.

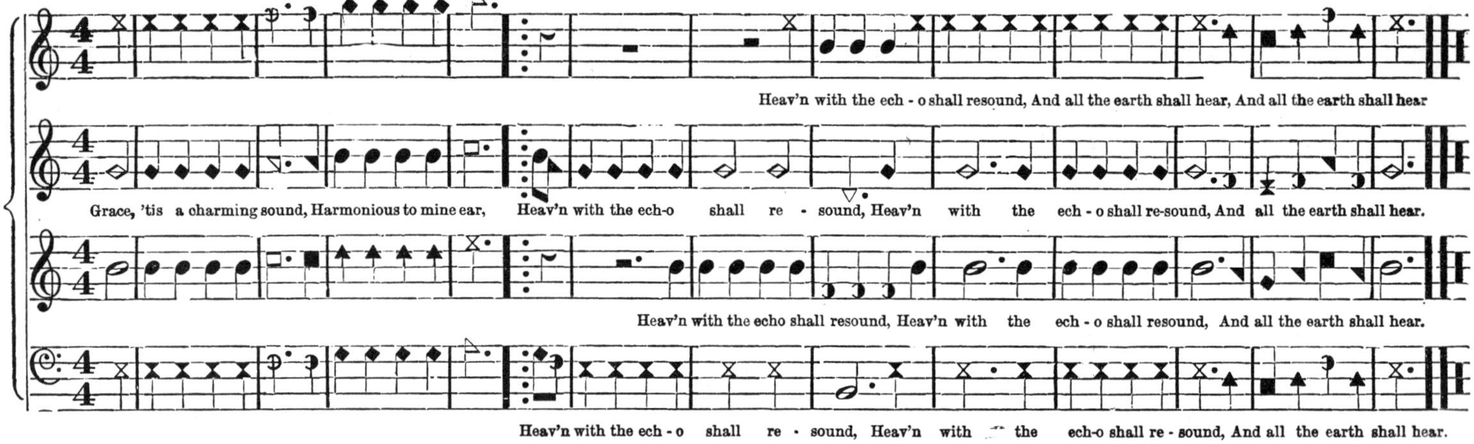

Heav'n with the ech - o shall resound, And all the earth shall hear, And all the earth shall hear
Grace, 'tis a charming sound, Harmonious to mine ear, Heav'n with the ech-o shall re - sound, Heav'n with the ech - o shall re-sound, And all the earth shall hear.
Heav'n with the echo shall resound, Heav'n with the ech - o shall resound, And all the earth shall hear.
Heav'n with the ech - o shall re - sound, Heav'n with the ech-o shall re - sound, And all the earth shall hear.

MARIETTA.

SWAN

Lo! on a narrow neck of land, 'Twixt two unbounded seas I stand, 'Twixt two un - bounded seas I stand, Yet how in-sen - si - ble!
A point of time, a moment's space, Removes me to yon heavenly place, Removes me to yon heavenly place, Or shuts me up in hell.

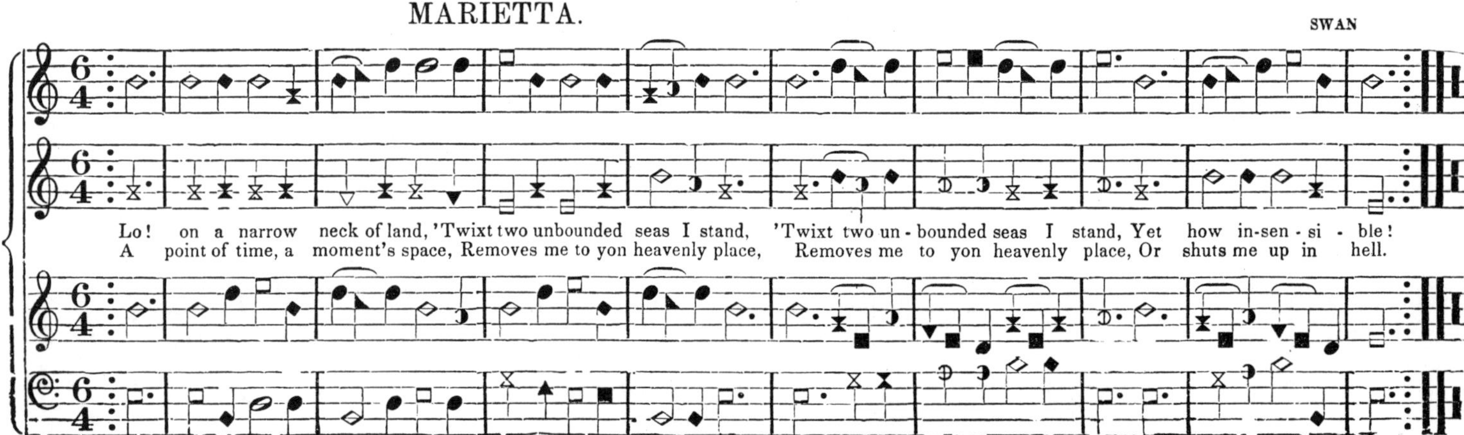

LANCASTER. 8,8,6 SWAN.

2.

Rejoicing now in earnest hope,
I stand, and from the mountain top
See all the land below:
Rivers of milk and honey rise,
And all the fruits of Paradise
In endless plenty grow.

3.

A land of corn, and wine, and oil,
Favour'd with God's peculiar smile,
With every blessing blest;
There dwells the Lord our righteousness,
And keeps his own in perfect peace
And everlasting rest.

92
DELAWARE. 7,6,7,6,7,7,7,6.
SWAN.
1. Rise my soul, and stretch thy wings, Thy bet-ter por-tion trace; Rise from tran-si - to - ry things, To heaven thy na - tive place; Sun, and moon, and
Brisk and Loud.
stars decay; Time shall soon this earth remove; Rise, my soul, and haste a-way, To seats prepared a - bove.
Rivers to the ocean run,
Nor stay in all their course;
Fire, ascending, seeks the sun:—
Both speed them to their source,
Thus, a soul, new-born of God,
Pants to view his glorious face,
Upward tends to his abode,
To rest in his embrace.
Fly, my riches! fly, my cares!
While I that coast explore,
Flattering world, with all your snares
Solicit me no more.
Pilgrims fix not here their home,
Strangers tarry but a night;
When the last bright morn shall come,
We'll rise to joyful light.
Cease, ye pilgrims, cease to mourn
Press onward to the prize;
Soon the Saviour will return,
Triumphant through the skies:
Yet a season, and you know
Happy entrance will be given
All your sorrows left below
And earth exchanged for heaven.

DEEP SPRING. C. M.
DOUGLASS.
As on the cross the Sa - viour hung, And wept, and bled, and died, He pour'd sal - va - tion on a wretch That lan-guish'd at his
side, that languish'd at his side, ... that languish'd at his side, He pour'd sal - va - tion on a wretch That languish'd at his side.

DEVIZES. C. M.

TUCKER.

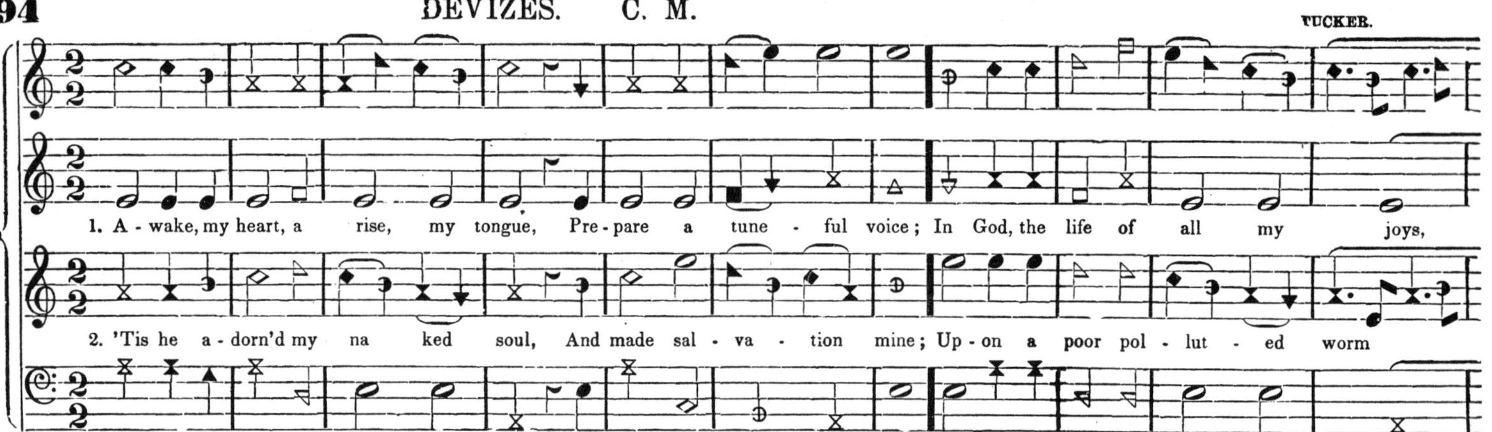

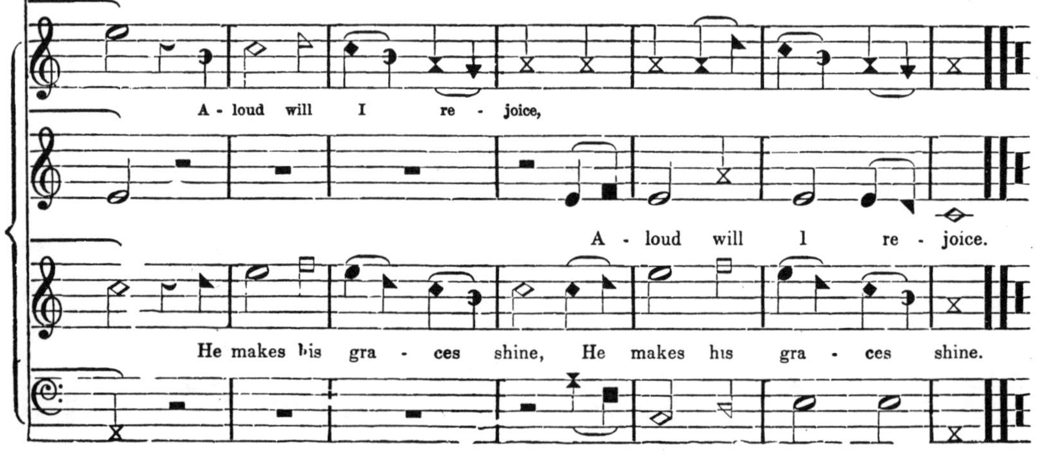

3. And lest the shadow of a spot
Should on my soul be found,
He took the robe the Saviour wrought,
And cast it all around.

4. How far the heavenly robe exceeds
What earthly princes wear!
These ornaments, how bright they shine.
How white the garments are!

5. The Spirit wrought my faith and love,
And hope, and every grace;
But Jesus spent his life to work
The robe of righteousness.

6. Strangely, my soul, art thou array'd
By the great Sacred Three:
In sweetest harmony of praise
Let all thy powers agree.

PARTING HAND. L. M

Counter by M. L. Swan.

WM. WALKER.

3. How sweet the hours have pass'd away,
Since we have met to sing and pray,
How loath we are to leave the place
Where Jesus shows his smiling face!

4. Oh! could I stay with friends so kind,
How would it cheer my drooping mind
But duty makes me understand,
That we must take the parting hand.

5 And since it is God's holy will
We must be parted for a while,
In sweet submission, all as one,
We'll say, our Father's will be done!

6. My youthful friends, in Christian ties,
Who seek for mansions in the skies,
Fight on! we'll gain that happy shore,
Where parting will be known no more.

7. How oft I've seen your flowing tears,
And heard you tell your hopes and fears!
Your hearts with love were seen to flame,
Which makes me hope we'll meet again.

8. Ye mourning souls, lift up your eyes,
To glorious mansions in the skies;
Oh! trust his grace—in Canaan's land,
We'll no more take the parting hand!

9. And now, my friends, both old and young,
I hope in Christ you'll still go on;
And if on earth we meet no more,
Oh! may we meet on Canaan's shore.

10. I hope you'll all remember me,
If you on earth no more I see;
An interest in your prayers I crave,
That we may meet beyond the grave.

11. Oh! glorious day, oh! blessed hope,
My soul leaps forward at the thought!
When, on that happy, happy land,
We'll no more take the parting hand.

12. But with our blessed, holy Lord,
We'll shout and sing with one accord;
And there we'll all with Jesus dwell,
So, loving Christians, fare you well!

HADDAM. H. M.
L. MASON.
1. The Lord Jehovah reigns; His throne is built on high; The garments he assumes Are light and majesty; His glories shine With beams so bright, No mor - tal eye Can bear the sight
2. The thunders of his hand Still keep the world in awe; His wrath and justice stand To guard his holy law: And where his love Resolves to bless, His truth con - firms And seals the grace.
WILMOT. 7s.
From C. M. von WEBER.
1. Heav'n - ly Fa - ther, sove - reign Lord, Be thy glorious name a-dored! Lord, thy mercies nev - er fail: Hail, ce - les - tial goodness, hail!
2. Though un - wor - thy, Lord, thine ear, Deign our humble songs to hear: Pu - rer praise we hope to bring When around thy throne we sing.

TEMPLE. 8s & 7s.
M. L. SWAN.
1. Cease, ye mourners, cease to languish O'er the graves of those you love,
Pain, and death, and night, and anguish, Enter not the world above.
2. While our silent steps are straying Lonely through night's deep'ning shade, Glory's brightest beams are playing Round th'
[spi - rit's head
3. Endless pleasure pain excluding, Sickness there no more can come;
There, no fear of woe intruding Sheds o'er heav'n a moment's gloom.
4. Now, ye mourners, cease to languish O'er the graves of those ye love: Far removed from pain and anguish, They are chanting hymns above
HERITAGE. 8, 6, 8, 8, 6.
M. L. SWAN.
1. There is an hour of peaceful rest To mourning wand'rers giv'n; There is a tear for souls distress'd. A balm for ev'ry wounded breast: 'Tis found a - lone in heav'n
2. There is a home for wea-ry souls, By sins and sorrows driv'n, When toss'd on life's tempestuous shoals, Where storms arise, and ocean rolls, And all is drear but heav'n.
G

LIBERTY. C. M.

WYTHE.

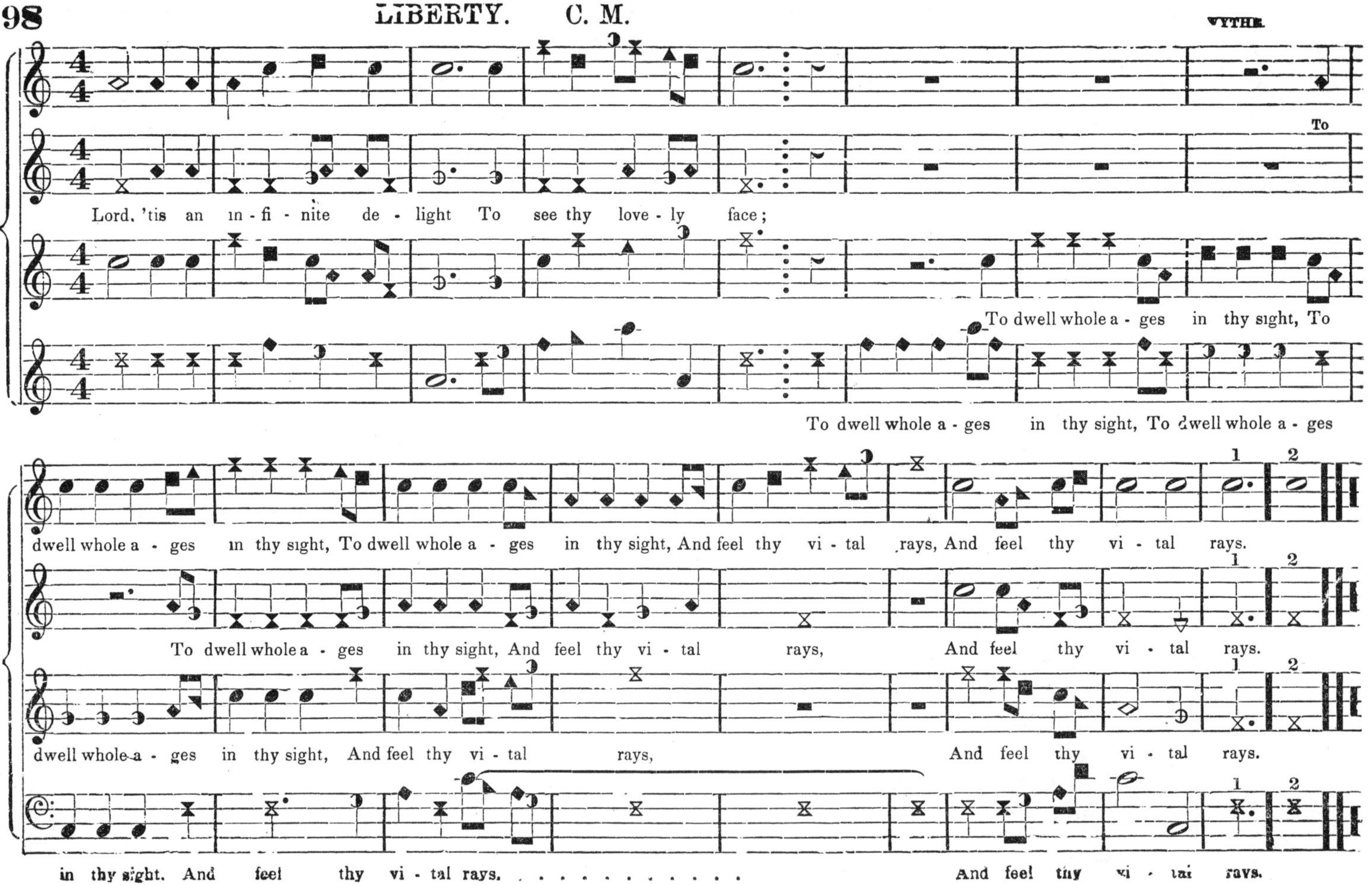

Counter by Swan.
MORNING TRUMPET.
CHORUS.
B. F. WHITE.
99
1. O when shall I see Je - sus, And reign with him a-bove? And shall hear the trumpet sound in that morn - ing.
And from the flow-ing foun-tain, Drink e - ver-lasting love? And shall hear the trumpet sound in that morn - ing.
Shout, Oh glo-
When shall I be de - li-vered From this vain world of sin? And shall hear the trumpet sound in that morn - ing.
And with my blessed Je - sus Drink endless pleasures in? And shall hear the trumpet sound in that morn - ing.
Shout, Oh glo-
ry! for I shall mount a-bove the skies, When I hear the trumpet sound in that morn - ing.
ry! for I shall mount a - bove the skies, When I hear the trumpet sound in that morn - ing.
2.
But now I am a soldier,
My Captain's gone before;
He's given me my orders,
And bids me ne'er give o'er,
His promises are faithful—
A righteous crown he'll give,
And all his valiant soldiers
Eternally shall live.
Shout, &c.
3.
Through grace I feel determined
To conquer, though I die,
And then away to Jesus,
On wings of love I'll fly:
Farewell to sin and sorrow,
I bid them both adieu!
And O my friends, prove faithful,
And on your way pursue.
Shout, &c.
4.
Whene'er you meet with troubles
And trials on your way,
Then cast your care on Jesus,
And don't forget to pray.
Gird on the gospel armour
Of faith, and hope, and love,
And when the combat's ended,
He'll carry you above.
Shout, &c.
5
O do not be discouraged,
For Jesus is your friend;
And if you lack for knowledge,
He'll not refuse to lend.
Neither will he upbraid you,
Though often you request;
He'll give you grace to conquer,
And take you home to rest.
Shout, &c.

PORTUGAL. L. M.

THORLEY.

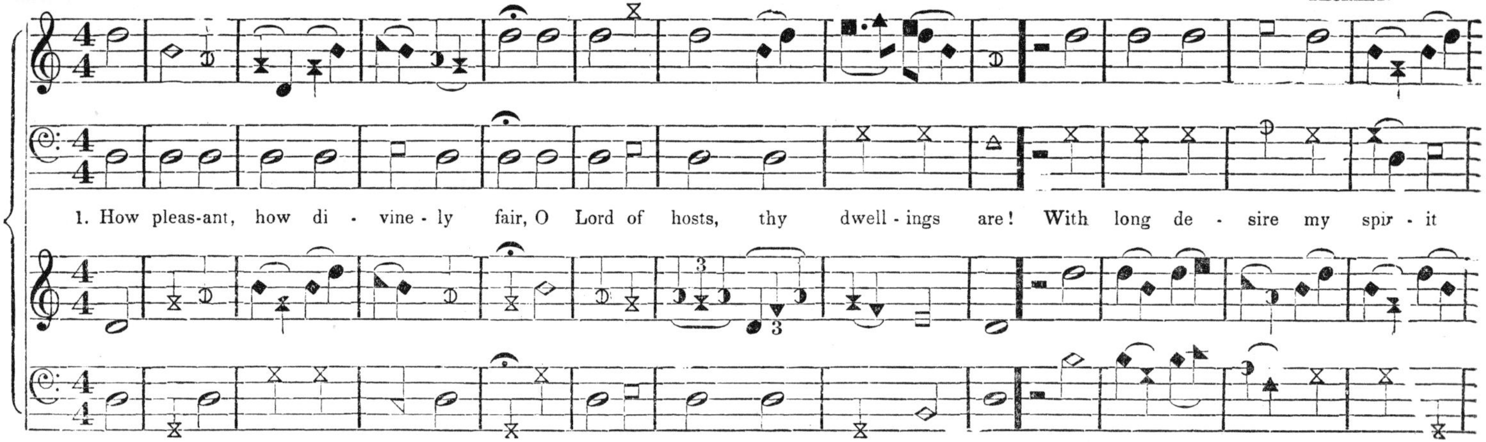

1. How pleas-ant, how di - vine - ly fair, O Lord of hosts, thy dwell - ings are! With long de - sire my spir - it

faints, To meet th' as - sem - blies of thy saints.

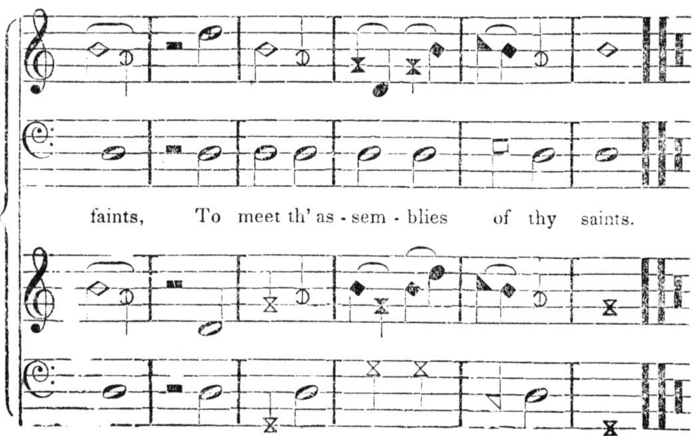

2.

My flesh would rest in thine abode,
My panting heart cries out for God;
My God, my King, why should I be
So far from all my joys, and thee?

3.

The sparrow chooses where to rest,
And for her young provides her nest;
But will my God to sparrows grant
That pleasure which his children want?

4.

Blest are the saints who sit on high,
Around thy throne of majesty;
Thy brightest glories shine above,
And all their work is praise and love.

5.

Blest are the souls that find a place
Within the temple of thy grace:
There they behold thy gentler rays,
And seek thy face and learn thy praise.

6.

Blest are the men whose hearts are set
To find the way to Zion's gate:
God is their strength, and through the road
They lean upon their helper, God.

7.

Cheerful they walk with growing strength
Till all shall meet in heaven at length;
Till all before Thy face appear,
And join in nobler worship there.

WINTER. C. M.

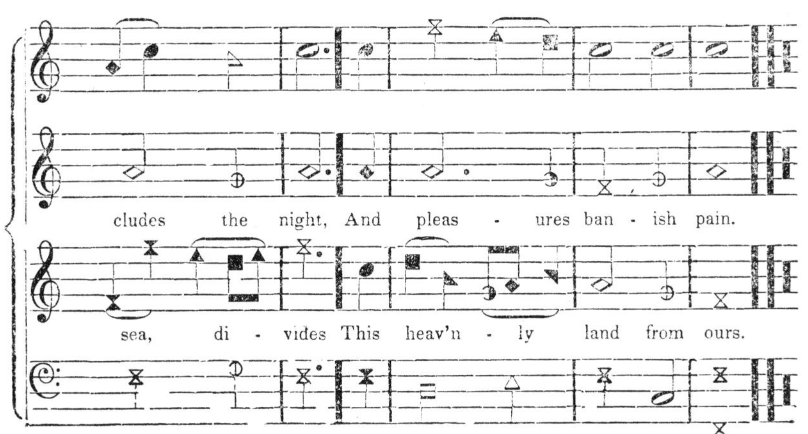

3. Sweet fields, beyond the swelling flood,
Stand dress'd in living green;
So to the Jews old Canaan stood,
While Jordan roll'd between.

4. But tim'rous mortals start and shrink
To cross this narrow sea,
And linger, shivering on the brink,
And fear to launch away.

5. Oh! could we make our doubts remove,
Those gloomy doubts that rise,
And see the Canaan that we love,
With unbeclouded eyes,

6. Could we but climb where Moses stood,
And view the landscape o'er;
Not Jordan's stream, nor death's cold flood
Should fright us from the shore!

FUNERAL THOUGHT. 12s & 11s.

CALDWELL

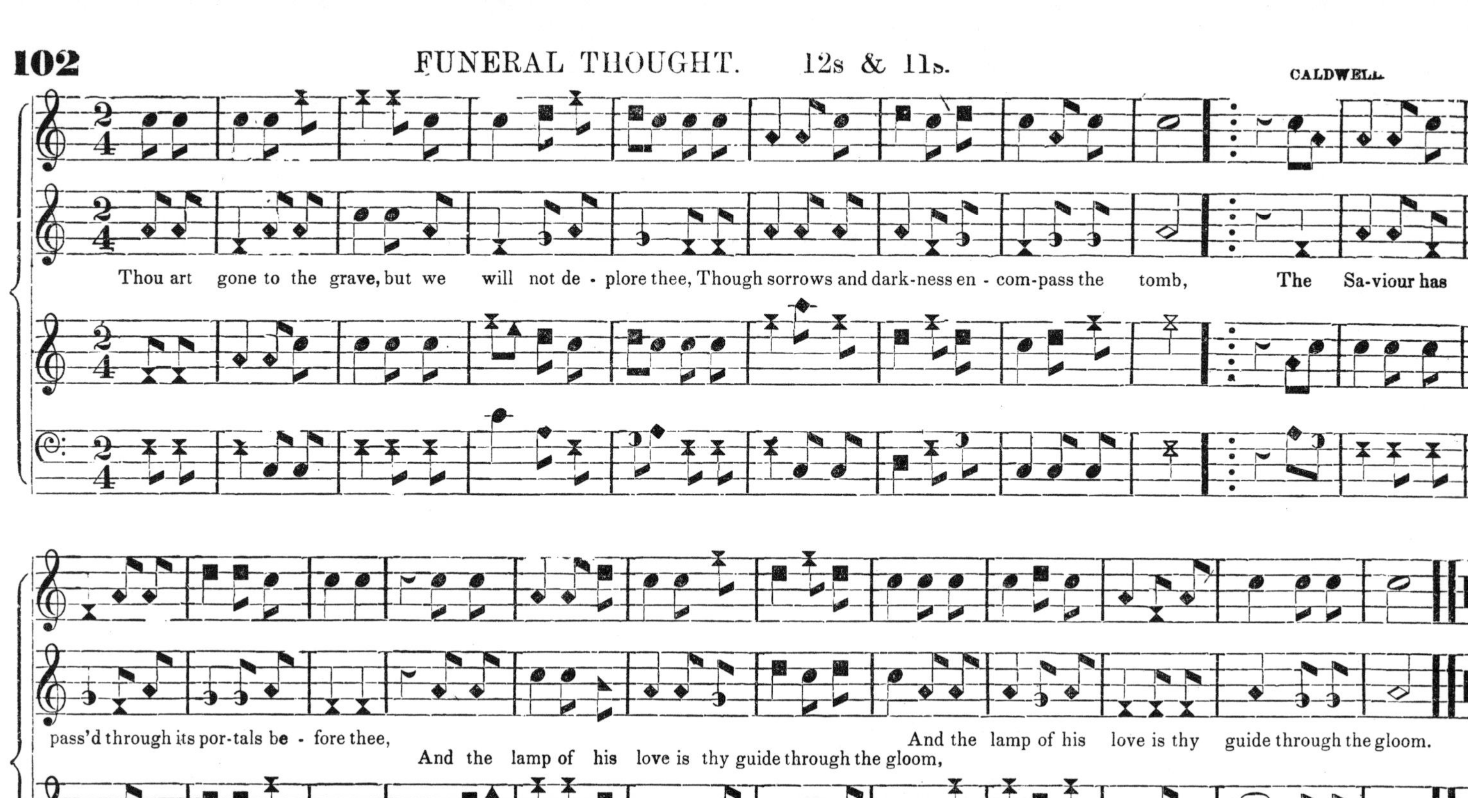

CANTON. 7s

CALDWELL.

3. Other refuge have I none,
Hangs my helpless soul on thee;
Leave, oh! leave me not alone,
Still support and comfort me!

4. All my trust on thee is stayed,
All my help from thee I bring;
Cover my defenceless head
With the shadow of thy wing.

5. Plenteous grace with thee is found,
Grace to pardon all my sins;
Let the healing streams abound,
Make and keep me pure within.

6. Thou of life the fountain art,
Freely let me take of thee;
Spring thou up within my heart,
Rise to all eternity!

MOUNT VERNON. 8s & 7s.
L. MASON.
Written, originally, on the death of a young Lady.
1. Sis - ter, thou wast mild and love - ly, Gen - tle as the sum - mer breeze, Plea - sant as the air of eve - ning When it floats a - mong the trees.
2. Peace - ful be thy si - lent slum - ber, Peace-ful, in the grave so low; Thou no more wilt join our num - ber, Thou no more our songs shalt know.
TAMWORTH. 8s, 7s & 4s.
LOCKHART.
1. Yes, we trust the day is break - ing; Joy - ful times are near at hand;
God, the migh-ty God, is speak - ing, By his word, in ev' - ry land.
When he choo - ses, When he choo - ses, Darkness flies, at his com - mand.

WOODS AND CALDWELL.

1. Lord, and is thine an-ger gone, And art thou pa - ci- fied,
After all that I have done, Dost thou no longer chide?
In - fi - nite thy mercies are, Beneath the weight I can - not move,
Oh! 'tis more than I can bear, The sense of pard'ning love.

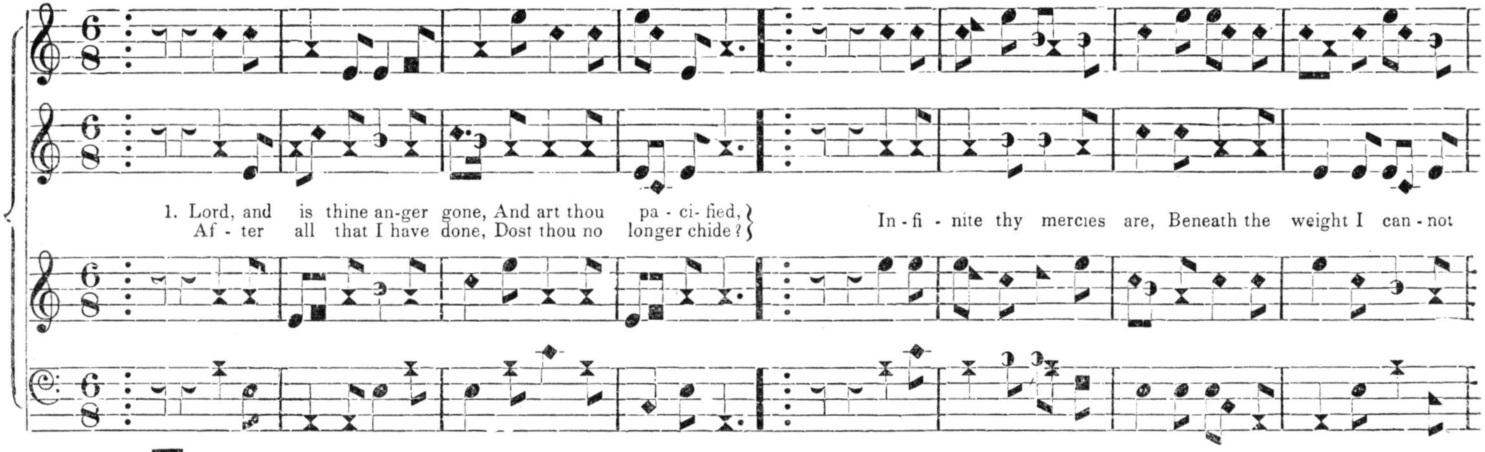

2. If I have begun once more,
Thy sweet return to feel,
If even now I find thy power,
Present my soul to heal;
Still and quiet may I lie,
Nor struggle out of thine embrace;
Never more resist or fly
From thy pursuing grace.

3. To the cross, thine altar, bind
Me with the cords of love;
Freedom let me never find
From thee, my Lord, to move;
That I never, never more
May with my much-loved Master part,
To the posts of mercy's door,
Oh! nail my willing heart!

OVERTON. L. M.

SWAN.

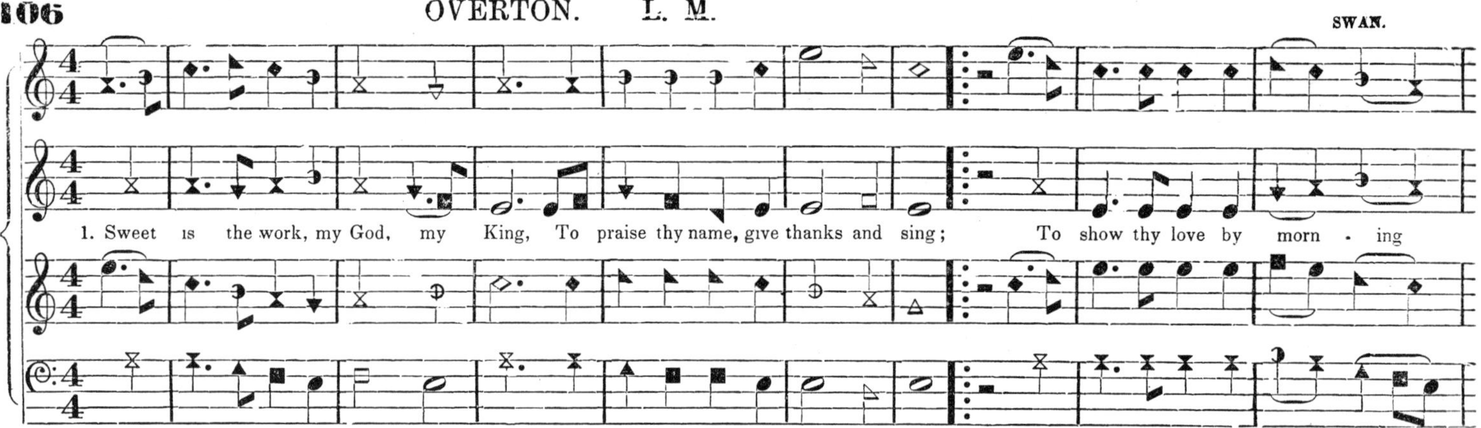

2. Sweet is the day of sacred rest,
No mortal cares shall seize my breast:
Oh may my heart in tune be found,
Like David's harp of solemn sound!

3. My heart shall triumph in my Lord,
And bless his works, and bless his word;
Thy works of grace, how bright they shine,
How deep thy counsels! how divine!

4. Fools never raise their thoughts so high;
Like brutes they live, like brutes they die,
Like grass they flourish, till thy breath
Blasts them in everlasting death.

5. But I shall share a glorious part,
When grace hath well refined my heart,
And fresh supplies of joy are shed,
Like holy oil, to cheer my head.

6. Sin, my worst enemy before,
Shall vex my eyes and ears no more;
My inward foes shall all be slain,
Nor Satan break my peace again.

7. Then shall I see, and hear, and know
All I desired or wished below;
And every power find sweet employ
In that eternal world of joy.

HOLY MANNA.

Jounter by Swan.

2. Brethren, see poor sinners round you,
Trembling on the brink of wo;
Death is coming, hell is moving,—
Can you bear to let them go?
See our fathers, see our mothers,
And our children sinking down·
Brethren, pray, and holy manna
Will be shower'd all around.

3. Sisters, will you join and help us?
Moses' sisters aided him;
Will you help the trembling mourners,
Who are struggling hard with sin?
Tell them all about the Saviour,
Tell them that he will be found;
Sisters, pray, and holy manna
Will be shower'd all around.

108
WAYNESVILLE. 8s, 7s & 4s.
1. Songs a - new of hon - or fra - ming, Sing ye to the Lord a - lone,
All his wondrous works pro - claim - ing,—Je - sus wondrous works hath done!
Glo - rious vic - t'ry His right hand and arm hath won.
HARWELL. 8s & 7s.
With Animation.
1. Hark! ten thousand harps and voices Sound the note of praise above:
Jesus reigns, and heav'n rejoices; Jesus reigns, the God of love.
See, he sits on yonder throne; Jesus rules the world a - lone. Halle - lu - jah! Halle - lu - jah! Halle - lu - jah! A - men.
2. Jesus, hail! whose glory brightens All above and gives it worth:
Lord of life, thy smile enlightens, Cheers, and charms thy saints on earth.
When we think of love like thine, Lord, we own it love di - vine. Halle - lu - jah! Halle - lu - jah! Halle - lu - jah! A - men.

Counter by Swan.

BRUCE'S ADDRESS. *Spiritualized.*

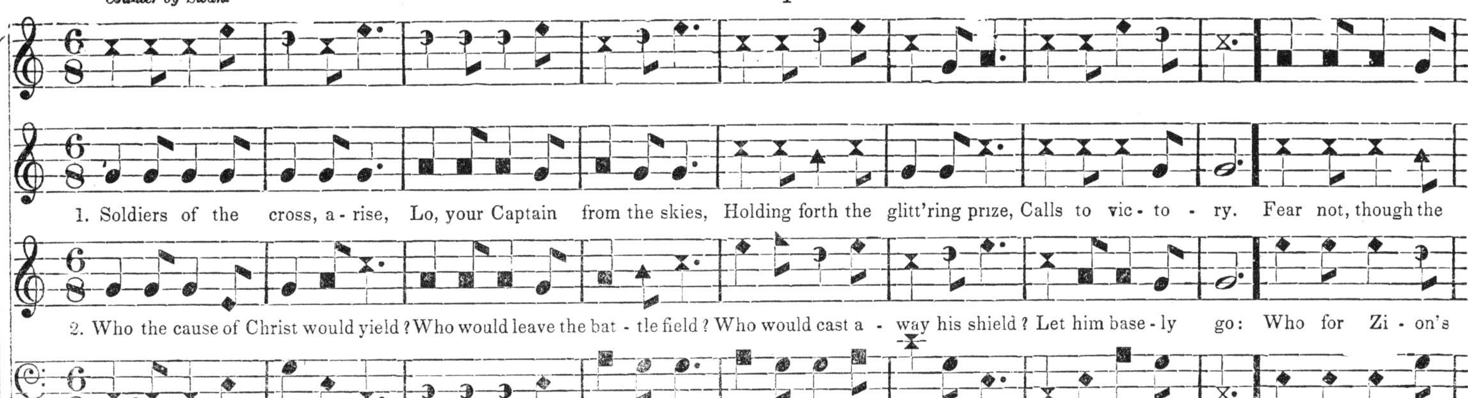

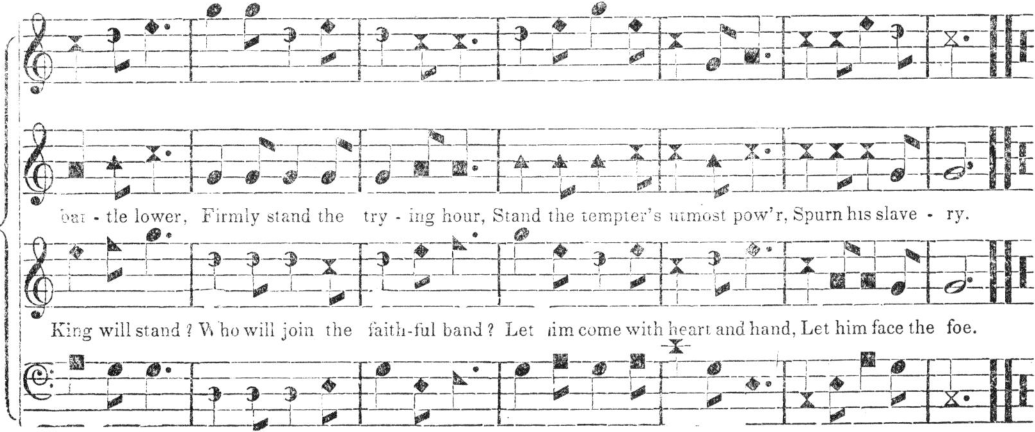

3.

By the mercies of our God,
By Emmanuel's streaming blood,
When alone for us he stood,
Ne'er give up the strife
Ever to the latest breath,
Hark to what your Captain saith;
"Be thou faithful unto death;
Take the crown of life."

4.

By the woes which rebels prove.
By the bliss of holy love,
Sinners, seek the joys above;
Sinners, turn and live!
Here is freedom worth the name;
Tyrant sin is put to shame;
Grace inspires the hallow'd flame;
God the crown will give.

Counter by Swan.

NORTH SALEM. C. M.

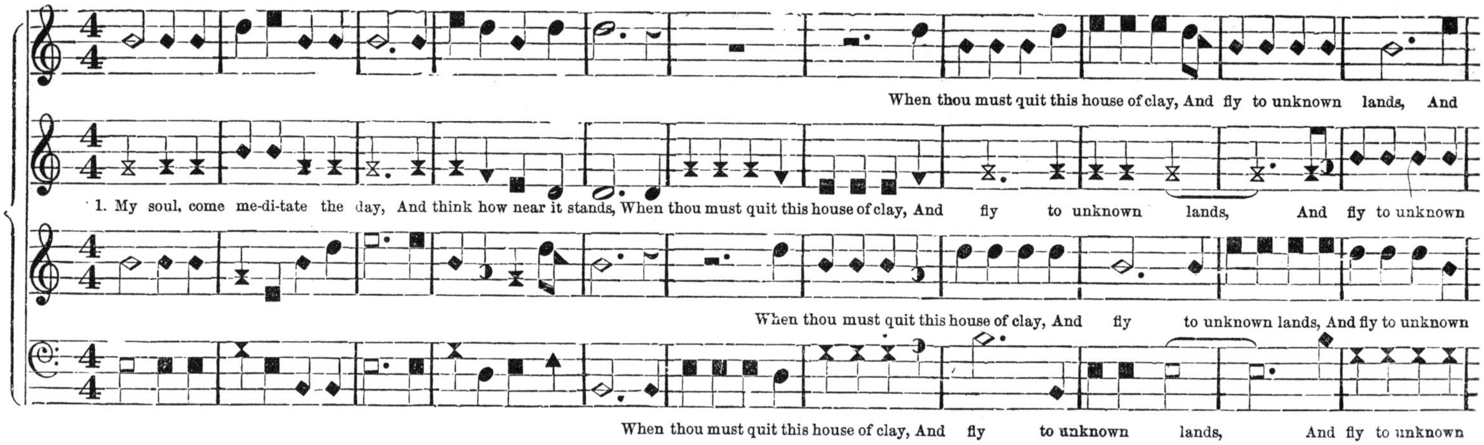

When thou must quit this house of clay, And fly to unknown lands, And

1. My soul, come me-di-tate the day, And think how near it stands, When thou must quit this house of clay, And fly to unknown lands, And fly to unknown

When thou must quit this house of clay, And fly to unknown lands, And fly to unknown

When thou must quit this house of clay, And fly to unknown lands, And fly to unknown

2. And you, mine eyes, look down and view
The hollow gaping tomb;
This gloomy prison waits for you
Whene'er the summons come.

3. Oh! could we die with those that die,
And place us in their stead;
Then would our spirits learn to fly,
And converse with the dead.

4. Then should we see the saints above,
In their own glorious forms.
And wonder why our souls should love
To dwell with mortal worms.

5. How we should scorn these clothes of flesh
These fetters, and this load;
And long for evening to undress,
That we may rest with God.

6. We should almost forsake our clay
Before the summons come,
And pray, and wish our souls away
To their eternal home.

SWAN.

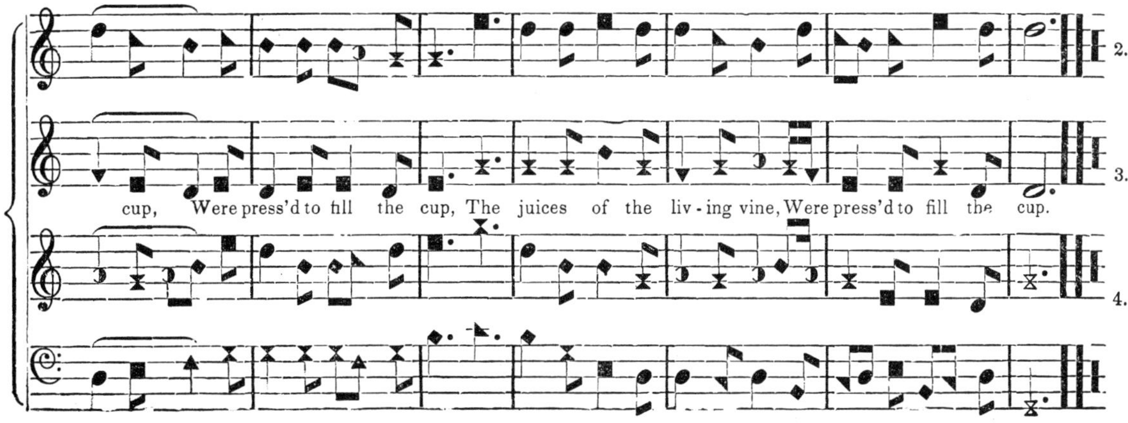

2. O bless the Saviour, ye that are
With royal dainties fed
Not heav'n affords a costlier fare,
For Jesus is the bread!

3. The vile, the lost, he calls to them,
"Ye trembling souls appear!"
The righteous in their own esteem
Have no acceptance here.

4. "Approach, ye poor, nor dare refuse
The banquet spread for you."
Dear Saviour, this is welcome news,
Then I may venture too.

HUMILITY. C. M.

CALDWELL.

3. "Jesus, the Son and heir of heav'n,
Thou spotless Lamb of God!
I see thee bathed in sweat and tears,
And welt'ring in thy blood.

4. "Yet quickly, from those scenes of wo,
In triumph thou shalt rise;
Burst through the gloomy shades of death,
And shine above the skies!

5. "Amid the glories of that world,
Dear Saviour, think on me;
And in the vict'ries of thy death,
Let me a sharer be."

6. His prayer the dying Jesus hears,
And instantly replies,
"To-day, thy parting soul shall be
With me in Paradise!"

SUTTON C. M
Save me, O God! the swelling floods, Break in upon my soul; I sink, and sorrows o'er my head Like mighty waters roll, like mighty waters roll.
LIVERPOOL. C. M.
1
2
Be-hold the man, threescore and ten, Up - on his dy ing bed, Has run his race and got no grace, An aw - ful sight in - deed.

ZION. 8s, 7s & 4s
1. On the mountain-top ap-pear-ing, Lo! the sa-cred herald stands,
Welcome news to Zi - on bear-ing, Zi - on long in hostile lands. Mourning cap - tive, God himself shall loose thy bands, Mourning cap - tive, God him-self shall loose thy bands.
2. Lo, thy sun is ris'n in glo - ry! God him - self appears thy friend;
All thy foes shall flee be - fore thee; Here their boasted triumphs end. Great de-liv'rance Zi - on's King will sure-ly send, Great de - liv'rance Zi - on's King will sure-ly send.
RICHMOND. 7s, 6s & 7s.
1. To the hills I lift my eyes, The ev - er - last-ing hills:
Streaming thence in fresh supplies, My soul the Spirit feels. Will he not his help afford? Help, while yet I ask, is given; God comes down, the God and Lord That made both earth and heav'n.

NORTHFIELD. C. M. INGOLS.

MILES' LANE. P. M

SHRUBSOLE.

1. All hail the pow'r of Je - sus' name, Let an - gels prostrate fall, Bring forth the roy - al di - a - dem,

Bring forth the roy - al di - a - dem, And crown him, crown him,

Bring forth the roy - al di - a - dem,

2. Crown him, ye martyrs of our God,
Who from his altar call:
Extol the stem of Jesse's rod,
And crown him—Lord of all.

3. Hail him, ye heirs of David's line,
Whom David Lord did call;
The God incarnate! Man Divine!
And crown him—Lord of all.

4. Ye chosen seed of Israel's race,
Ye ransom'd from the fall,
Hail him who saves you by his grace,
And crown him—Lord of all.

5. Sinners, whose love can ne'er forget
The wormwood and the gall,
Go, spread your trophies at his feet,
And crown him—Lord of all.

6. Let every kindred, every tribe,
On this terrestrial ball,
To him all majesty ascribe,
And crown him—Lord of all.

7. Oh, that with yonder sacred throng,
We at his feet may fall;
We'll join the everlasting song,
And crown him—Lord of all

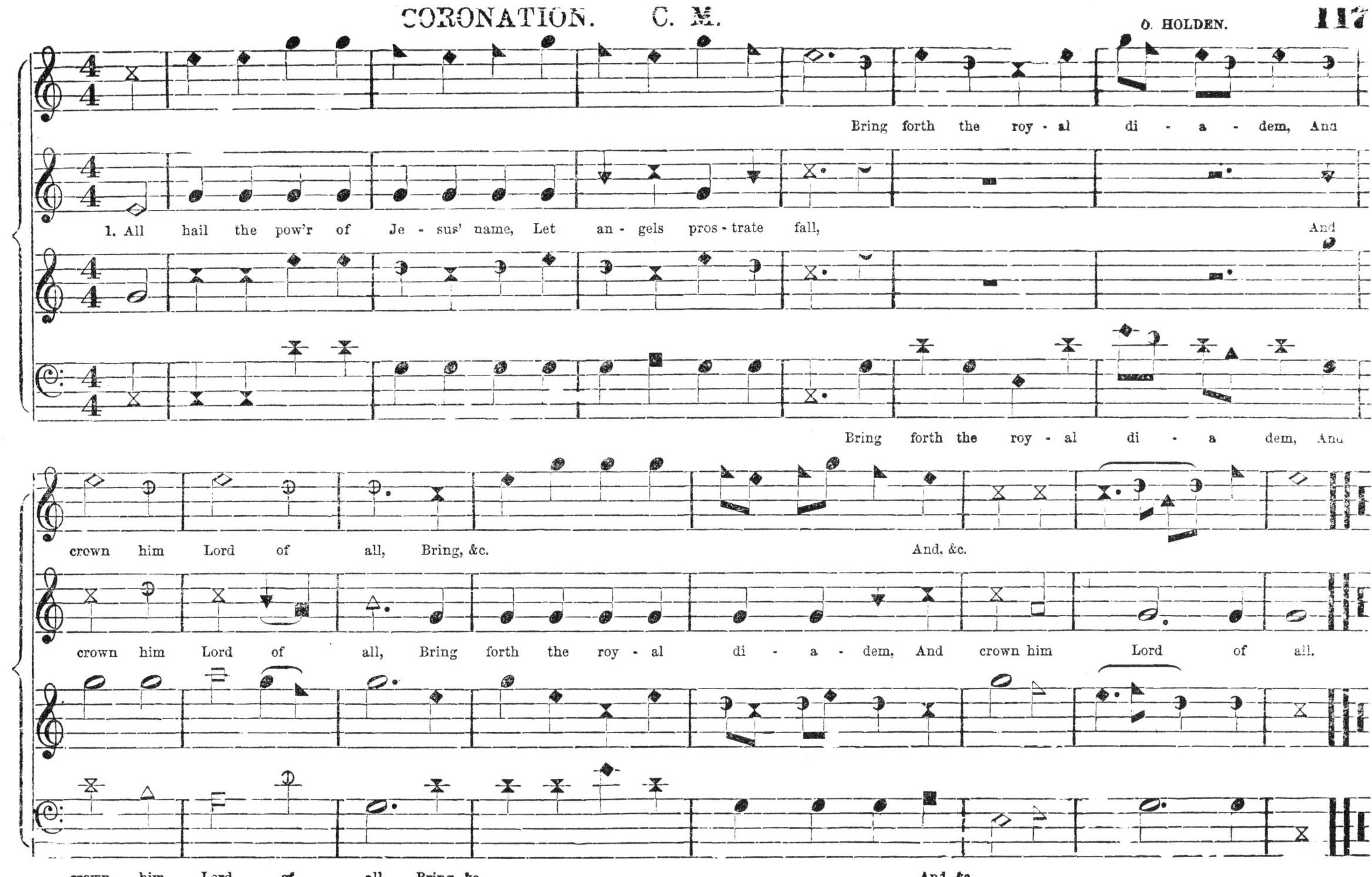
CORONATION. C. M.
O. HOLDEN.
Bring forth the roy - al di - a - dem, And
1. All hail the pow'r of Je - sus' name, Let an - gels pros - trate fall, And
Bring forth the roy - al di - a dem, And
crown him Lord of all, Bring, &c. And, &c.
crown him Lord of all, Bring forth the roy - al di - a - dem, And crown him Lord of all.
crown him Lord of all, Bring, &c. And, &c

CELEBRATION. 7s & 6s.

SWAN

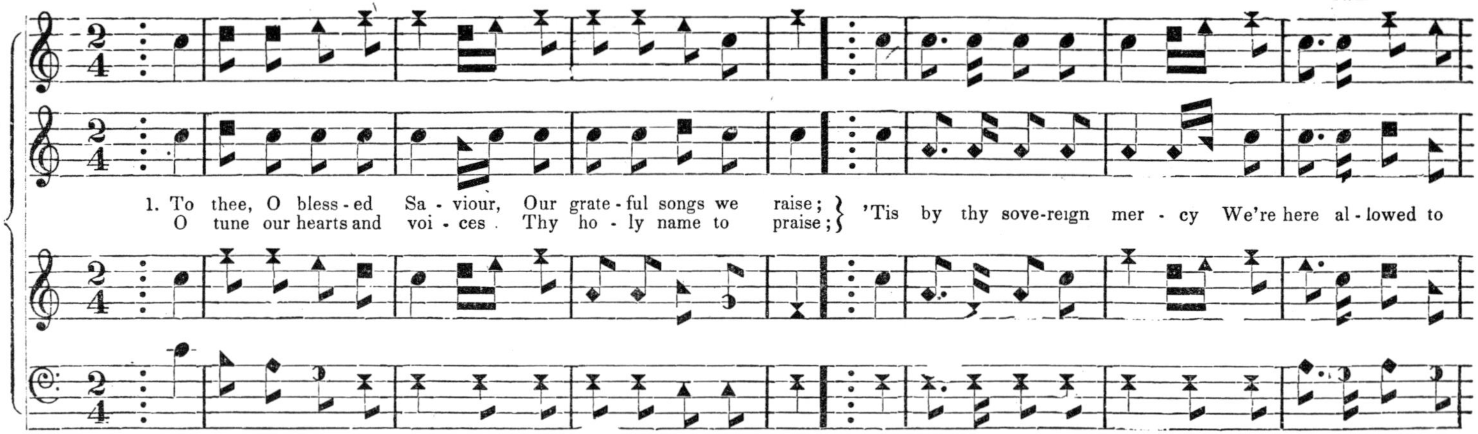

1. To thee, O bless - ed Sa - viour, Our grate - ful songs we raise; }
O tune our hearts and voi - ces . Thy ho - ly name to praise; }
'Tis by thy sove-reign mer - cy We're here al - lowed to

meet: To join with friends and teach - ers, Thy bless - ing to en - treat.

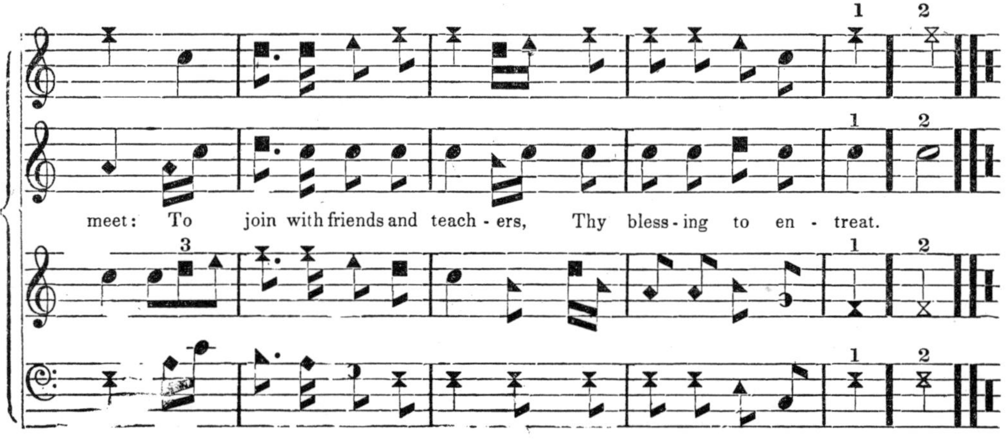

2. Lord, guide and bless our teachers
Who labour for our good,
And may the holy Scriptures
By us be understood;
Oh may our hearts be given
To thee, our glorious King!
That we may meet in heaven,
Thy praises there to sing.

3. And may the precious gospel
Be published all abroad,
Till the benighted heathen
Shall know and serve the Lord;
Till o'er the wide creation
The rays of truth shall shine,
And nations now in darkness
Arise to light divine.

HOLY ARMY. L. M. SWAN.

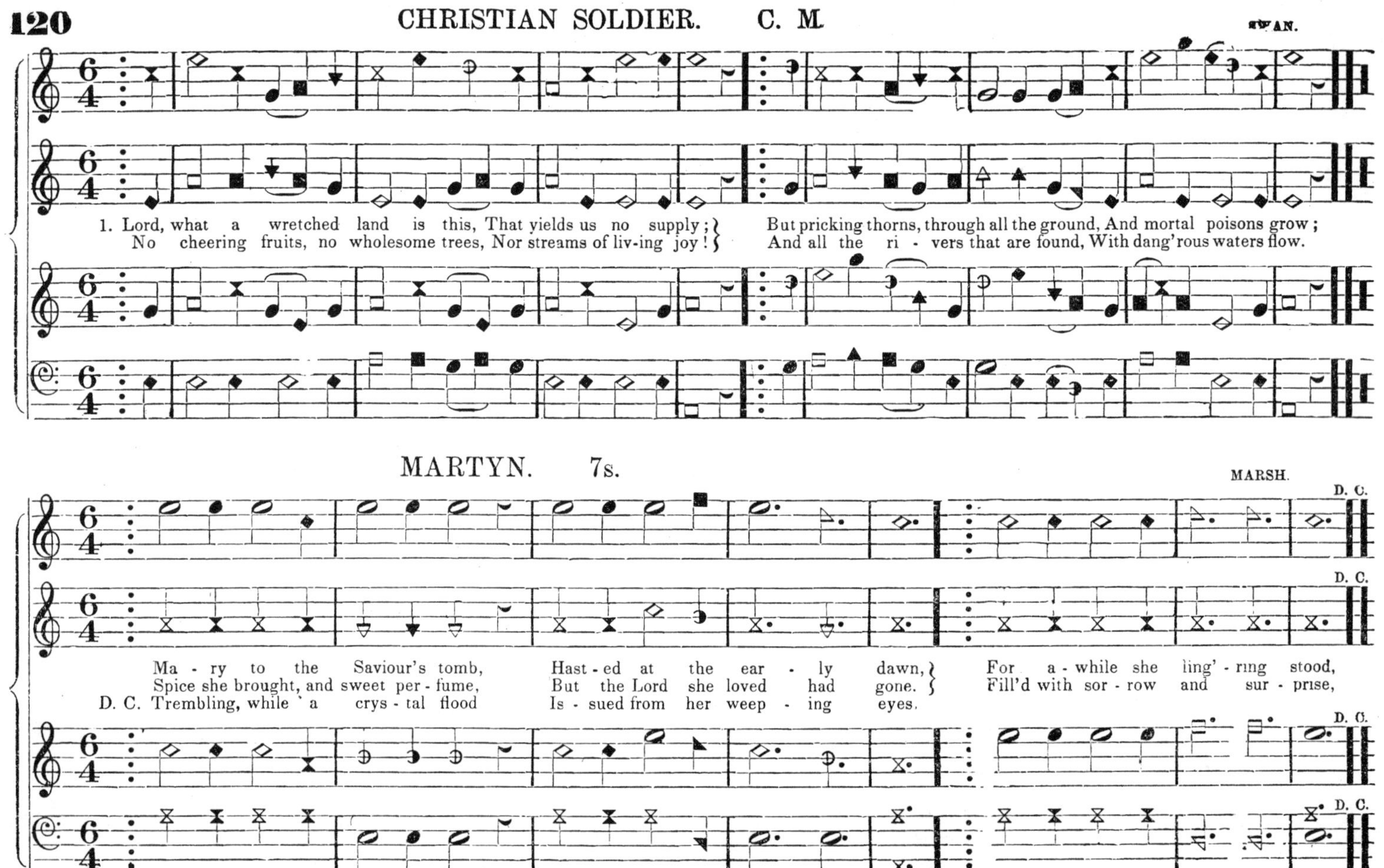
CHRISTIAN SOLDIER. C. M.
SWAN.
1. Lord, what a wretched land is this, That yields us no supply; No cheering fruits, no wholesome trees, Nor streams of liv-ing joy!
But pricking thorns, through all the ground, And mortal poisons grow; And all the ri - vers that are found, With dang'rous waters flow.
MARTYN. 7s.
MARSH.
D. C.
Ma - ry to the Saviour's tomb, Hast - ed at the ear - ly dawn,
Spice she brought, and sweet per - fume, But the Lord she loved had gone.
D. C. Trembling, while a crys - tal flood Is - sued from her weep - ing eyes.
For a - while she ling' - ring stood, Fill'd with sor - row and sur - prise,

SEAMAN 12 SWAN.

UMMER. 11s

WAN.

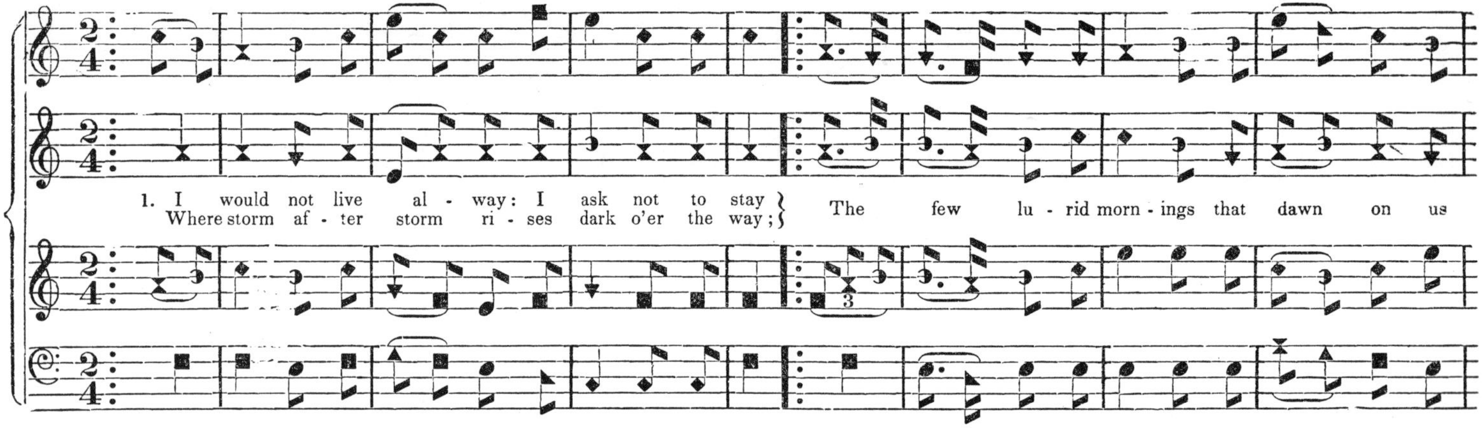

1. I would not live al - way: I ask not to stay
Where storm af - ter storm ri - ses dark o'er the way;
The few lu - rid morn - ings that dawn on us

here, Are e-nough for life's woes— full e - nough for its cheer.
1
2

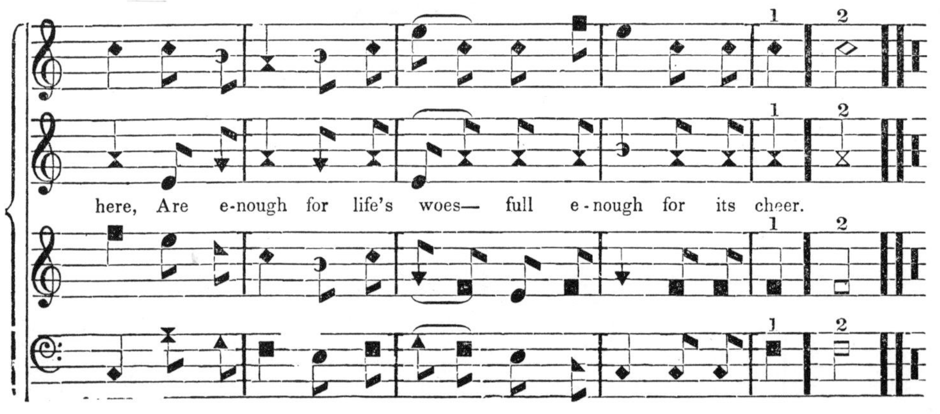

2. I would not live alway: no—welcome the tomb,
Since Jesus hath lain there, I dread not its gloom;
There, sweet be my rest, till he bid me arise,
To hail him in triumph descending the skies.

3. Who, who would live alway, away from his God,
Away from yon heaven, that blissful abode,
Where the rivers of pleasure flow o'er the bright plains,
And the noontide of glory eternally reigns?

4. Where the saints of all ages in harmony meet,
Their Saviour and brethren transported to greet;
While the anthems of rapture unceasingly roll,
And the smile of the Lord is the feast of the soul.

1
2
Come a - way to the skies, My be - lov - ed, a - rise, And re - joice in the day thou wast born! On this
fes - ti - val day, Come ex - ult - ing a - way, And with sing - ing to Zi - on re - turn.

THE SAINT'S ADIEU

M. L. SWAN.

1. What's this that steals, that steals up - on my frame, Is it death, is it death? That soon will quench, will quench, this vital flame, Is it death, is it death? If this be death, I soon shall be From every pain and

2. Weep not my friends, my friends, weep not for me, All is well, All is well. My sins are pardon'd, pardon'd, I am free, All is well, All is well. There's not a cloud that doth arise, To hide my Je - sus

3. Tune, tune your harps, your harps, ye saints in glory,
All is well, all is well.
I will rehearse, rehearse the pleasing story,
All is well, all is well.
Bright angels are from glory come,
They're round my bed, they're in my room,
They wait to waft my spirit home.
All is well, all is well.

4. Hark, hark, my Lord, my Lord and Master calls me!
All is well, all is well;
I soon shall see, shall see his face in glory
All is well, all is well,
Farewell, my friends, adieu, adieu,
I can no longer stay with you,
My glittering crown appears in view;
All is well, all is well.

5. Hail, hail, all hail, all hail, ye blood-wash'd throng,
Saved by grace, saved by grace,
I come to join, to join your rapturous song,
Saved by grace, saved by grace.
All, all is peace and joy divine,
And heaven and glory now are mine,
Ah! hallelujah to the Lamb,
All is well, all is well.

THOU ART PASSING AWAY. 11s.

Arranged by Rev. George Coles from Russell's "Mind of the Winter Night."

LUCAS. 5s, 6s & 11s.

1. Come, let us a - new Our journey pur-sue, Roll round with the year, And nev - er stand still till the Mas - ter ap-pear; His a - do - ra - ble

2. Our life is a dream, Our time as a stream Glides swiftly a - way, And the fu - gi - tive moment re - fu - ses to stay. The ar - row is

will Let us gladly ful - fil, And our tal - ents im-prove By the patience of hope and the la - bor of love, By the pa - tience of hope and the la - bor of love.

flown, The moment is gone, The moment is gone, The mil - len - ni - al year rushes on to my view, And e - ter - ni-ty's here, And e - ter - ni - ty's here.

THE ROCK. 11s.

Harmony by M. L. Swan.

IANTHE.

CALDWELL.

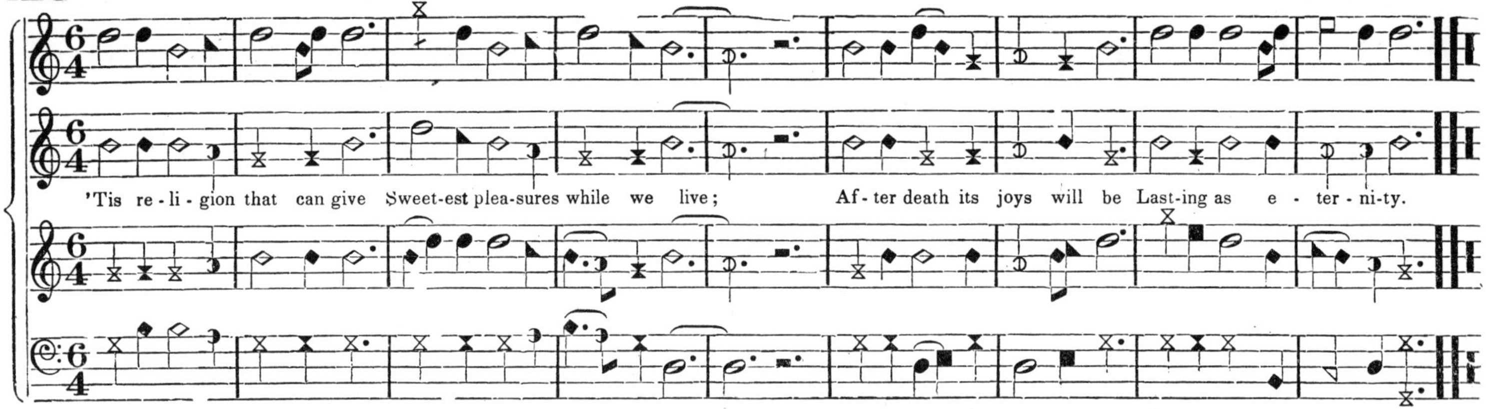

'Tis re - li - gion that can give Sweet-est plea-sures while we live; Af - ter death its joys will be Last-ing as e - ter - ni-ty.

ORTONVILLE. C. M.

Oh! for a closer walk with God, A calm and heav'nly frame; A light to shine up - on the road That leads me to the Lamb, That leads me to the Lamb.

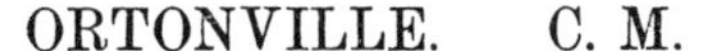

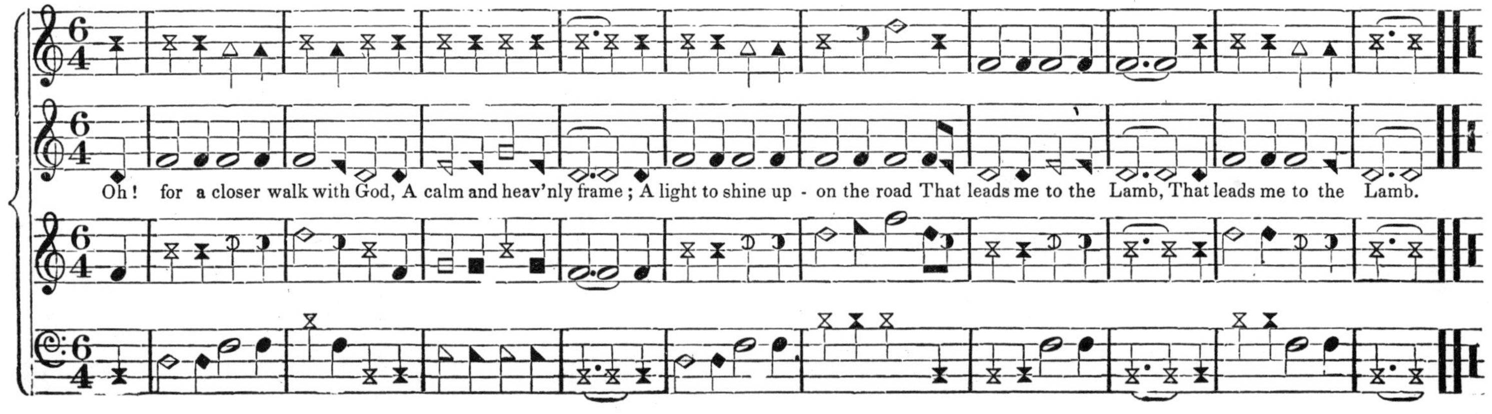

DUBLIN. C. M

Lord, what is man, poor fee-ble man? Born of the earth at first; His life a sha-dow, light and vain, Still hast'ning to the dust.
Counter by Swan.
WATCHMAN. C. M.
A charge to keep I have, A God to glo ri - fy; A nev - er dy - ing soul to save, And fit it for the sky.

ANTIOCH. C. M.

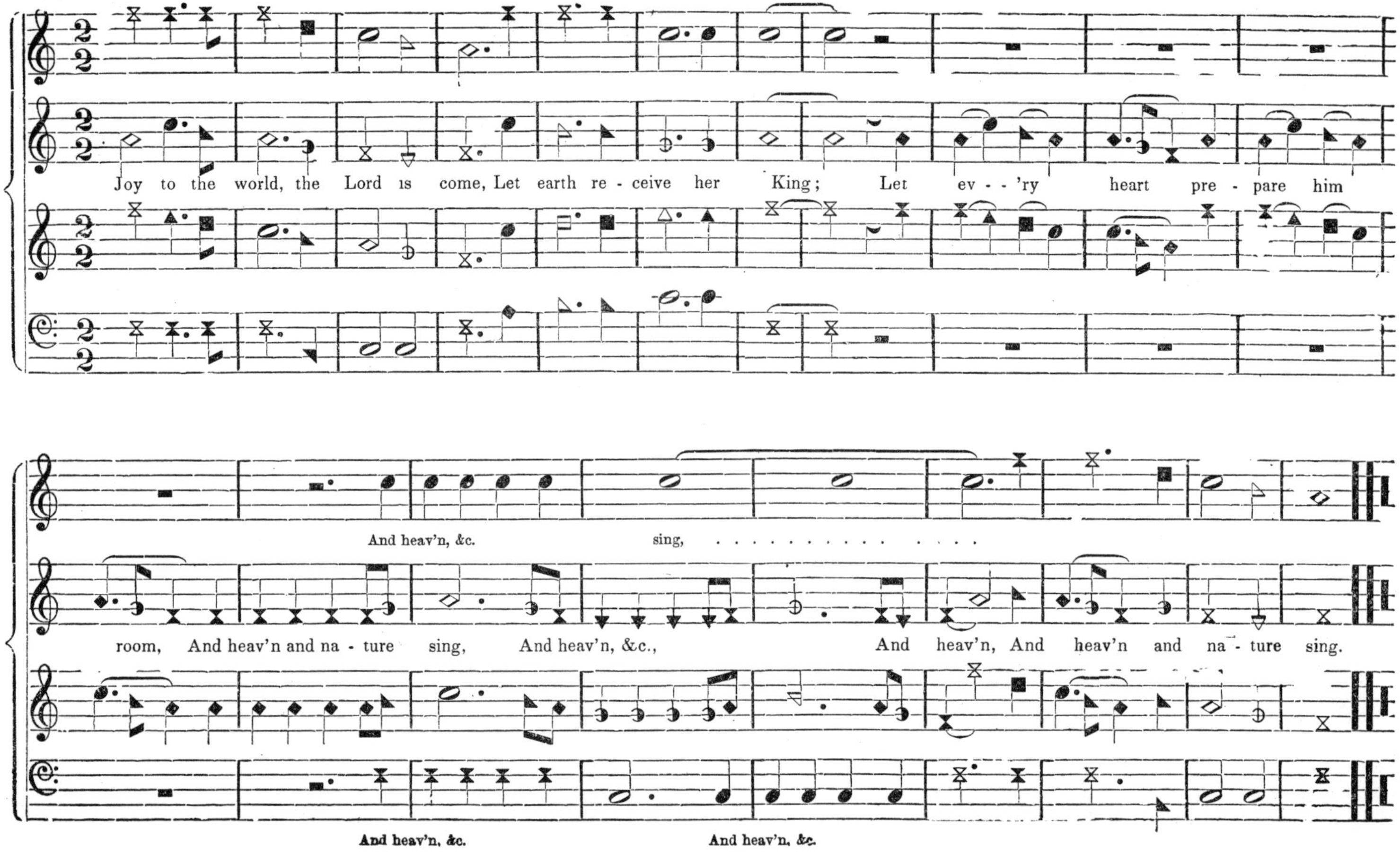

Joy to the world, the Lord is come, Let earth re - ceive her King; Let ev - - 'ry heart pre - pare him

MARSTON. 6's.

COLLIER.

1. O gracious Lord of all, Thy little children see, And mer-ci-ful-ly call Our wand'-ring hearts to thee.

2. Oh let thy pow'r-ful grace Our souls' at-ten-tion draw, And on our mem'-ries trace Thy ne-ver-chang-ing law.

BROOMFIELD. S. M.

SWAN.

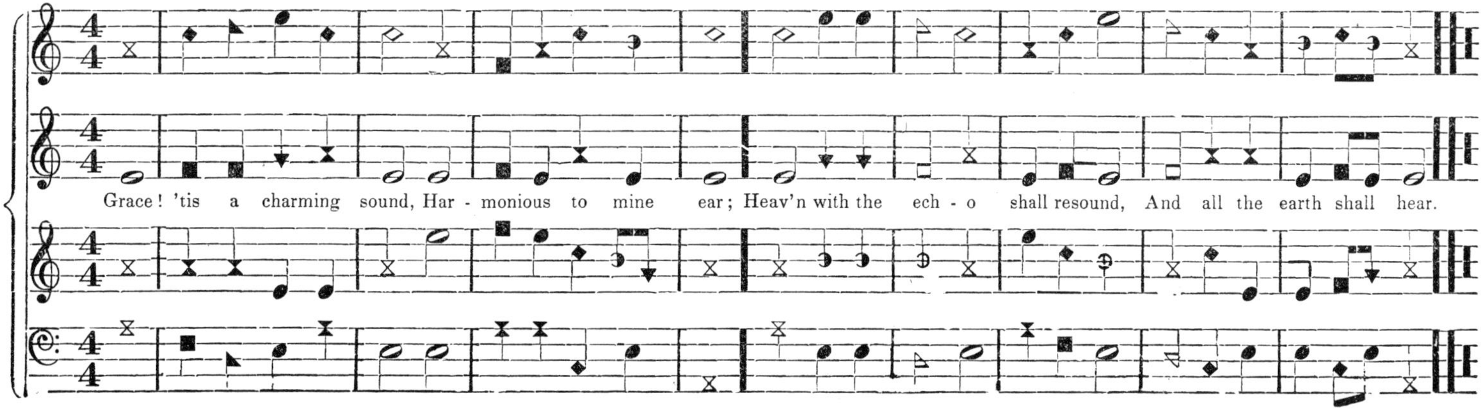

Grace! 'tis a charming sound, Har-monious to mine ear; Heav'n with the ech-o shall resound, And all the earth shall hear.

LISCHER. H. M

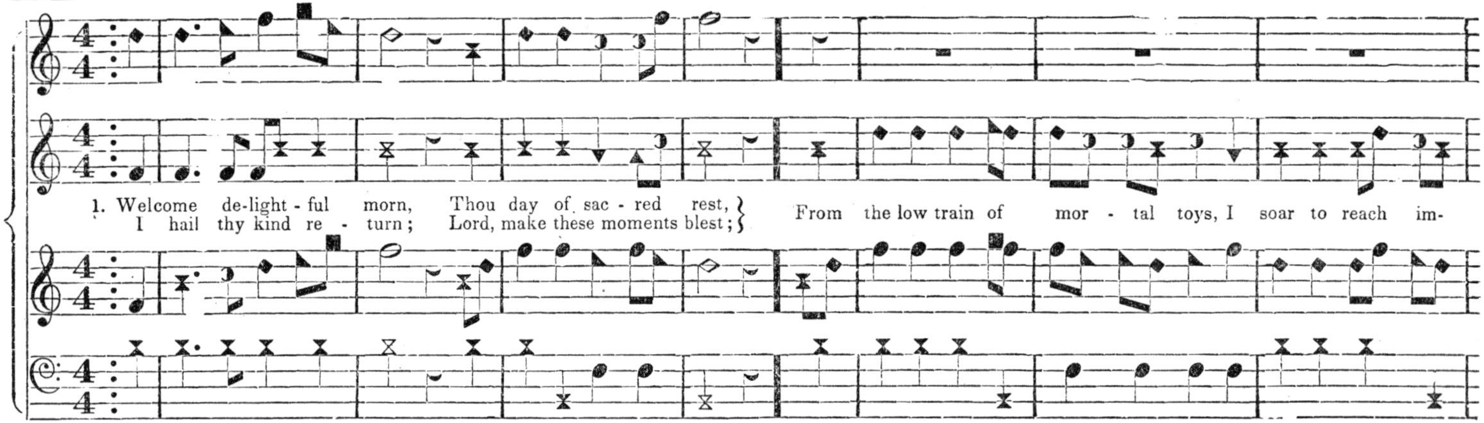

1. Welcome de-light - ful morn, Thou day of sac - red rest,
I hail thy kind re - turn; Lord, make these moments blest;
From the low train of mor - tal toys, I soar to reach im-

I soar, &c.
mor - tal joys, I soar to reach im - mor - tal joys.
I soar, &c.

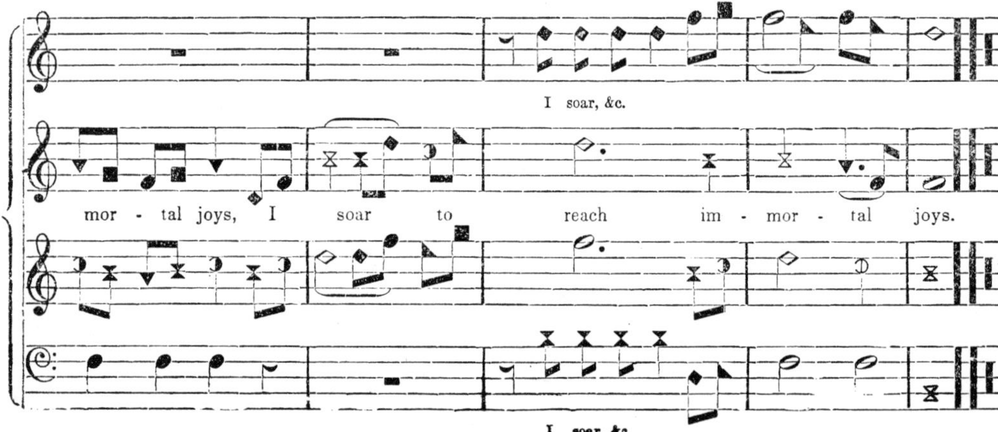

2.

Now may the king descend,
And fill his throne of grace!
Thy sceptre, Lord, extend,
While saints address thy face:
Let sinners feel thy quick'ning word,
And learn to know and fear the Lord.

3.

Descend, celestial Dove,
With all thy quick'ning powers;
Disclose a Saviour's love,
And bless these sacred hours:
Then shall my soul new life obtain,
Nor Sabbaths be indulged in vain

TO-DAY. 6s & 4s.
1. To-day the Saviour calls, Ye wand rers come! O ye be-night-ed souls, Why long-er roam?
2. To-day the Saviour calls, Oh hear him now! With-in these sa-cred walls, To Je-sus bow.
3. To-day the Saviour calls, For ref-uge fly! The storm of Jus-tice falls, And death is nigh.
PERU. C. M.
SWAN.
1. Sal-va-tion! Oh the joy-ful sound! 'Tis pleasure to our ears; A sovereign balm for every wound, A cor-dial for our fears.
2. Bur-ied in sorrow and in sin, At hell's dark door we lay, But we arise by grace divine, To see a heav'nly day.
3. Sal-va-tion! let the ech-o fly, The spacious earth around, While all the armies of the sky Conspire to raise the sound.

Counter by Swan.

INDIAN'S FAREWELL. 7s

2. Though in distant lands we sigh,
Parch'd beneath the hostile sky;
Though the deep between us rolls,
Friendship shall unite our souls;
And in fancy's wide domain,
There shall we all meet again.

3. When our burnish'd locks are gray,
Thinn'd by many a toil-spent day,
When around the youthful pine
Moss shall creep and ivy twine;
Long may the loved bow'r remain,
Ere we all shall meet again.

4. When the dreams of life are fled,
When its wasted lamps are dead;
When in cold oblivion's shade,
Beauty, wealth and fame are laid,
Where immortal spirits reign,
There may we all meet again

SPRING PLACE. L. P. M. or 6 lines 8s. SWAN.

2. Why should I make a man my trust?
Princes must die and turn to dust;
Vain is the help of flesh and blood:
Their breath departs, their pomp and power
And thoughts all vanish in an hour,
Nor can they make their promise good.

3. Happy the man whose hopes rely
On Israel's God: he made the sky,
And earth and seas, with all their train;
His truth for ever stands secure;
He saves th' opprest, he feeds the poor,
And none shall find his promise vain.

4. The Lord hath eyes to give the blind;
The Lord supports the sinking mind;
He sends the labouring conscience peace:
He helps the stranger in distress,
The widow and the fatherless,
And grants the prisoner sweet release.

THE PEARL. 7,6,7,6,8,8,6,6.

SWAN.

3. The road that many travel
Is not the road for me;
It leads to death and sorrow,
In it I would not be.
But there's a road that leads to God,
'Tis mark'd by Christ's most precious blood,
The passage here is free,
Oh that's the road for me.

4. The hope that sinners cherish
Is not the hope for me;
Most surely will they perish
Unless from sin made free.
But there's a hope which rests in God,
And leads the soul to keep his word,
And sinful pleasures flee;
Oh that's the hope for me

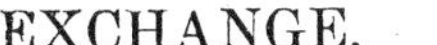

EXCHANGE. C. M.

SWAN.

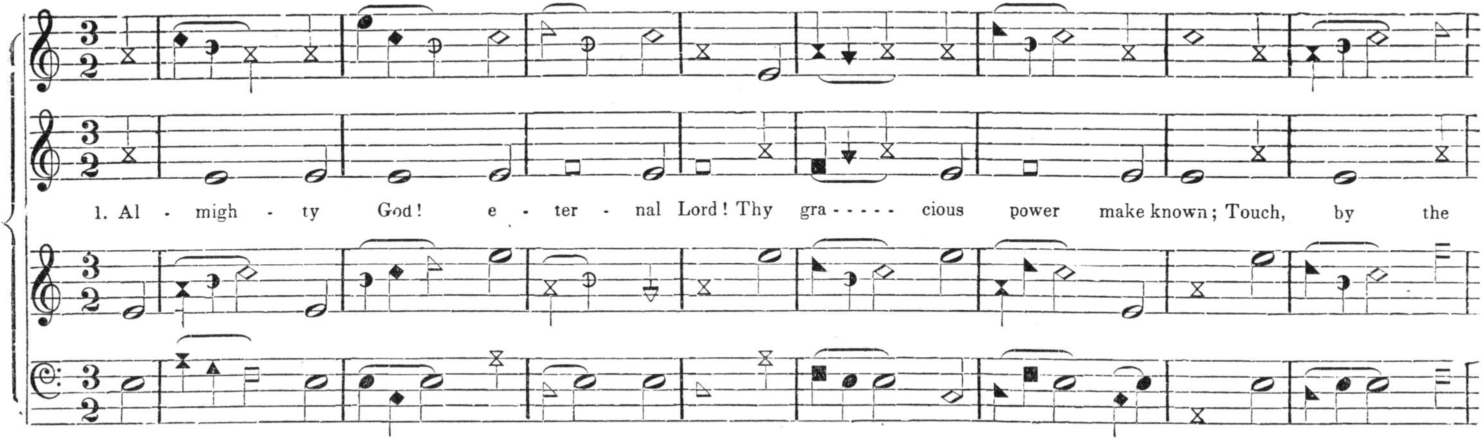

1. Al - migh - ty God! e - ter - nal Lord! Thy gra - - - - - cious power make known; Touch, by the

vir - - - - - tue of thy word, And melt . . . . . the heart of stone.

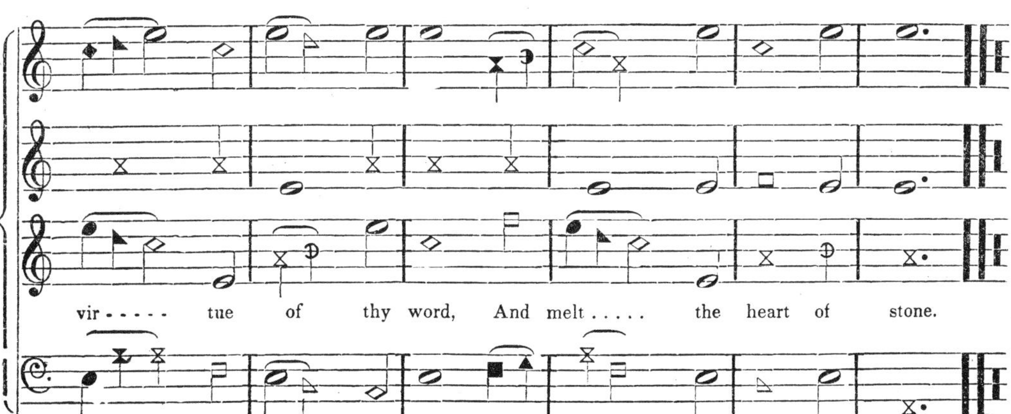

2. Speak with a voice that wakes the dead
   And bid the sleeper rise;
And let his guilty conscience dread
   The death that never dies.

3. Let us receive the word we hear,
   Each in an honest heart;
Lay up the precious treasure there,
   And never with it part.

4. Now let our darkness comprehend
   The light that shines so clear;
Now the revealing Spirit send,
   And give us ears to hear.

CARDIPHONIA

Music by SWAN.
Words by Thos. Mackellar.

1. Far dis - tant from my Father's house I would no long - er stay; But gird my soul and hast - en

2. The skies are dark, the thunders roll,
   And lightnings round me play;
   Let me but feel my Saviour near,
   I'll sing upon the way! And sing! &c.

3. The night is long and drear, I cry;
   Oh when will come the day?
   I see the morning star arise,
   And sing upon the way!

4. When care and sickness bow my frame,
   And all my powers decay,
   I'll ask Him for His promised grace,
   And sing upon the way!

5. He'll not forsake me when I'm old
   And weak, and blind, and gray;
   I'll lean upon his faithfulness,
   And sing upon the way!

6. When grace shall bear me home to God—
   Disrobed of mortal clay,
   I'll enter in the pearly gates,
   And sing upon the way!
   And sing! and sing!
   An everlasting day!

MEDITATION. C. M. D

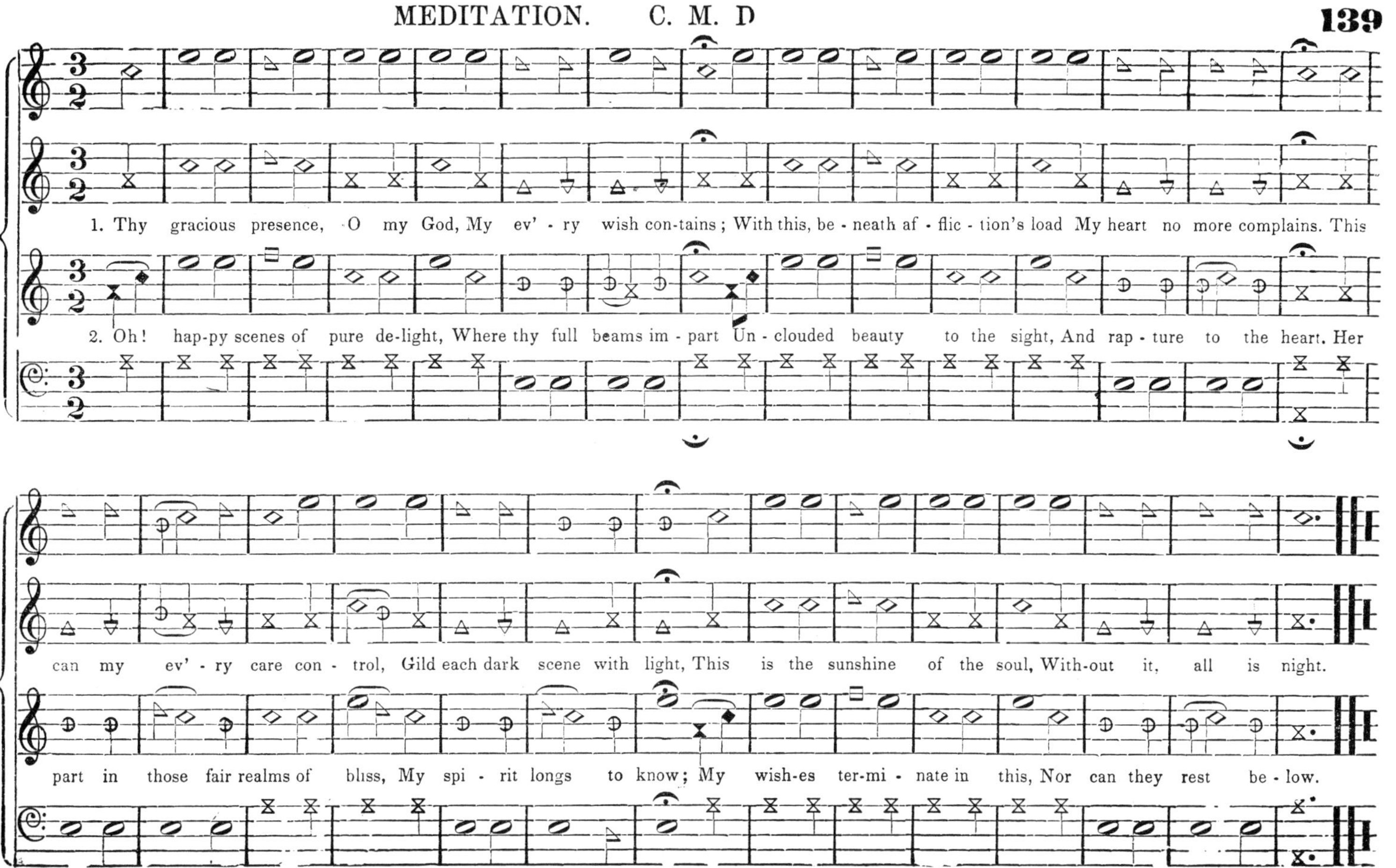

HASTEN, SINNER, TO BE WISE. 7s.

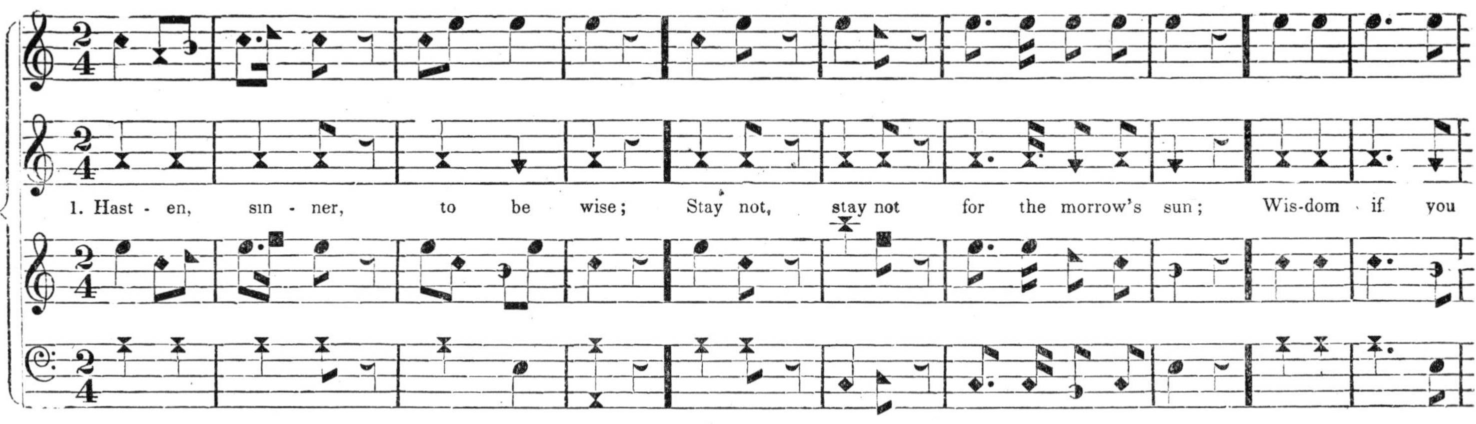

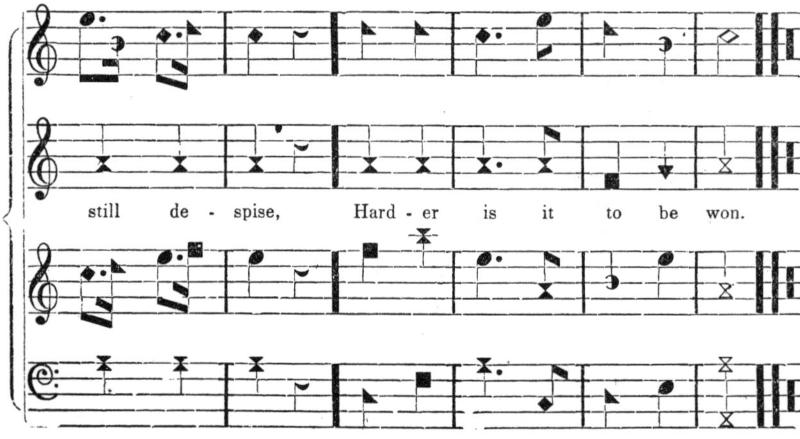

2. Hasten mercy to implore;
Stay not, stay not for the morrow's sun,
Lest thy season should be o'er,
Ere this evening's course be run.

3. Hasten, sinner, to return;
Stay not, stay not for the morrow's sun,
Lest thy lamp should cease to burn,
Ere salvation's work is done.

4. Hasten, sinner, to be bless'd;
Stay not, stay not for the morrow's sun,
Lest perdition thee arrest,
Ere the morrow is begun.

5. Lord, do thou the sinner turn;
Rouse him, rouse him from his senseless state;
Let him not thy counsel spurn,
And lament his choice too late.

PART II.

CONSISTING PRINCIPALLY OF PIECES USED IN SCHOOLS AND SOCIETIES.

JOYFUL. C. M.

fought to win the prize, And sail'd thro' bloody seas? Oh! that will be joy - ful, joy - ful, joy - ful, Oh! that will be joy - ful, to meet to part no
more, To meet to part no more, On Canaan's hap - py shore, We all shall meet at Je - sus' feet, With those who've gone be - fore.

WONDROUS LOVE. 12,9,6,6,12.9.

CHRISTOPHER.

ROWLEY. 6s & 9s, or 5s & 8s.

OLIPHANT. 8,7,4.

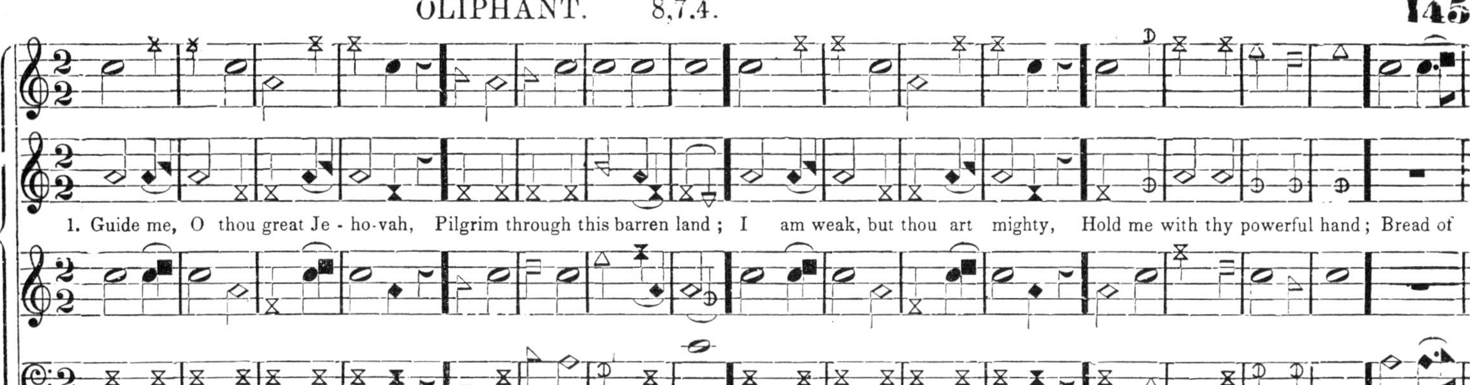

2.

When I tread the verge of Jordan
Bid my anxious fears subside;
Bear me through the swelling current;
Land me safe on Canaan's side:
Songs of praises,
I will ever give to thee.

3.

Open now the crystal fountain,
Whence the healing streams do flow;
Let the fiery, cloudy pillar
Lead me all my journey through:
Strong Deliv'rer,
Be thou still my strength and shield.

EDOM. C. M.

With songs . . . and hon-ours sound-ing loud, Ad-dress . . . . the Lord on high, ... O-ver the heav'ns he spreads his clouds,
And wa-ters veil the
And wa-ters veil the

sky, ... And wa-ters veil . . . the sky. He sends his show'rs of bless-ings down, To
sky, And wa- . . . ters veil the sky. He sends his show'rs of bless-ings down, To cheer the plains be - low; . . . .
sky, ... And wa - ters veil . . . . . the sky. He sends his show'rs of bless-ings down, To cheer the plains be - low; . . .

EDOM. *Concluded*

MEXICO. 7s & 6s.

SWAN.

D. C.

How lost was my con - di-tion, Till Je-sus made me whole,
There is but one phy - si-cian Can cure my sin - sick soul!
The worst of all dis - eases Is light compared with sin,
D. C. On eve - ry part it seizes, But rages most with - in.

D. C.

D. C.

FRANCE. 7s & 6s.

SWAN

place; Pray, where-fore are you smil - ing, While tears run down your face? We soon shall cease from toil - ing, And reach that heav'nly place.

OLNEY. S. M.

The Spi - rit in our hearts Is whis-p'ring, "Sin - ner, come," The bride, the church of Christ, pro - claims To all his chil - dren "Come."

EGYPT. 8s

SWAN.

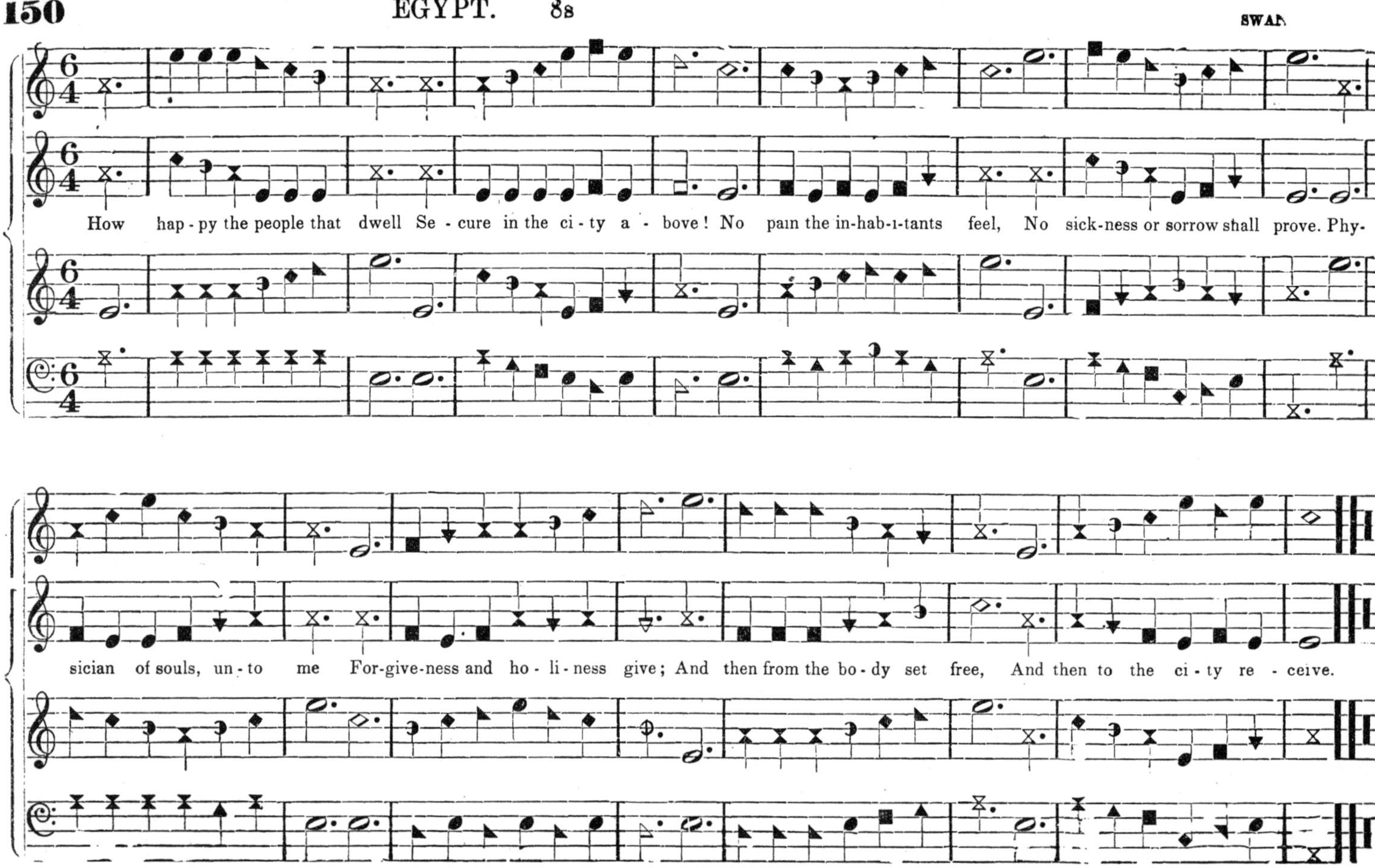

While thee I seek, pro - tect-ing Power, Be my vain wish - es still'd; And may this con - se - cra - ted hour With bet - ter hopes be fill'd!
Thy love the power of thought bestow'd, To thee my thoughts would soar, Thy mercy o'er my life has flow'd, That mer - cy I a - dore.

152
MILFORD. C. M.
STEPHENSON.
If an-gels sung . . a Saviour's birth, If angels, &c. On that au - spi-cious morn,
If an-gels sung . . a Sa - viour's, Sa-viour's birth, On that au - spi-cious morn,
If an-gels sung . . . a Sa - viour's birth, If an-gels sung a Sa - - viour's, Sa - viour's birth, On that au - spi-cious morn, We
If an-gels sung . . . . a Sa viour's birth, If an-gels sung a Sa - viour's birth, On that au - spi-cious morn, We well may imi-
We well may imi - tate their mirth, Now he a-gain is born, Now he a-gain is born, Now he, &c.
We well may im-i - tate . . . . . their mirth, Now he again is born, ... Now he a-gain, Now he a-gain , is born.
well may im - i -tate their mirth, We well, &c. Now he a-gain is born, Now he again is born.
tate their mirth. We well &c. Now he a-gain is born, Now he a - gain . . . is born.

Counter by Swan.

SHARON. P. M.

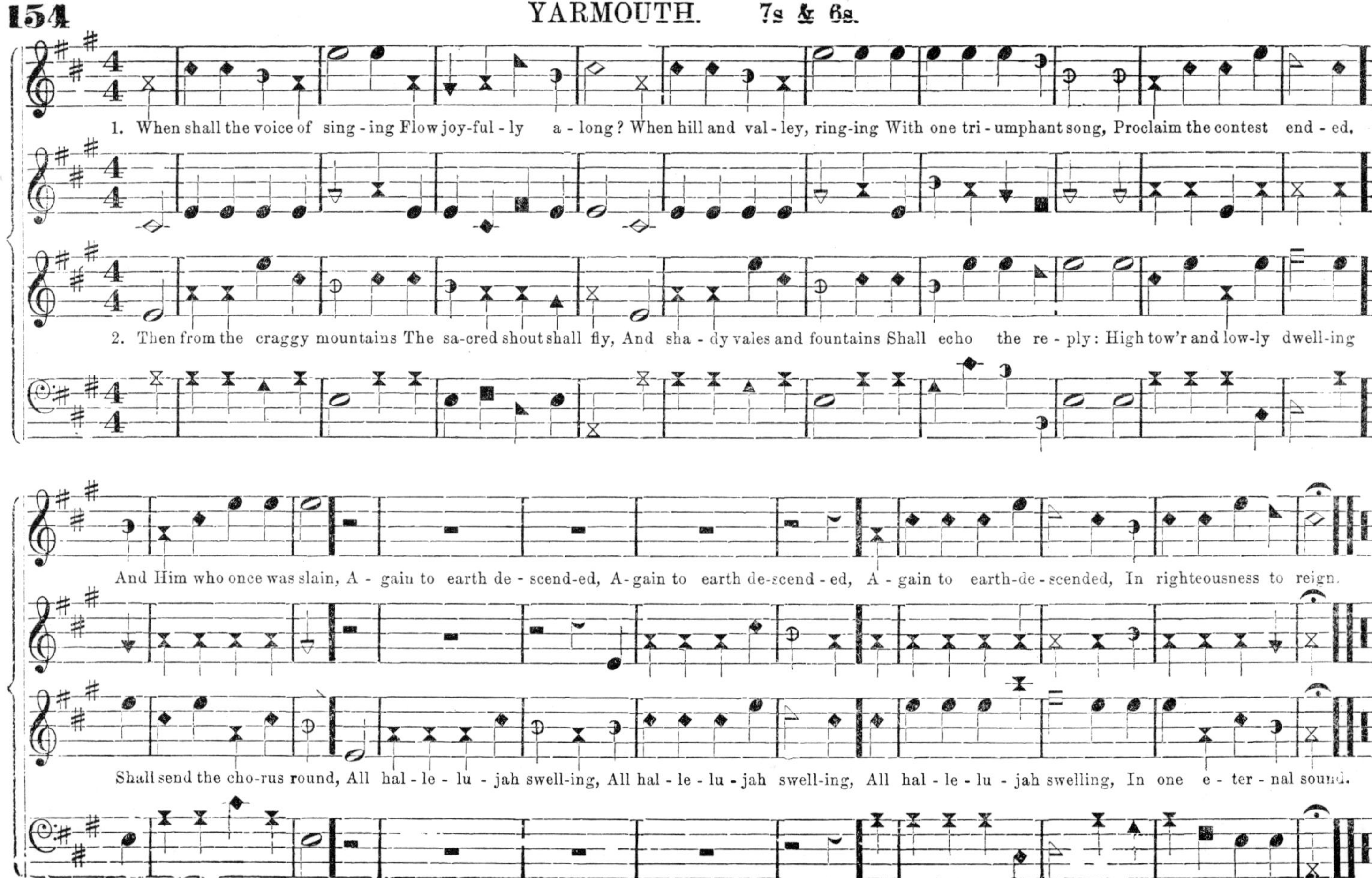
YARMOUTH. 7s & 6s.
1. When shall the voice of sing - ing Flow joy-ful - ly a - long? When hill and val - ley, ring-ing With one tri - umphant song, Proclaim the contest end - ed,
2. Then from the craggy mountains The sa-cred shout shall fly, And sha - dy vales and fountains Shall echo the re - ply: High tow'r and low-ly dwell-ing
And Him who once was slain, A - gain to earth de - scend-ed, A- gain to earth de-scend - ed, A - gain to earth-de - scended, In righteousness to reign.
Shall send the cho-rus round, All hal - le - lu - jah swell-ing, All hal - le - lu - jah swell-ing, All hal - le - lu - jah swelling, In one e - ter - nal sound.

EXHORTATION. L. M.

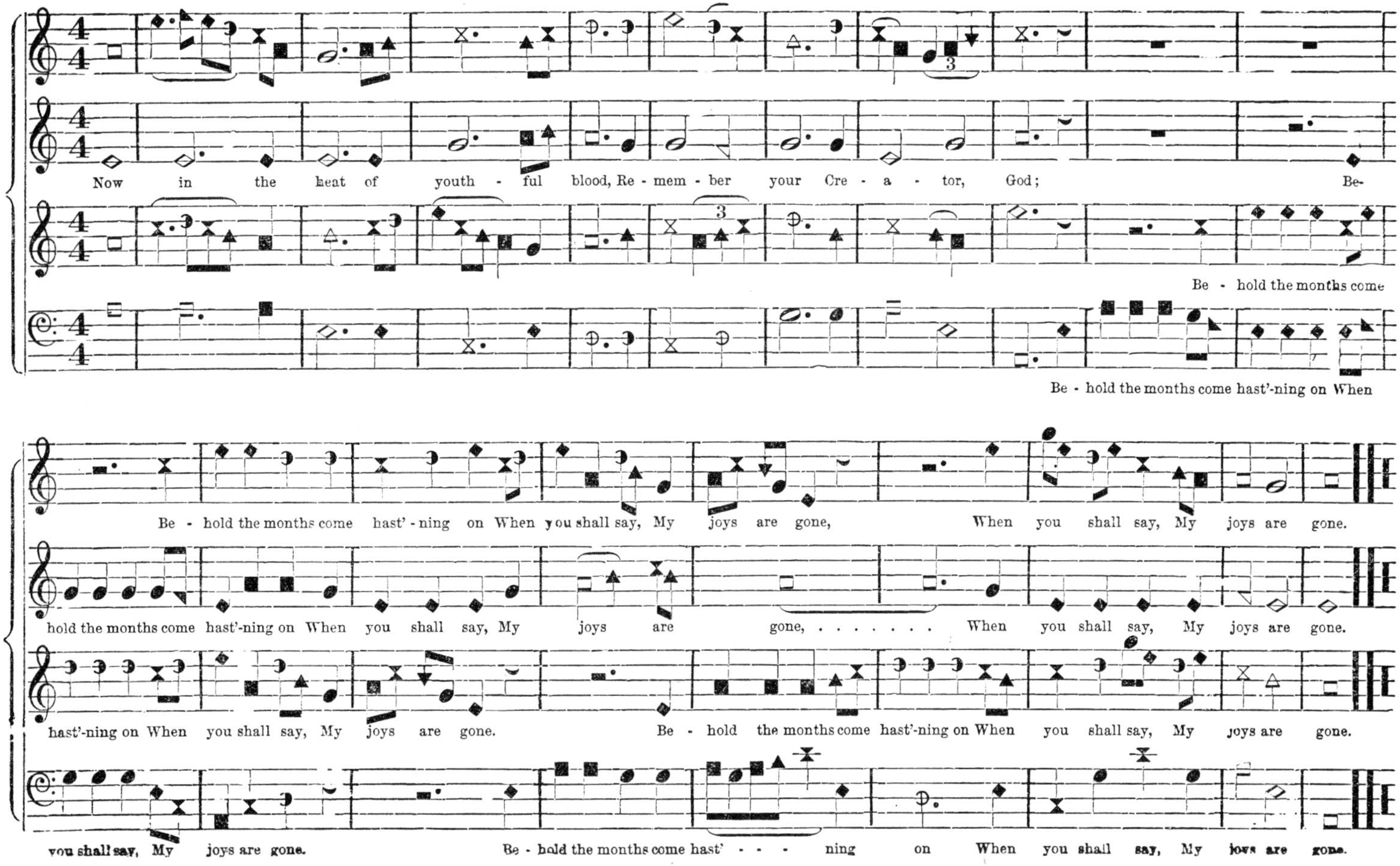

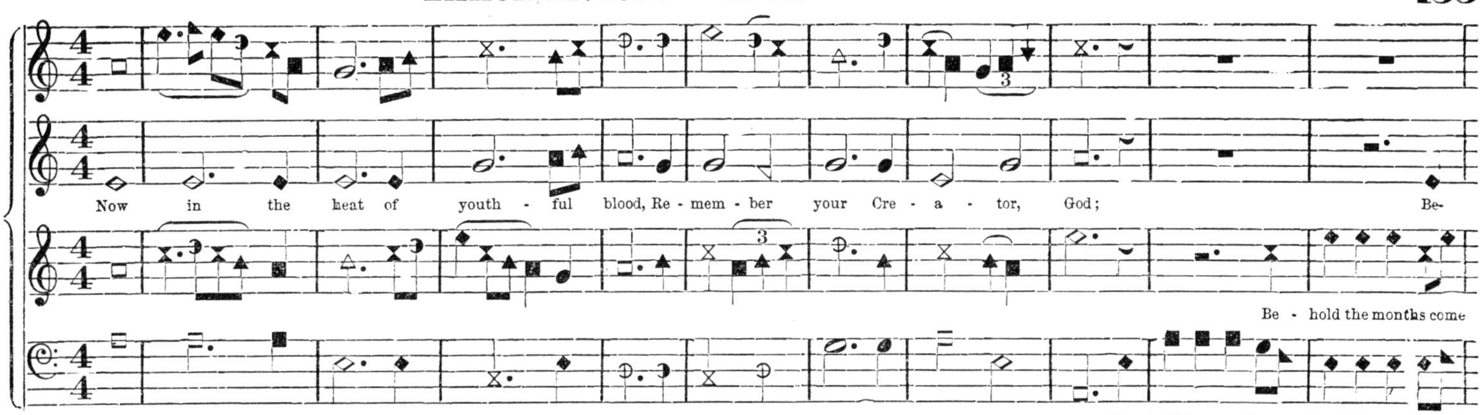

Be - hold the months come hast' - ning on When you shall say, My joys are gone, When you shall say, My joys are gone.

hold the months come hast'-ning on When you shall say, My joys are gone, ... When you shall say, My joys are gone.

hast'-ning on When you shall say, My joys are gone. Be - hold the months come hast'-ning on When you shall say, My joys are gone.

you shall say, My joys are gone. Be - hold the months come hast' - - - ning on When you shall say, My joys are gone.

CUBA. 10s & 11s.

SWAN.

2.

God ruleth on high, Almighty to save;
And still He is nigh, his presence we have.
The great congregation his triumphs shall sing,
Ascribing salvation to Jesus our King.

3

Salvation to God, who sits on the throne,
Let all cry aloud, and honour the Son:
The praises of Jesus, the angels proclaim,
Fall down on their faces, and worship the Lamb.

4.

Then let us adore and give Him his right,
All glory, and power, and wisdom, and might,
All honour and blessing, with angels above,
And thanks never ceasing, for infinite love

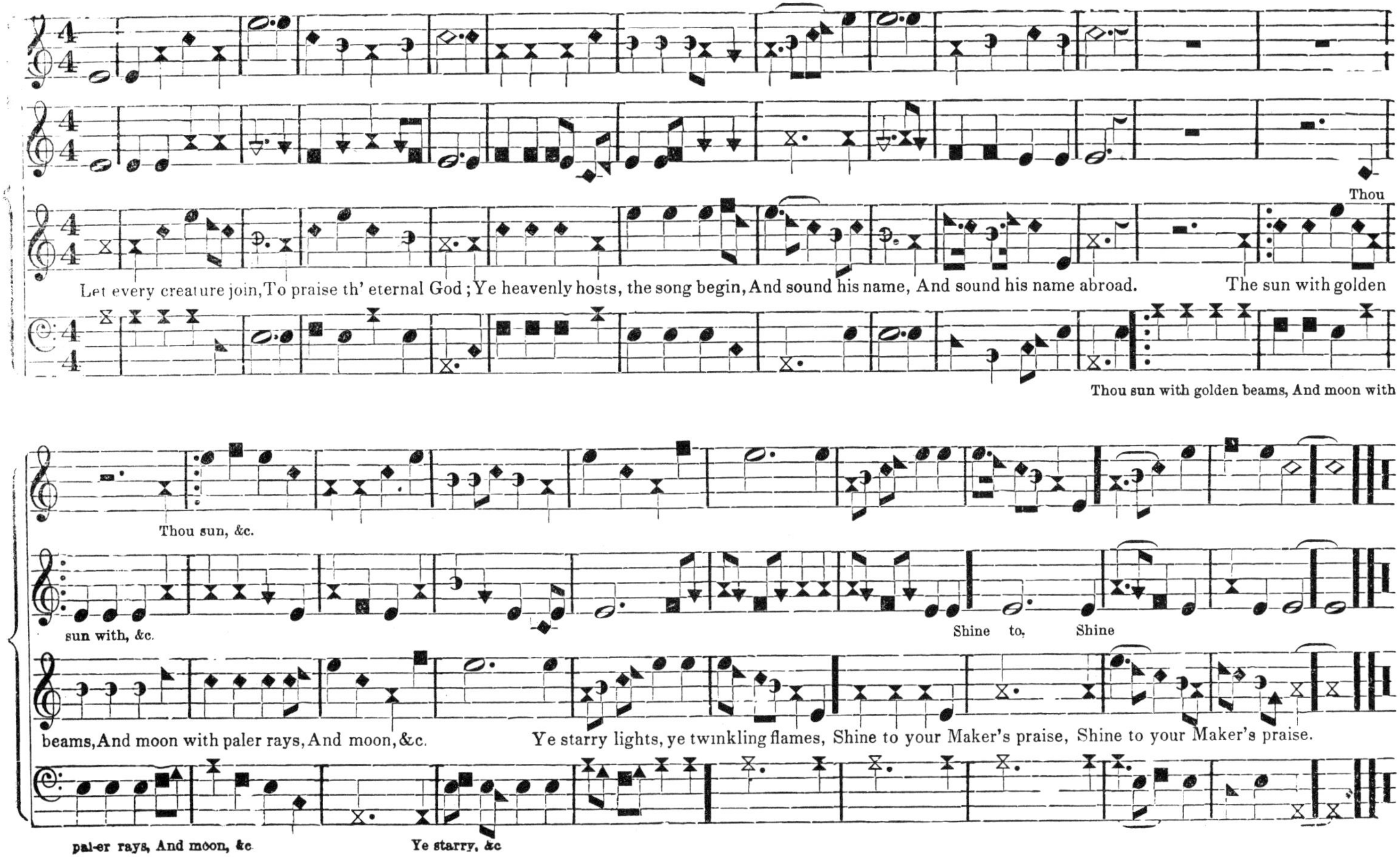

CREATION. S. M.

SHUMWAY.

Thou

Let every creature join, To praise th' eternal God; Ye heavenly hosts, the song begin, And sound his name, And sound his name abroad. The sun with golden

Thou sun with golden beams, And moon with

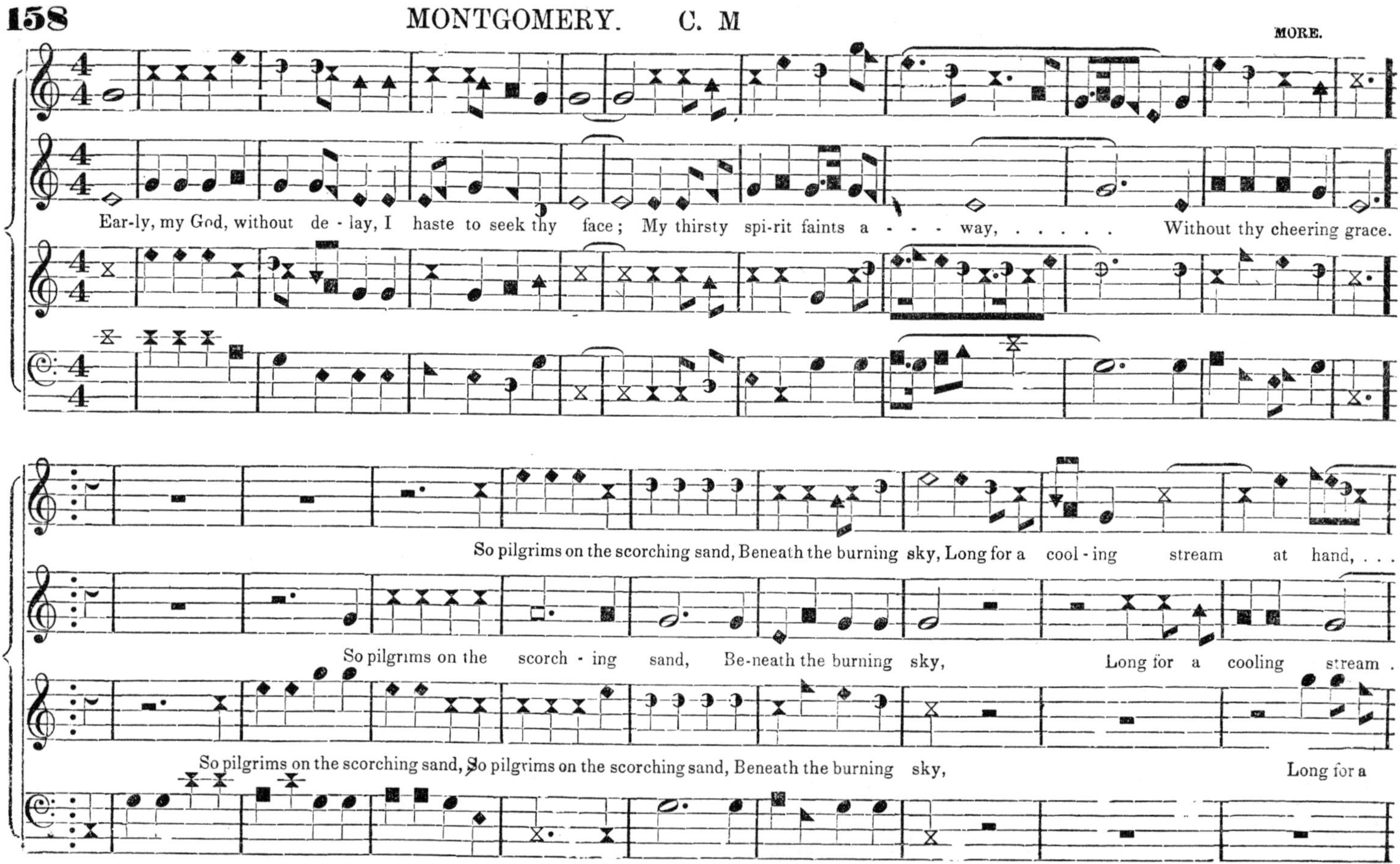
MONTGOMERY. C. M
MORE.
Ear-ly, my God, without de - lay, I haste to seek thy face; My thirsty spi-rit faints a - - - way, ... Without thy cheering grace.
So pilgrims on the scorching sand, Beneath the burning sky, Long for a cool - ing stream at hand, . . .
So pilgrims on the scorch - ing sand, Be-neath the burning sky, Long for a cooling stream .
So pilgrims on the scorching sand, So pilgrims on the scorching sand, Beneath the burning sky, Long for a
So pilgrims on the scorching sand, So pilgrims on the scorch - ing sand Be-neath the burning sky,

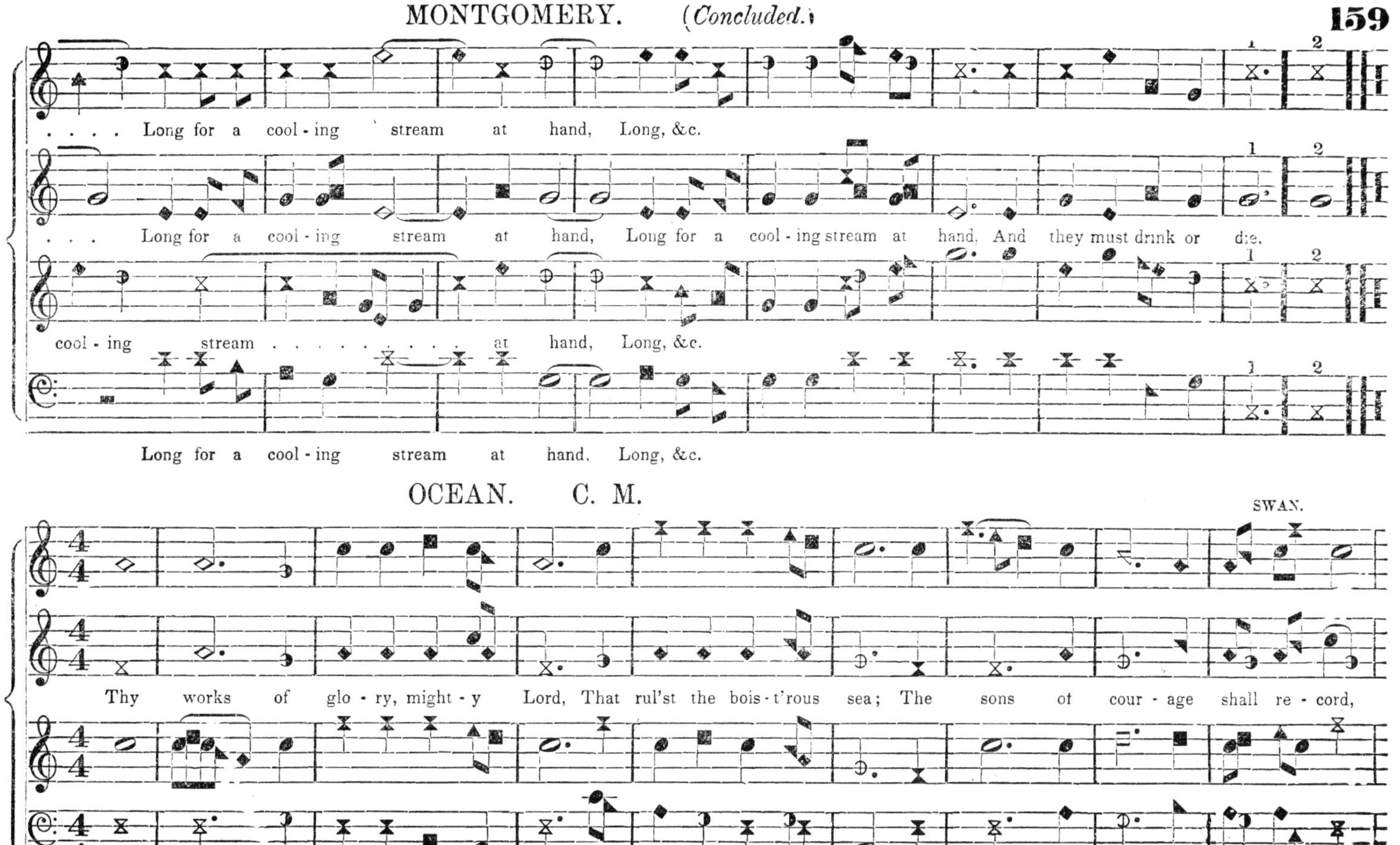
MONTGOMERY. (Concluded.)
1
2
. . . . Long for a cool - ing stream at hand, Long, &c.
. . . Long for a cool - ing stream at hand, Long for a cool - ing stream at hand. And they must drink or die.
cool - ing stream . . . . at hand, Long, &c.
Long for a cool - ing stream at hand. Long, &c.
OCEAN. C. M.
SWAN.
Thy works of glo - ry, might - y Lord, That rul'st the bois - t'rous sea; The sons of cour - age shall re - cord,

At thy command the winds a-rise, And swel. . . .
Who tempt the dangerous way. At thy command the winds a-rise, And swell the tow'ring waves; . . . .
At thy command the winds a-rise, And swell the tow-'ring waves;
At thy command the winds a-rise, And swell the tow'ring waves . . . .
. . the tow-'ring waves;
The men, as-ton-ish'd, mount the skies, And sink in gap - - - - ing graves.
1
2

BALLSTOWN. L. M.

MERDIN. 7s, 6s & 7s.

NEW TOPIA. P. M.

Young peo-ple, all at - tention give, And hear what I do say; I want your souls in Christ to live, In ev - er-last-ing day; Remember, you are hast'ning on To death's dark, gloomy
Re-member, you are hast'ning on To death's dark, gloomy

Remember, you are hast'ning on To death's dark, &c.
shade;
Your joys on earth will soon be gone, Your flesh in dust be laid, Your joys on earth will soon be gone, Your flesh in dust be laid.
Remember, you are hast'ning on To death's dark, &c.
shade,
Your joys on earth, &c.

MARION. S. M
SWAN
1. The hill of Zi - on yields A thou - sand sa - cred sweets, Be - fore we reach the heav'n - ly fields, Or walk the gold - en streets.
EUSEBIA. 7s & 6s.
SWAN.
1. From Greenland's i - cy moun - tains, From India's co - ral strand,
Where Af - ric's sun-ny foun - tains Roll down their golden sand;
From ma-ny an an - cient riv - er, From ma - ny a palm - y plain,

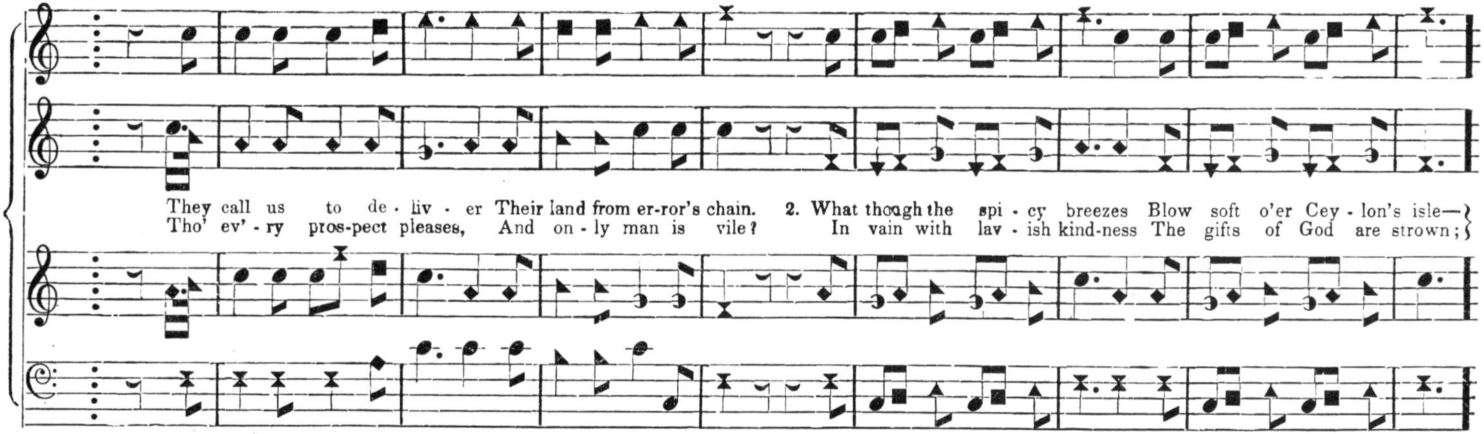

They call us to de - liv - er Their land from er-ror's chain. 2. What though the spi - cy breezes Blow soft o'er Cey - lon's isle—
Tho' ev' - ry pros-pect pleases, And on - ly man is vile? In vain with lav - ish kind-ness The gifts of God are strown;

The heath-en in his blind-ness Bows down to wood and stone, Bows down to wood and stone.

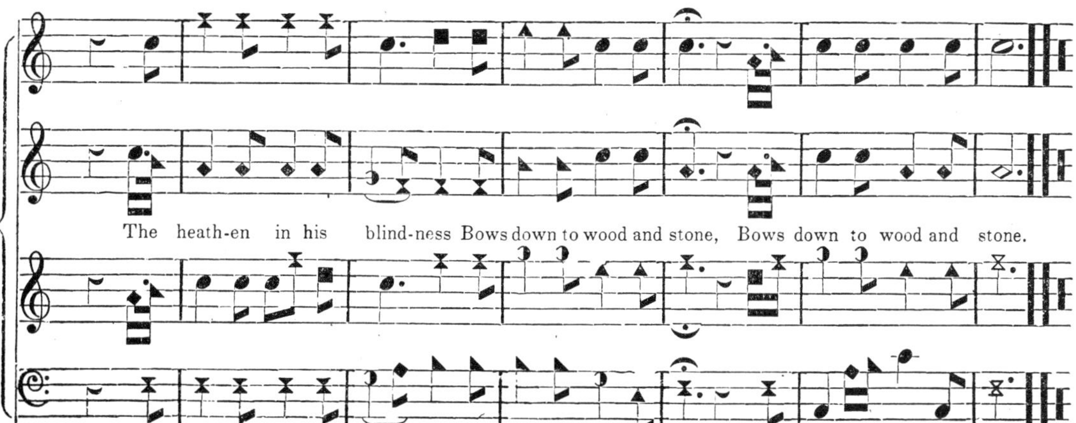

3. Shall we, whose souls are lighted
With wisdom from on high—
Shall we, to men benighted,
The lamp of life deny?
Salvation! oh, salvation!
The joyful sound proclaim,
Till earth's remotest nation
Has learn'd Messiah's name.

4. Waft, waft, ye winds, his story,
And you, ye waters, roll,
Till, like a sea of glory,
It spreads from pole to pole;
Till o'er our ransom'd nature
The Lamb for sinners slain,
Redeemer, King, Creator,
In bliss returns to reign.

MINSTREL. 8s. SWAN.

clay, His cheeks bloom with ro - ses no more, Since death call'd his spi - rit a - way, Since death call'd his spi - rit a - way, Since
death call'd his spi - rit a way. His cheeks bloom with ro - ses no more, Since death call'd his spi - rit a - way.

WHEN SHALL WE MEET AGAIN? (Hymn.)

Alto by M. L. SWAN.

AMSTERDAM. 7s & 6s.

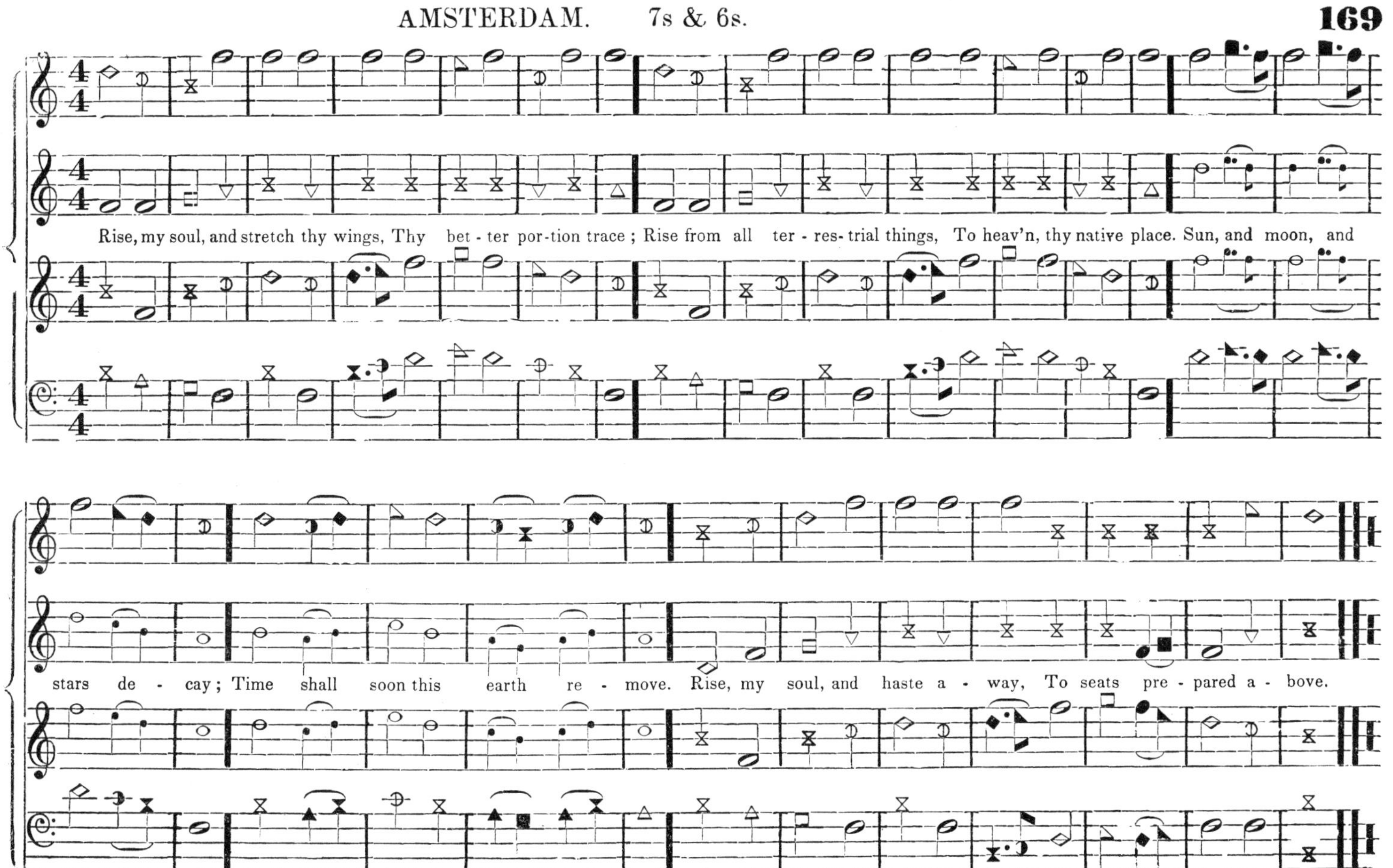

SPRING. P. M.

Counter by Swan.

2.

The voice of my beloved sounds,
While o'er the mountain top he bounds;
He flies exulting o'er the hills,
And all my soul with transport fills.
Rise, my soul, and come away,
Gently doth he chide my stay.

URMUND. 8s & 4s.

2.

Hail! all-virtuous, conquering Lord!
Be thou by all thy works adored,
Who undertook, for sinful man,
And brought salvation through thy name,
That we with thee may ever reign
In endless day.

3.

Fight on, ye conquering souls, fight on,
And when the conquest you have won,
Then palms of victory you shall bear,
And in his kingdom have a share,
And crowns of glory ever wear
In endless day.

Hail the day that . . . saw him rise, Rav - ish'd from our wish-ful eyes; Christ, a - while to mor-tals given,
Re - - - - - a - scends his na-tive heaven.
There the pomp-ous tri-umph waits, Lift your heads, e - ter - nal gates, ... Wide un-fold the ra - diant scene, Take the King of glo - ry in.

THE RIVULET

SWAN.

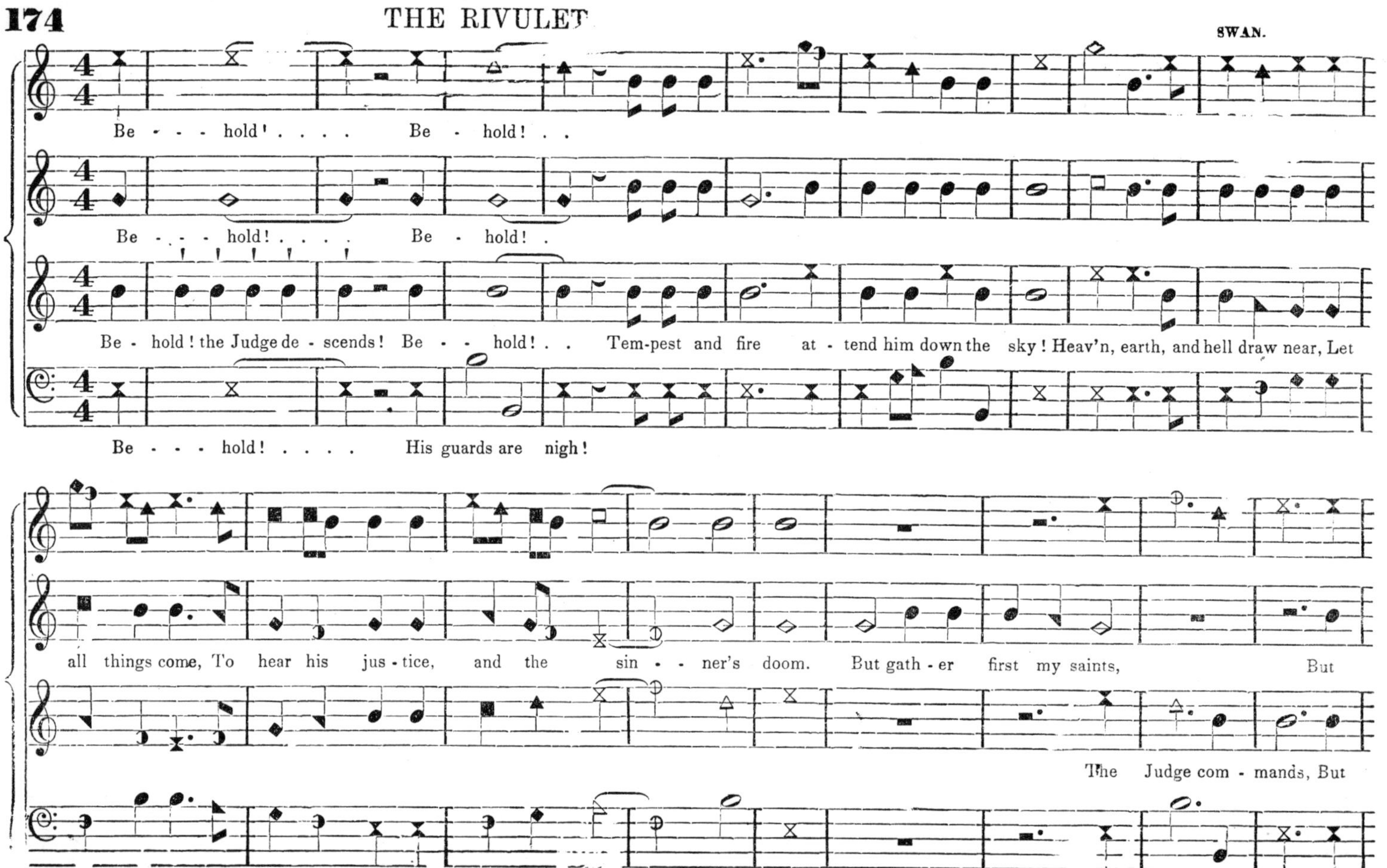

HUNTINGDON. L. M.

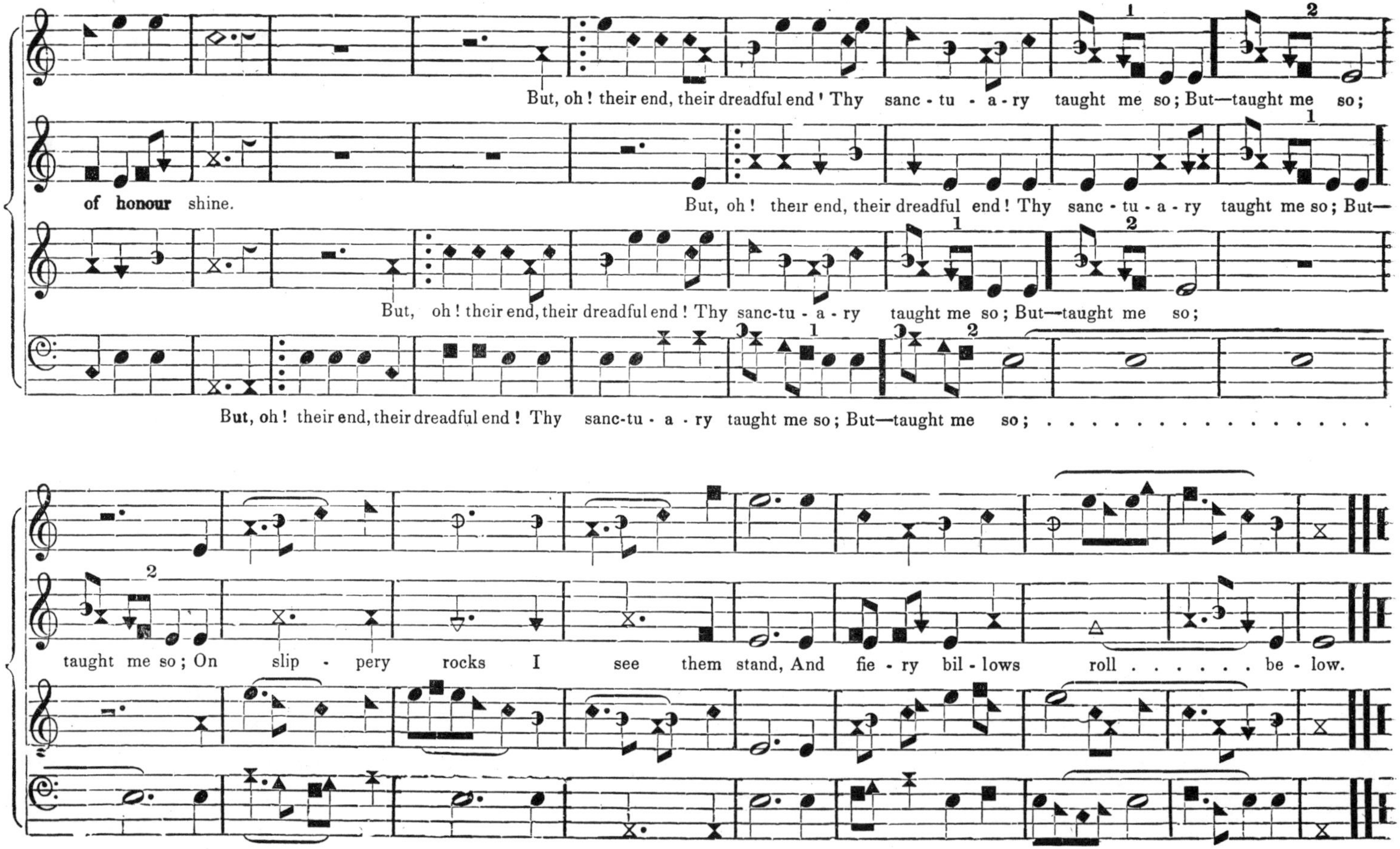

But, oh! their end, their dreadful end' Thy sanc - tu - a - ry taught me so; But—taught me so;

of honour shine. But, oh! their end, their dreadful end! Thy sanc - tu - a - ry taught me so; But—

But, oh! their end, their dreadful end! Thy sanc-tu - a - ry taught me so; But—taught me so;

But, oh! their end, their dreadful end! Thy sanc-tu - a - ry taught me so; But—taught me so; . . . .

Counter by Swan.

JORDAN'S SHORE. C. M.

J. T. WHITE.

IOWA.

SWAN.

INVITATION. L. M.

KIMBOL.

Come, my be - lov-ed, haste a-
nigh, From caves of darkness and of doubt, He gent-ly speaks and calls us out.
Come, my be-
Come, my be - lov-ed, haste a - way, Cut short the
Come, my be-lov-ed, haste a - way, Cut short the hours of thy .
way, Cut short the hour of thy de - lay; Fly like a youth - ful hart or roe, O - ver the hills where spi - - - ces grow.
lov-ed, haste a - way, Cut short the hours of thy de - lay; Fly like a youthful hart or roe, O - ver the hills where spi-ces grow.
hours of thy de - lay; Fly like a youthful hart . . . . or roe, O - - - ver the hills . . where spi - - - ces grow.
. . de - lay; Fly like a youthful hart . or roe. . . . O - ver the hills where spi - - - ces grow

WHITESTOWN. L. M.

WARD.

WHITESTOWN. *Concluded.*

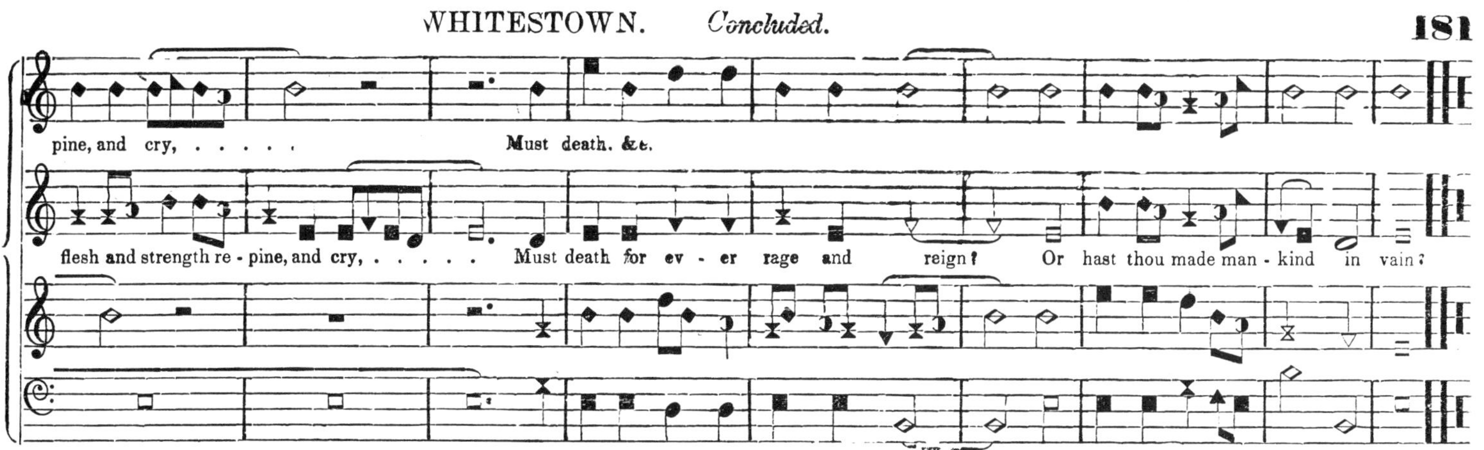

BOYLSTON. S. M.

L. MASON.

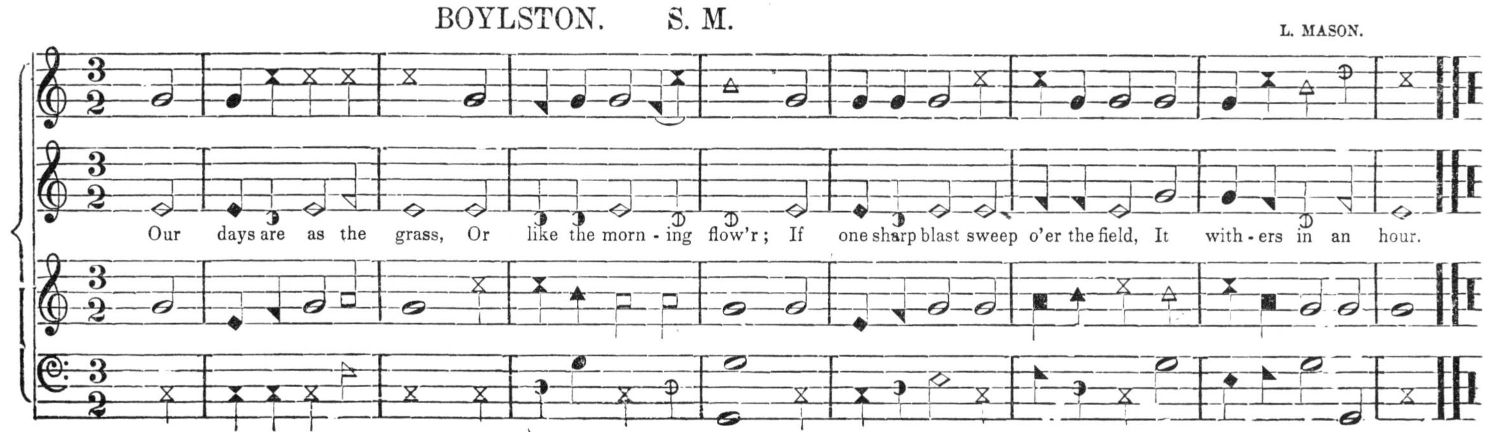

ORNAN. 8s & 7s

1. Yes, my na-tive land, I love thee, All thy scenes, I love them well; Friends, con-nec-tions, hap-py coun-try, Can I bid you all fare-well?
2. Home, thy joys are pass-ing love-ly, Joys no stranger's heart can tell; Hap-py home, in-deed I love thee; Can I, can I say fare-well?
Can I leave you, can I leave you, Far in hea-then lands to dwell? Can I leave you, can I leave you, Far in hea-then lands to dwell?
Can I leave thee, can I leave thee, Far in hea-then lands to dwell? Can I leave thee, can I leave thee, Far in hea-then lands to dwell?

LONG AGO. 10,4,4,10,4,4,10,10,10,4,3.

M. L. SWAN.

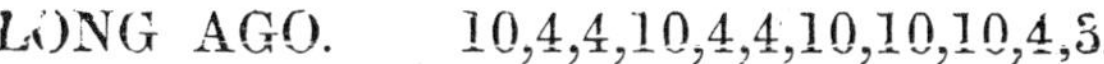

1. Where are the friends, that to me were so dear, Long, long a - go, Long, long a - go? {Friends that I loved, in the grave are laid low—}
Where are the hopes, that my heart used to cheer, Long, long a - go, Long, long a - go? {Hopes that I cherish'd, are fled from me now.}

I have been taught there's no joys here be - low, Long, long a - go, Long a - go.

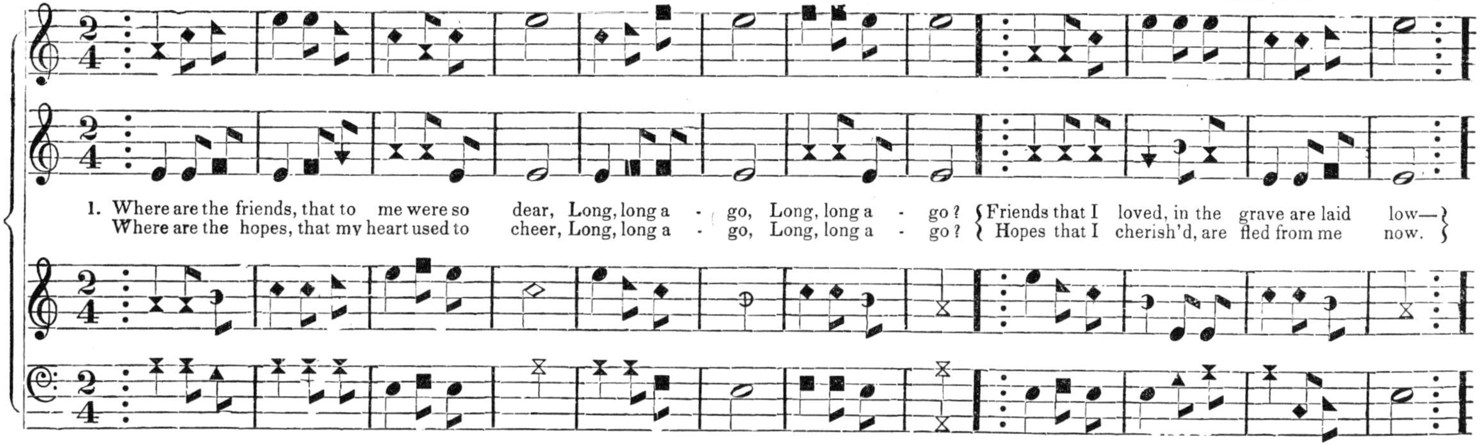

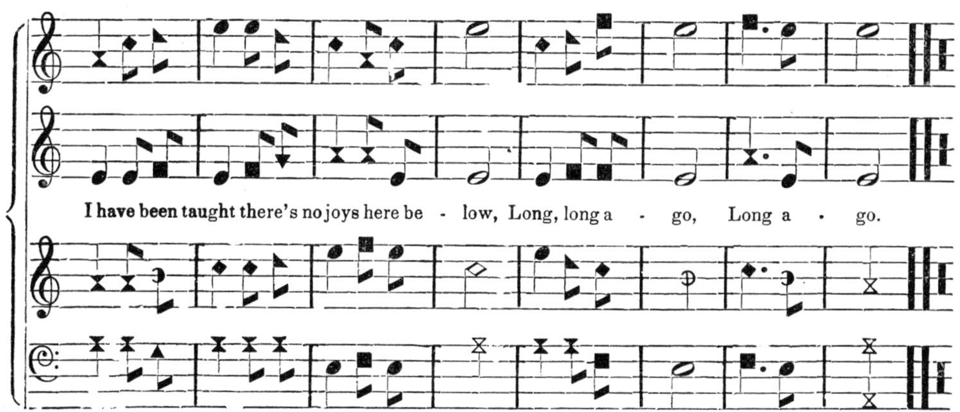

2. Jesus, the Saviour, has died on the cross,
Long, long ago—long, long ago;
Told me believe in his name, or be lost,
Long, long ago—long, long, ago;
Had I repented and turned to the Lord,
Trusted his grace and believed in his word,
Pleasures for me had been placed on record,
Long, long ago—long ago.

WATCHMAN! TELL US OF THE NIGHT.
Missionary or Christmas Hymn.
L. MASON.
Tenor Voice.
Treble Voice.
1. Watchman! tell us of the night, What its signs of pro - mise are: Trav'ler! o'er yon mountain's height, See that glo - ry - beam-ing star.
2. Watchman! tell us of the night; High-er yet the star as - cends: Trav'ler! bless - ed - ness and light, Peace and truth, its course portends.
3. Watchman! tell us of the night, For the morning seems to dawn: Trav'ler! dark - ness takes its flight, Doubt and ter - ror are withdrawn.
Tenor Voice.
Treble Voice.
Watchman! does its beauteous ray Aught of hope or joy fore - tell? Trav'ler! yes! it brings the day, Promised day, of Is - ra - el.
Watchman! will its beams a - lone Gild the spot that gave them birth? Trav'ler! a - ges are its own: See, it bursts o'er all the earth!
Watchman! let thy wand'rings cease; Hie thee to thy qui - et home: Trav'ler! lo! the Prince of Peace, Lo! the Son of God, is come.
CHORUS to 1st and 2d verses.—All voices.
CHORUS to 3d verse.
Trav'ler! yes! it brings the day, Promised day, of Is - ra - el!
Trav'ler! a - ges are its own: See, it bursts o'er all the earth!
Trav'ler! lo! the Prince of Peace, Lo! the Son of God, is come! Lo! the Son of God is come!

PART III.

CONTAINING ODES AND ANTHEMS.

CHRISTIAN SONG.

SOFT AND SLOW.
BRISK.
Oh! what is this drawing my breath, And stealing my senses away? O tell me, :‖: :‖: O tell me, my soul, is it death Releasing me
kindly from clay? Now, mounting, my soul shall descry The regions of pleasure and love; My spirit triumphant shall fly, And dwell with my Saviour above.
VERY BRISK.

Be hold, thou art fair, my love; Be - hold, thou art fair; thou hast dove's eyes within thy locks: thy hair is as a flock of goats, that ap-

pear from mount Gil-e-ad. Thy teeth are like a flock of sheep that are even shorn, which came up from the washing; whereof every one bear twins,

and none is bar-ren a-mong them. Thy lips are like a thread of scar-let, and thy speech is comely: thy temples are like a
piece of a pomegranate with - in thy locks. Thy neck is like the tow - er of Da - vid build-ed for an ar - mo - ry, where-

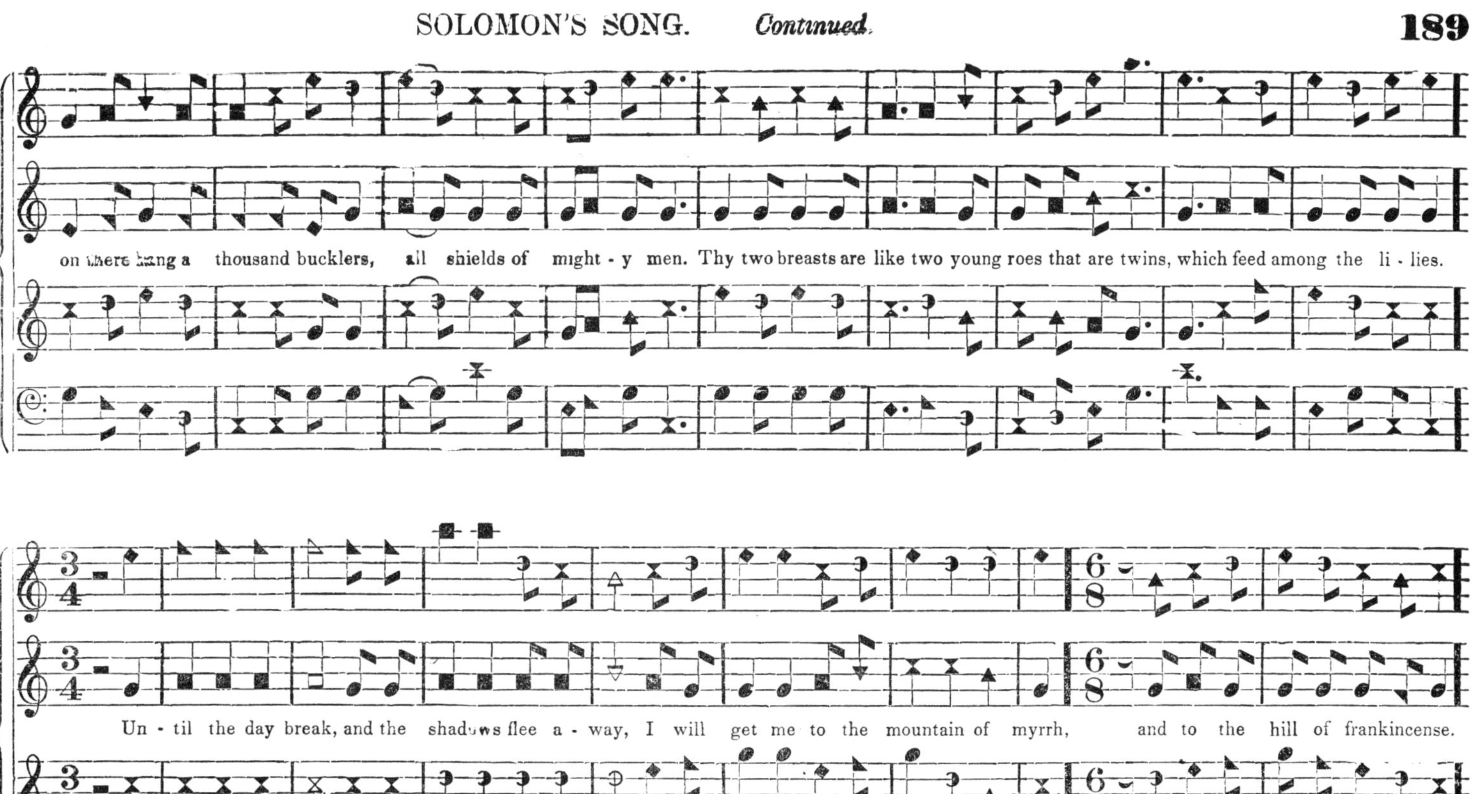
on there hang a thousand bucklers, all shields of might - y men. Thy two breasts are like two young roes that are twins, which feed among the li - lies.
Un - til the day break, and the shadows flee a - way, I will get me to the mountain of myrrh, and to the hill of frankincense.

Thou art all fair, my love; there is no spot in thee. Come with me from Le - ba - non, my spouse, with me from Le-ba-non:
look from the top of A - ma - na, from the top of She - nir and Her-mon, from the li - ons' dens, from the mountains of the leopards.

Thou hast ravish'd my heart, my sis-ter, my spouse; thou hast ravish'd my heart with one of thine eyes, with one chain of thy neck.
How fair is thy love,
How fair is thy love, my sis - ter, my spouse! how much better is thy love than wine! and the smell of thine ointments than all spi - ces!

Thy lips, O my spouse, drop as the honeycomb: honey and milk are un - der thy tongue; and the smell of thy garments is like the smell of Le - ba - non.
A garden enclosed is my sis-ter, my spouse; a spring shut up, a fountain seal'd. Thy plants are an orchard of pomegranates, with plea - sant fruits;

camphire, with spikenard, spikenard and saffron; ca - la - mus and cin - na - mon, with all trees of frank - in - cense; myrrh and
a - loes, with all the chief spi - ces: A fountain of gardens, a well of liv - ing waters, and streams from Le - ba - non.

A-wake, a - wake, O north wind; and come, thou south, a - wake, a - wake, O north wind; and come, thou south; blow upon my garden,
and come, thou south;
that the spi - ces there-of may flow out. Let my be - lov - ed come in - to his gar-den, And eat his pleas-ant fruits.

EASTER ANTHEM.

Hal - le - lu - jah, The Lord is risen in - deed, Hal - le - lu - jah,

The Lord is risen in - deed,

Now is Christ ris - en from the

Now is Christ ris - en from tne dead, And be - come the firs uits of them that slept.

dead, and be - come the first-fruits of them that slept, Hal - le - lu - jah, Hal - le - lu - jah, Hal - le - lu - jah.
And did he rise? And did he rise? . . .
And did he rise? Did he rise? Hear it, ye nations! hear it, O ye dead!
And did he rise? And did he rise? . . .
And did he rise? . . . . And did he rise? . . . .

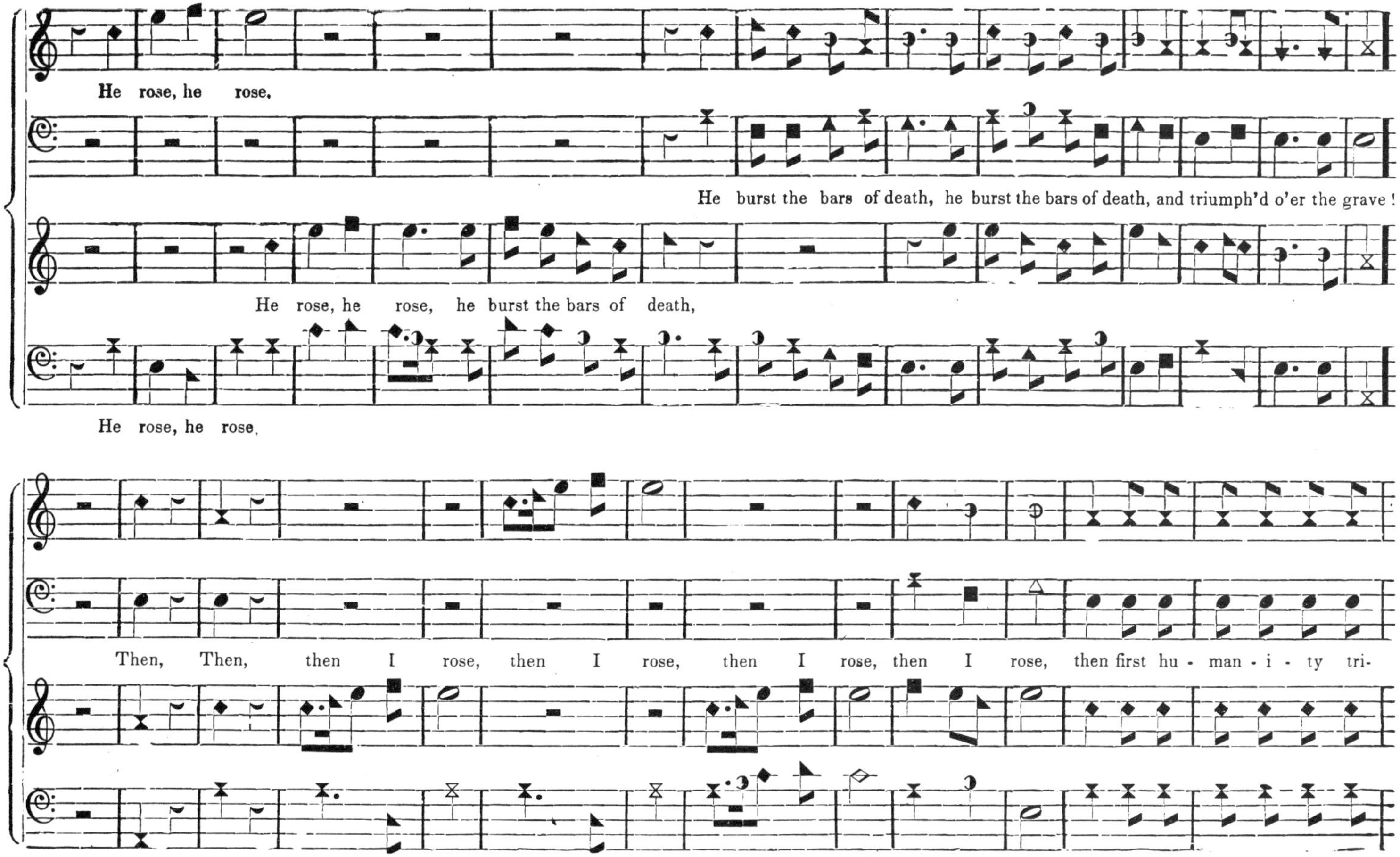

He rose, he rose,

He burst the bars of death, he burst the bars of death, and triumph'd o'er the grave !

He rose, he rose, he burst the bars of death,

He rose, he rose,

1
2
umph-ant pass'd the crys - tal ports of light, And seized e - ter - nal youth.
Man, all im-mor- tal, hail! Hail,
Heaven! all lav-ish of strange gifts to man,
Thine's all the glo - ry, man's the boundless bliss.
Thine's all the glo - ry, man's the boundless bliss.

ROSE OF SHARON.

BILLINGS.

So is my be - lov - ed a - mong the sons.
As the ap - ple tree, the ap - ple tree a - mong . . . . the trees . . . of the wood, so is my be - lov - ed a - mong the sons.
I sat down un - der his sha - dow with great de - light, and his
I sat down un - der his sha dow with great de - light,
So is my be - lov - ed a - mong the sons. I sat down un - der his sha - dow with great de - light,
I sat down an - der his sha - dow with great de light, and his

fruit . . . . was sweet to my taste. And his fruit, And his fruit was sweet to my taste.
And his fruit, And his fruit was sweet to my taste.
And his fruit . . . . was sweet to my taste.
fruit, and his fruit was sweet to my taste. And his fruit, and his fruit was sweet to my taste. He brought me to the
Stay me with
banqueting house, his ban - ner o - ver me was love. He brought me to the banqueting house, His ban-ner o - ver me was love.

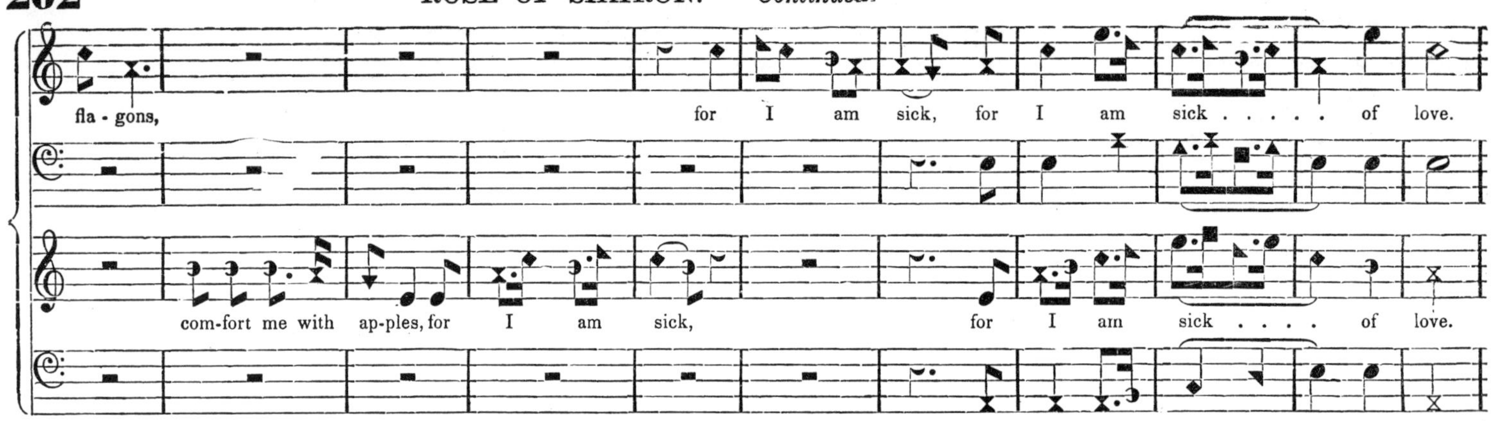
fla - gons, for I am sick, for I am sick, for I am sick . . . . . of love.
com-fort me with ap-ples, for I am sick, for I am sick . . . . of love.

I charge you, O ye daugh-ters of Je - ru sa - lem, by the roes, and by the hinds of the field,
I charge you, O ye daugh-ters of Je - ru - sa - lem, by the roes, and by the hinds of the field, that ye stir not up,

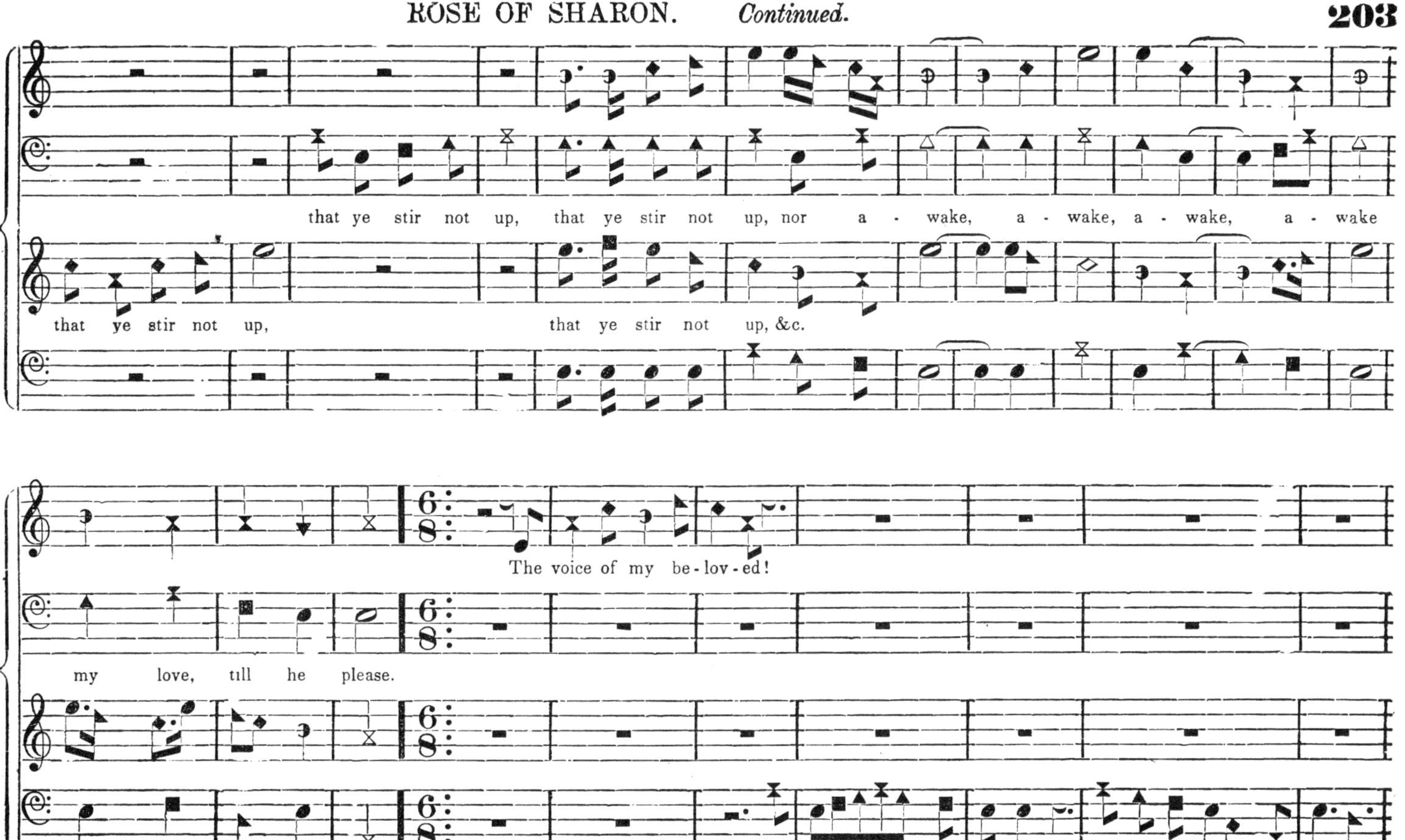
that ye stir not up, that ye stir not up, nor a - wake, a - wake, a - wake, a - wake
that ye stir not up, that ye stir not up, &c.
The voice of my be - lov - ed!
my love, till he please.
be - hold, . . . he cometh leap - ing up - on the mountains,

skipping, leap-ing up-on the moun-tains, skipping up-on the hills. and said un-to
skip-ping,
skipping, skip-ping, leaping up-on the moun-tains, skip-ping up-on tne hills. My be-lov-ed spake,
me, Rise up, my love, my fair one, and come a-way. For lo, the win-ter is
Rise up,
Rise up, Rise up, Rise up, . . . my love, my fair one, and come a-way. For lo, the win-ter is

past, the rain is o-ver and gone.
For lo, the win-ter is past, the rain is o-ver and gone, the rain is o-ver, the
past, the rain is o-ver and gone. For lo, the win-ter is past, the rain is o-ver and gone, the rain is o-ver, the
rain is o-ver, the rain is o-ver and gone. For lo, the win-ter is past, the rain is o-ver and gone.

WESTERN MOUNT PLEASANT. C. M.

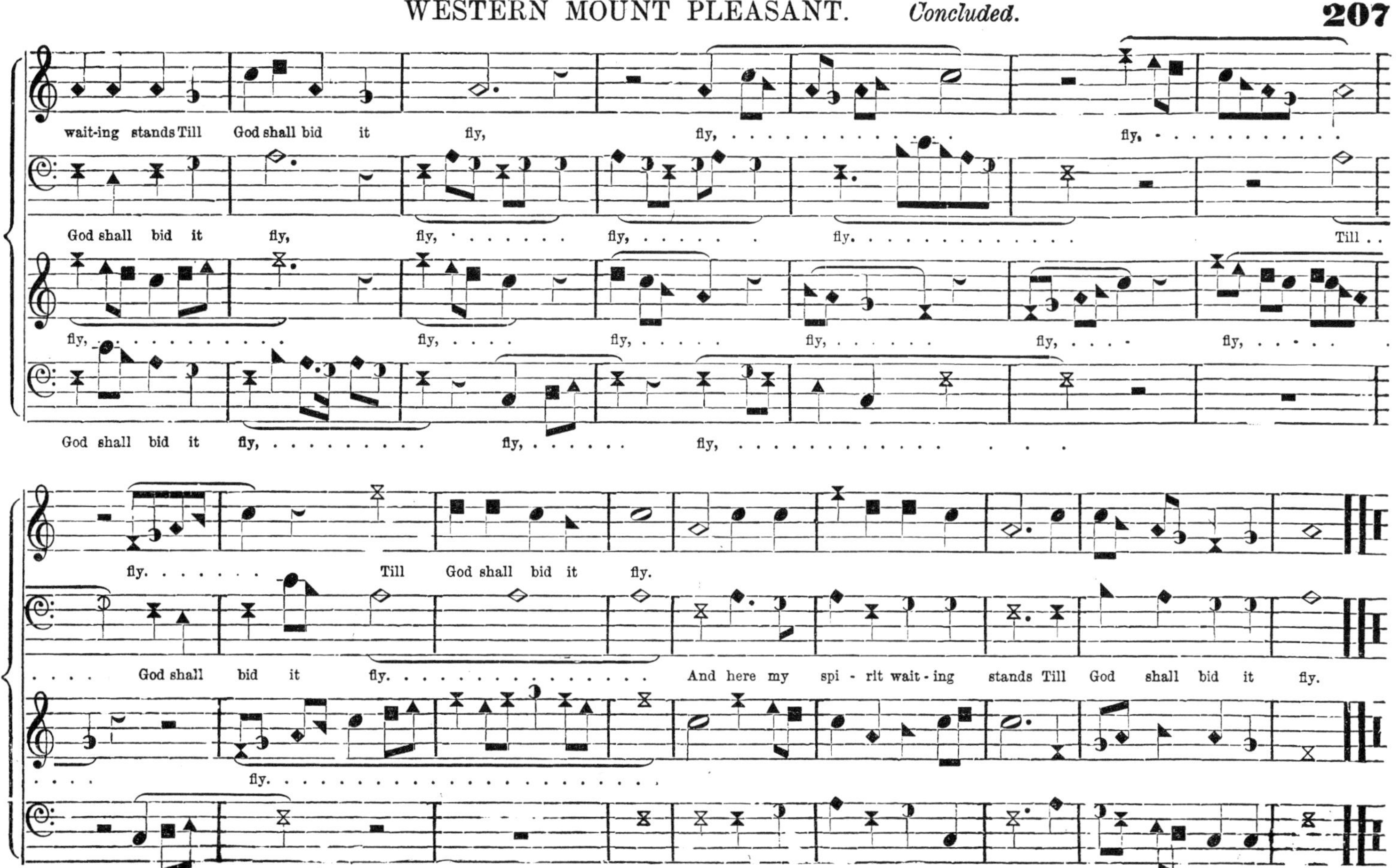
wait-ing stands Till God shall bid it fly, fly, ... fly, ...
God shall bid it fly, fly, ... fly, ... fly. . . . . Till . .
fly, ... fly, ... fly, ... fly, ... fly, ... fly, ...
God shall bid it fly, ... fly, ... fly, ...
fly. . . . . Till God shall bid it fly.
. . . . God shall bid it fly. . . . . And here my spi - rit wait - ing stands Till God shall bid it fly.
. . . . fly. . . . .
fly, fly

The morn - ing sun shines from the east, And spreads his glo - ries to the west: All na - tions with his
beams are blest, Wher - e'er the ra - diant light ap - pears: So sci-ence spreads her lu - cid ray O'er lands which

long in darkness lay; She vi - sits fair Co - lum - bi a, And sets her sons a - mong the stars.
1
2
Fair Freedom, her at tend - ant, waits To bless the por - tals of her gates, To crown the young and ris - ing state With

lau - rels of im - mor - tal date! The Bri - tish yoke, the Gal - lic chain Was urged up - on our
necks in vain: All haugh-ty ty - rants we dis dain, And shout, Long live A - me - ri - ca!
1
2
1
2
1
2
1
2

CLAREMONT.

Slow.
Trembling, hoping, ling - 'ring, fly - ing, fly - ing, fly - ing,
Vi - tal spark of heav'nly flame, Quit, oh quit this mor-tal frame! Trembling, hoping, ling - 'ring, fly - ing, fly - ing, fly - ing,
Ling - 'ring, fly - ing,
Trembling, hop-ing, ling - 'ring, fly - ing, fly - ing, fly-ing,
Cease, fond na - ture, cease thy strife,
Oh, the pain, the bliss of dy-ing! And let me languish in - to life, And let me languish in - to life.
Cease, fond na - ture, cease thy strife,

CLAREMONT. *Continuea.*

Loud.
Tell me, my soul, &c.
Tell me, my soul, &c.
my breath, Tell me, my soul, can this be death? Tell me, my soul, can this be death? Tell me, my soul, can this be death?
Tell me, my soul, &c.
Soft.
The world re - cedes—it dis - ap - pears, Heav'n o - pens on my eyes, Mine ears, &c.
Mine ears with sounds se - raph - ic ring, Mine ears with sounds se - raph - ic
The world re - cedes, &c.

Slow.
Brisk.
ring, ... Mine ears with sounds se - raph - ic ring. Lend, lend your wings, I mount, I fly, I mount, I fly, O
grave! where is thy vic - to - ry, thy vic - to - ry? O grave! where is thy vic - to - ry, thy vic - to - ry? O death! where is thy sting? Lend,

lend your wings, I mount, I fly . . . . I mount, I fly, I mount, I fly, I fly, O grave! where is thy vic - to-
ry? O death! where is thy sting? I mount, I fly, I mount, I fly, O grave! where is thy vic - to - ry? O death! where is thy sting?

O PRAISE GOD IN HIS HOLINESS.

praise him up - on the lute and
praise him in the sound of the trump - et, in the sound of the trump - et; praise him up - on the lute, up - on the lute and
praise him up - on the lute and
harp; Praise him in the cym - bals, in the cym - bals and dances; praise him on strings, on

Let
strings and pipes; Let ev' - ry thing that hath breath, let ev' - ry thing that hath
Let ev' - ry thing that hath breath, let ev' - ry thing that hath breath, ...
Let ev' - ry thing that hath
ev' - ry thing that hath breath
breath, that hath breath praise the Lord, that hath breath praise the Lord. Praise the Lord, Praise the Lord.

FAREWELL ANTHEM.

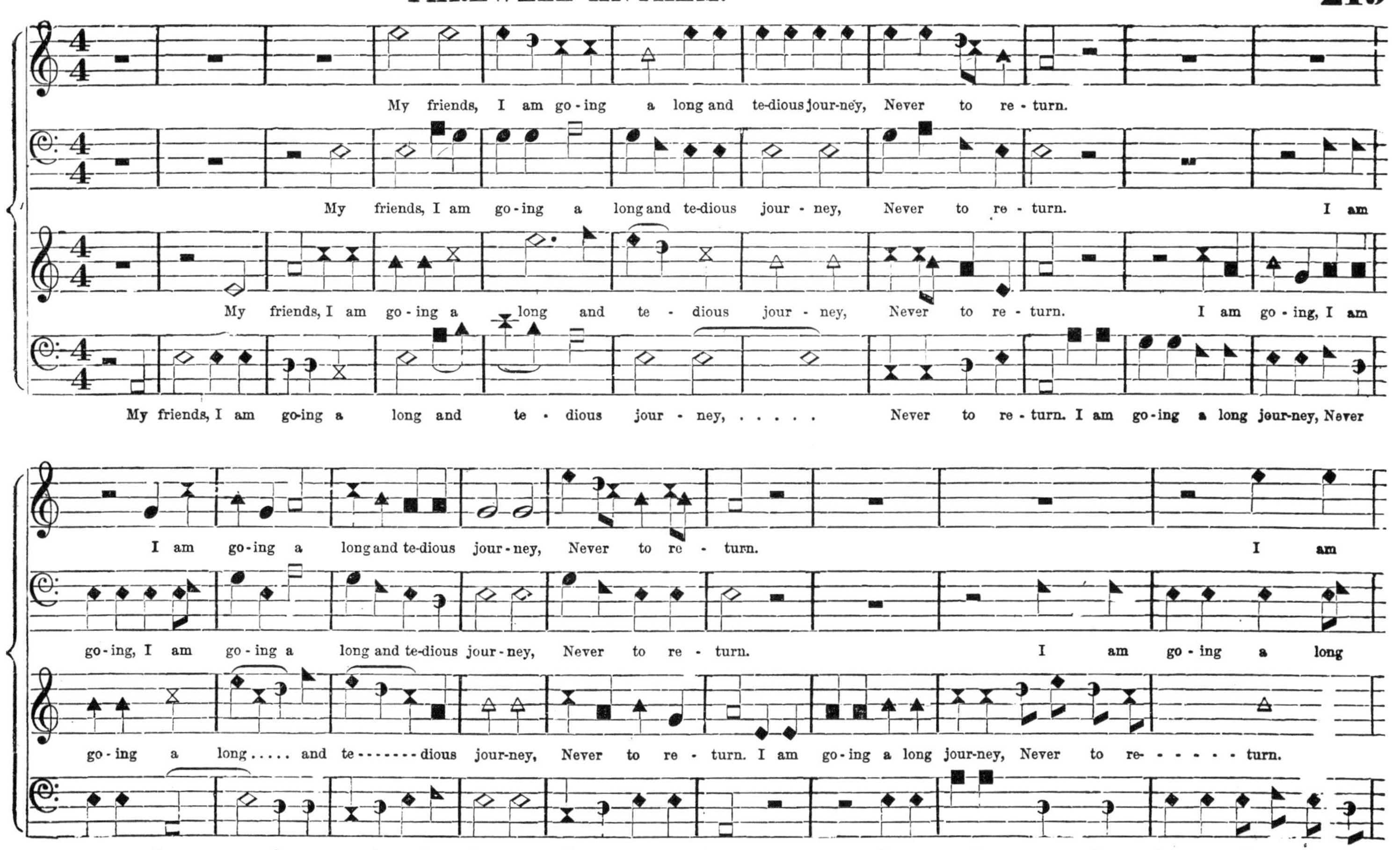

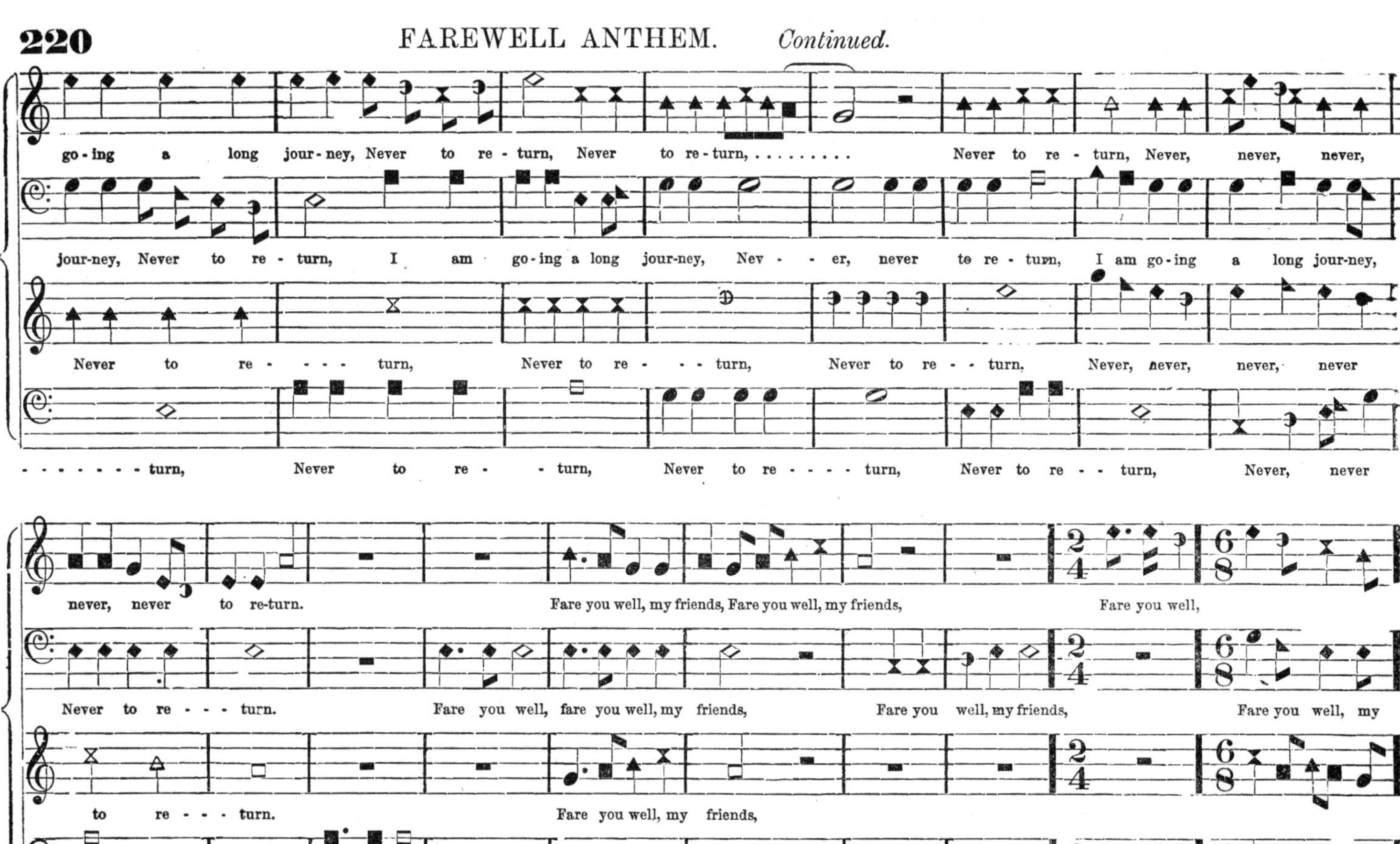
go-ing a long jour-ney, Never to re-turn, Never to re-turn, ... Never to re - turn, Never, never, never,
jour-ney, Never to re - turn, I am go-ing a long jour-ney, Nev - - er, never to re - turn, I am go-ing a long jour-ney,
Never to re - - - - turn, Never to re - - - turn, Never to re - - turn, Never, never, never, never
- - - - - - - - turn, Never to re - - turn, Never to re - - - - turn, Never to re - - turn, Never, never
never, never to re-turn. Fare you well, my friends, Fare you well, my friends, Fare you well,
Never to re - - - turn. Fare you well, fare you well, my friends, Fare you well, my friends, Fare you well, my
to re - - - turn. Fare you well, my friends,
to re - - - turn. Fare you well, Fare you well, my friends.
2
4
6
8

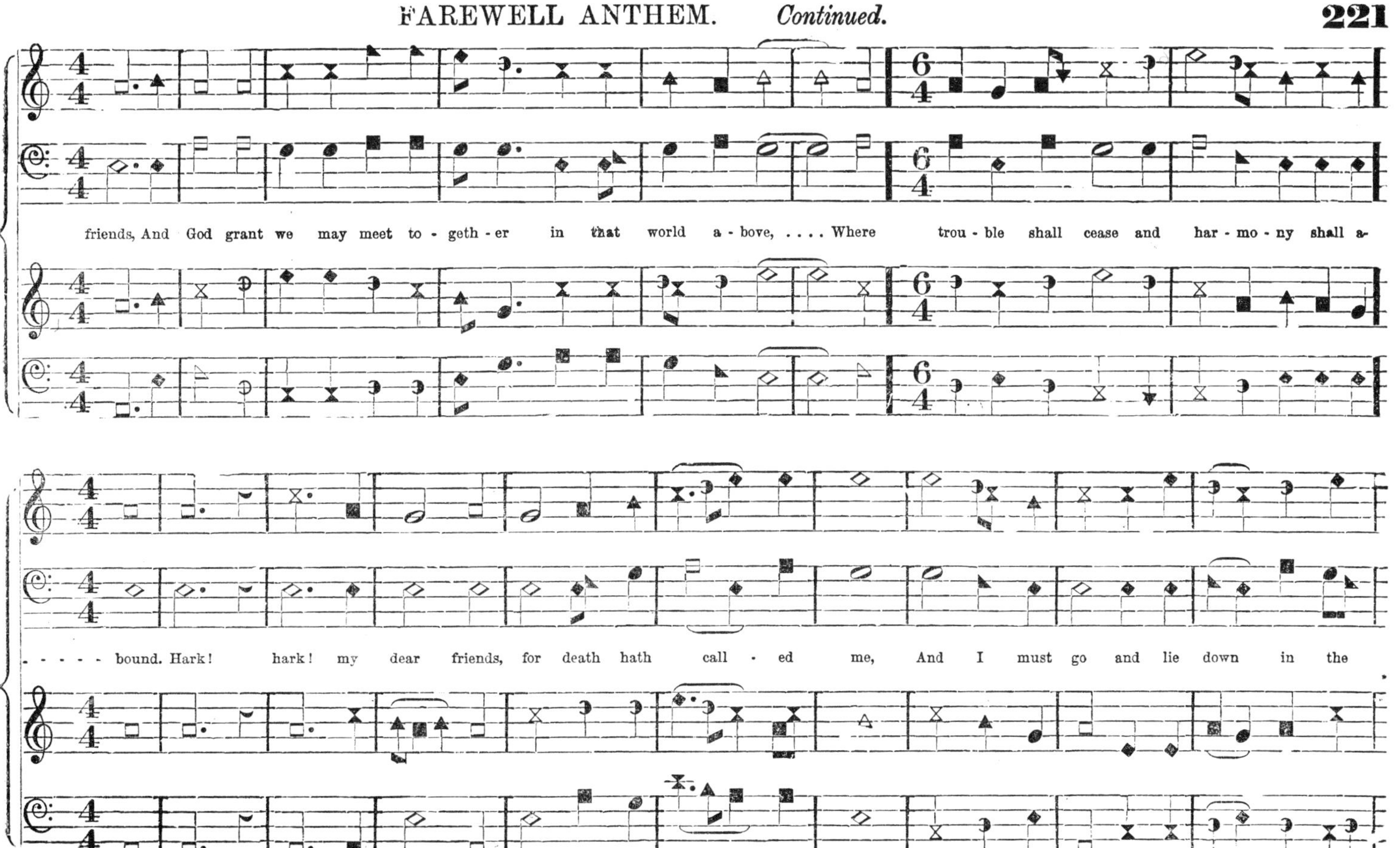
friends, And God grant we may meet to - geth - er in that world a - bove, ... Where trou - ble shall cease and har - mo - ny shall a-
- - - - - bound. Hark! hark! my dear friends, for death hath call - ed me, And I must go and lie down in the

cold and si - lent grave. There the mourn - ers cease from mourn-ing, And the pris' - ner is set free; Where the rich and the
poor are both a - like. Fare you well, Fare you well, Fare you well, Fare you well, Fare you well, my friends.

ALPHABETICAL INDEX.

ANTHEMS.

METRICAL INDEX.

INDEX OF FIRST LINES

(Compiled by Ron Petersen)